"Godless Communists"

"Godless Communists"

Atheism and Society in Soviet Russia
1917–1932

William B. Husband

NORTHERN ILLINOIS UNIVERSITY PRESS DeKalb 2000

© 2000 by Northern Illinois University Press
Published by the Northern Illinois University
Press, DeKalb, Illinois 60115
Manufactured in the United States using acid-
free paper
All Rights Reserved
Design by Julia Fauci

Library of Congress

Cataloging-in-Publication Data

Husband, William.

Godless communists : atheism and society

in Soviet Russia, 1917–1932 / William B.

Husband.

p.   cm.

Includes bibliographical references

and index.

ISBN 0-87580-257-5 (alk. paper)

1. Atheism—Soviet Union—History.

2. Soviet Union—Religion. I. Title.

BL2765.S65H87 2000

211'.8'0947—dc21   99-33412

CIP

To the Memory of Tom Renehan

There are some who can rise above blind faith,

Others just can't seem to pray,

Then there are those condemned by the gods to write,

They sparkle and fade away.

—*Ray Wylie Hubbard*

Contents

Acknowledgments

It is a pleasure to acknowledge publicly the many who have helped make this book possible. Inverting the usual protocol, but moving in order of importance, I thank Jeffrie. Why she gave up a perfectly sensible life in West Texas and New Mexico to throw in her lot with a historian of Russia remains a mystery to me even after twenty-nine years, but I am glad she did. I have also enjoyed the unfailing support of Bill Husband, Sr., and of Jimmie Emmons.

I could never have finished the project without the help of numerous friends and colleagues. Gregory L. Freeze has been a mentor, guide, critic, and supporter. Best of all, he and ChaeRan have been loyal and valued friends. Donald J. Raleigh has also provided unstinting professional support, good advice, and friendship for which I cannot adequately thank him. Orest Pelech came to Oregon for three days of virtually uninterrupted discussion of Russian Orthodoxy, which took place largely, in the Russian style, around my kitchen table. David LaFrance alerted me to important sources outside my specialization and generally kept me from taking myself too seriously. Daniel Peris showed patience and good spirit in debating Russian atheism with me. And I cannot begin to express my gratitude for the generosity of spirit shown me by Kirill L. Shepelev and Galina A. Ippolitova. Other friends—Edith and Rich Dallinger, Bess Beatty, Jim Foster, Roy Robson, Barbara Clements, Christine Worobec, Ed Roslof, Kate Transchel, and Greta Bucher—provided many of the good times that made this book a joy to write.

Various institutions and individuals generously supported this project. I am grateful for a National Endowment for the Humanities Fellowship for College Teachers; a Fulbright-Hays Fellowship for Faculty Research Abroad; an International Research and Exchanges Board (IREX) Long-Term Advanced Research Fellowship; a Research Grant from the Oregon Council for the Humanities; an NEH Summer Seminar for College Teachers; and various grants from Oregon State University. I especially benefited from the professionalism of the staff of the European Division of the Library of Congress and of the Slavic Division of the Library of the University of Illinois; my research at the latter was made possible through two fellowships from the University of Illinois Summer Research Laboratory. I owe deep gratitude to the Russian National Library, the Russian State Historical Library, the Russian State Library, and the various archives listed in the introduction of this book. I also thank the Dawson Center and the Moody Library of Baylor University; the Suzzallo Library of the University of Washington; the Knight Library of the University of Oregon; and Heather A. Shannon of the Firestone Library of Princeton University. The Oregon State University Center for the Humanities and its director, Peter Copek, twice provided opportunities for uninterrupted work on the manuscript. And of course I thank my department colleagues and its chair, Paul L. Farber.

Others helped in a variety of ways. Lynne Viola, Barbara Evans Clements, Julie Hessler, Paul Steeves, and Anne E. Gorsuch made valuable comments on various parts of the manuscript; the two anonymous referees for NIU Press gave the book an especially insightful reading. I thank each of them, while taking full responsibility for whatever mistakes and flaws remain. The University of Chicago Press allowed me to incorporate material from my essay, "Soviet Atheism and Russian Orthodox Strategies of Resistance, 1917–1932," *Journal of Modern History* (March 1998): 74–107 (© 1998 by The University of Chicago—all rights reserved). Ray Wylie Hubbard generously granted permission to quote lyrics from his *Ballad of the Crimson Kings* in the dedication, and I thank Judy Hubbard for her role in making this possible. And certainly not least, Mary Lincoln and her staff at Northern Illinois University Press have exhibited exemplary professionalism in every one of my dealings with them.

Finally, I thank the late Tom Renehan for his friendship. This gentle man and scholar left us far too soon, and to his memory I affectionately dedicate this book.

—*Austin, Texas*

Introduction

Holy Russia and Antireligion

"Do you remember your expression that 'An atheist can't be a Russian,' that 'An atheist at once ceases to be a Russian?' Do you remember it?"—Fëdor Dostoevsky, *The Devils*

"In our country there's nothing surprising about atheism," said Berlioz with diplomatic politeness. "Most of us have long ago and quite consciously given up believing in all those fairy tales about God."
—Mikhail Bulgakov, *The Master and Margarita*

Why do Russians act the way they do? This basic question ultimately underlies every attempt to understand Russia and to place its past and present in broader context. It is the denominator common to Russians' efforts to make sense of their shared experience and to ventures by non-Russians to fathom the unfamiliar. Those who have tried to answer even a part of it have filled lecture halls and the shelves of libraries, created a celebrated Russian national literature, touched off debates around countless kitchen tables, and turned taxi drivers into political philosophers. For centuries, Russian intellectuals as well as the rank and file have vigorously debated what it means to be Russian and, with even greater passion, what the mission of Russia *ought* to be. The resultant array of competing prescriptions has undoubtedly enriched the country's intellectual life and reverberated strongly beyond its borders, but it has also failed to produce anything resembling consensus. The worst cases have led to persecution and bloodshed.

This book examines one highly significant chapter in the ongoing contention over collective behavior in Russia: the promotion of Soviet atheism during 1917–1932. The study of belief systems—religious, ideological, philosophical, scientific, occult—provides important insight into every society, of course, and Russia is by no means unique in having experienced calamity and carnage when one group tried to alter the basic views and actions of another. Long before Marxism, efforts to eliminate heresy and apostasy, variously defined, and to control the social environment punctuated Russian history no less than the rest of the violent and intolerant premodern world. By the nineteenth century, ideas from Europe helped foment intellectual, political, and spiritual discord in Russia, and the socioeconomic displacement and secularizing influences that everywhere accompany industrial modernization challenged tsarist institutions no less fundamentally than other monarchies and landholding aristocracies. But the cultivation of atheism in Soviet Russia also possessed distinct characteristics, none more important than the one most obvious: atheism was an integral part of the world's first large-scale experiment in communism.

The promotion of an antireligious society therefore constitutes an important development in Soviet Russia and in the social history of atheism globally. Bolshevik leaders, following their seizure of political authority in October 1917, believed that long-term success depended in large measure on their ability to inculcate a new social consciousness in the country and to create a model for future revolutionary societies abroad. From this perspective, transforming Russia would require more than the exercise of political power and a reshaping of the national economy. It also made imperative the appearance of a more enlightened citizenry. This "new Soviet man" was to understand human existence in material and scientific terms and be fully emancipated from faith in spiritual forces and the expectation of direct supernatural intercession in worldly affairs. The Soviet state accordingly became the first modern government—the anticlericalism of the French Revolution and the radical secularism of the Paris Commune and the Mexican Revolution notwithstanding—to promote the rejection of all religious deities as a sustaining national ideal.

As happened with many objectives of the Russian Revolution, officially sanctioned atheism entered an environment frequently inhospitable when not altogether hostile. We should not underestimate the importance of this during 1917–1932, when the fledgling revolutionary state was not yet the powerful dictatorship it became at the height of Stalinism. Students of the early years of Soviet rule have thoroughly documented the fragility of the regime that launched a Marxist revolution in what was still a predominantly agrarian country. They have alerted us to the continuing influence of the rivals of Bolshevism long after the revolution, the far-reaching unpopularity of the state, the manifold limitations on its actual authority, and the vulnerability of a ruling party weakened by the debilitating loss of its founding leader and by ongoing factionalism in its ranks. Throughout 1917–1932, economic shortfalls and shortages of goods eroded public confidence and patience, while mass political support proved unreliable, class antagonisms unremitting, and the sway of tradition persistent.[1]

Against such a backdrop, early Soviet atheism cannot be properly understood only in the oversimplified terms of state oppression versus church resistance that have dominated much of previous historical discussion. Both certainly played important roles, but the divergent cultural perceptions and aspirations that coexisted within Russian society, often antagonistically, make the story both more inclusive and more nuanced than the volatile yet ultimately narrow categories of oppression and resistance can accommodate.[2] For its part, the revolutionary regime made a conscious and deliberate decision to reconfigure social and cultural habits. In practice, though, the Bolsheviks frequently talked past their intended audience, and the state could not yet accomplish with force what it failed to gain through propaganda.[3] Conversely, the social rank and file—this work concentrates on followers of Russian Orthodoxy—often reacted reflexively to what they perceived not just as attacks on church officials and institutions, but as assaults on a consecrated order of earthly and heavenly affairs. This should not cause surprise. Russian Orthodoxy had been the state religion of the tsarist empire and was the leading denomination in most ethnically Russian areas of Soviet territory. But it was much more than this. Deeply embedded in Russian culture, Orthodoxy shaped rituals of hospitality and celebration, rites of passage, the ordering of daily and seasonal routines, and household organization.[4] It helped inform popular wisdom, rumor, proverbs, and folklore. And Russian Orthodoxy provided a symbol of national identity even for those who were lax about religious observance. To the majority in society, therefore, the status quo was more a preordained order than an intellectual or even a personal choice, and perpetuating familiar rhythms of life was all but instinctive.

So the history of early Soviet atheism illuminates a critical aspect of Bolshevism in practice and highlights patterns of behavior that were to resonate throughout the communist period of Russian history. In examining those phenomena, this book will, first of all, bring into sharper focus the multiple tensions that existed between the Bolsheviks' commitment to Marxist ideology and their political pragmatism. As extensive previously published documentation makes clear, the revolutionary state marshaled all available resources, including but by no means limited to coercion, in its efforts to undermine the institutional and economic bases of Russian Orthodoxy. Mass mobilization and the use of force have been the most widely publicized parts of this story, but Bolshevism proved to be something more than a single-minded monolith determined to eradicate religion as an end in itself and at all cost. Thus, although the Soviet regime certainly committed itself in principle to the elimination of all religious influences in society, in the larger schema atheism was but one of a series of interconnected social objectives being pursued in the interest of inculcating a new, materialist worldview in the country. In reality, the uncertainty of popular support limited the range of Bolshevik tactical options in seeking these goals, and political realism influenced the more moderate leaders to try to restrain the most militant antireligious activists. They experienced at best mixed success in this, but even the attempt fed the discontent of those in the ranks who already felt that the tempo of revolutionary transformation was too slow.

Second, this work will explain the variety of strategies that members of society employed to cope with new realities. Bolshevik initiatives provoked defiance and circumvention, to be sure, but they also gave rise to accommodation, compliance, obedience, apathy, resignation, the pursuit of self-interest, and outright acceptance. Scholars have rightly paid particular attention to overt resistance and its variations in society, where the motivations behind responses to Soviet atheism could be transparently simple or highly complex.[5] Thousands of Orthodox believers certainly fought Bolshevik antireligious actions out of sincere religious conviction and a legitimate sense of violation. But Soviet citizens also showed themselves capable of framing their objections to any unwanted policy in religious terms, and they became skilled at using religious rationales to perpetuate what was preferable largely because it was familiar. Resistance thus deserves emphasis, but it was only one strategy among several. No less significant were those who acquiesced in Soviet programs and still others who actively gave support. Without both, there would be no story to tell.

This book therefore gives a central place to strategies normally not emphasized in discussions of atheism versus Orthodoxy in Russia: degrees of nonmilitant religious and antireligious commitment. Although the contention between activist believers and militant atheists was strident and often violent, the deciding voice in the religious future of Soviet Russia belonged to neither. The critical mass who stood between the extremes, and whose allegiance both church and state ardently sought, ultimately did far more to shape the outcome. This majority was vastly more numerous than either Orthodox or Bolshevik activists; their variegated agendas, in combination with their collective inertia, could and did overwhelm religious and antireligious proselytizing alike.

Thus, whereas activists grounded their respective strategies in the un-compromising acceptance or rejection of belief, for the mass an attitude pro or con toward religion never became the single, overarching issue in their lives. Unlike militants of both persuasions, most citizens exten-sively integrated their feelings toward religion and atheism with other, nonspiritual concerns. This by no means suggests neutrality. Many who chose not to defend the church militantly still considered themselves fully Orthodox; Russians who harbored strong anticlerical sentiments might also revere the faith and observe its rituals; few, regardless of be-lief, failed to recognize Orthodoxy as a fundamental symbol of Russian identity; attacks on church rituals and institutions regularly stimulated a rise in religious observance; and the party made no secret of the lack of antireligious enthusiasm among a communist rank and file who other-wise accepted the general Bolshevik line. In short, the priorities of many individual citizens proved to be conditional, even situational. The issue of religion versus atheism consequently pivoted not on a choice between unwavering piety and unalloyed materialism, but on shades of religious and antireligious commitment within the full spectrum of per-sonal and collective concerns.

Viewed in this way, nonmilitant religious strategies—which encom-passed the full range of attitudes and behaviors toward collective belief short of the combative promotion and defense of either organized reli-gion or atheism—ultimately proved more important than activism in early Soviet society. During 1917–1932, these ranged from a personal but politically uninvolved atheism through a passive, nonpracticing, or even partial identification with Orthodoxy to a position of complete lack of involvement with religious and antireligious issues. These strategies accommodated the youth who professed one faith at home and another in public, the peasant who believed in and praised God but resented priests and opposed any new religious expenditures, the worker who had received religious training in childhood but passively and without visible regret became resigned to "the new way" after the revolution, the so-called protoproletarian who failed to attend church regularly or fulfill Easter obligations but clung tenaciously to the right to celebrate church holidays, the party member who observed both reli-gious and civil rites, and those who considered the conflict between re-ligion and antireligion beneath their notice.

In sum, this study of early Soviet atheism will demonstrate that—in addition to the well-documented clashes of political parties, classes, na-tionalities, and interest groups—the intensity of competing cultural per-ceptions and aspirations in Russian society played an instrumental role in shaping the aftermath of the revolution. When one gives this cultural dimension full consideration, both the experimental aspect of the Bolshevik Revolution and the bounds of tradition that inhibited its progress emerge as far more important factors in the history of Soviet Russia than we have previously appreciated. Moreover, the experience of 1917–1932 laid the foundation for behaviors that would continue to shape relations between state and society until the end of the Soviet period. Therefore, whatever one's personal view of the phenomenon Russians literally call godlessness [*bezbozhie*],[6] atheism was a historical reality of the Soviet period—a belief system that millions accepted as literal truth and with which millions more reached an accommodation. This book explores the historical roots of those circumstances.

This work attempts the elusive balance of presenting a new interpretation for professional specialists in a form accessible to nonspecialists, interested lay readers, and students. Its documentation draws extensively on the holdings of the State Archive of the Russian Federation (GARF) (formerly Central State Archive of the October Revolution and the Central State Archive of the RSFSR), the Russian Center for the Preservation and Study of Documents on Recent History (RTsKhIDNI) (formerly the Central Archive of the Communist Party), the Archive of the State Museum of the History of Religion (GMIR), the Central State Archive of the Moscow Region (TsGAMO), the Central State Archive of the City of Moscow (TsGIAgM), the Archive of the State Museum of the Political History of Russia (GMPIR), the Smolensk Archive, and the Nicolaevsky Collection of the Hoover Institution Archive; to a lesser extent, it refers to the Archive of the State Museum of the Ethnography of the Peoples of the USSR (GME).[7] It also rests on a broad range of published documents, ethnographic materials, Russian journals and newspapers, and pertinent secondary sources. This research strategy has made it possible to take full advantage of Russian archives opened since 1991 without diminishing the importance of printed sources, which also provide often unique information. And this book attempts to allow the Russians who lived through the events of 1917–1932 to speak for themselves to the degree possible.

Ultimately, neither this nor any other work of history will fully answer the question posed at the outset: Why do Russians act as they do? *"Godless Communists"* will pursue the much more modest objective of explaining the promotion of an atheistic society in early Soviet Russia. To that end, it will argue that the cultural middle ground between militant religious and antireligious positions proved far more important than the more highly publicized confrontations between state and church. By the end of the Cultural Revolution, therefore, the religious future of Soviet Russia lay not in the outcome of episodes of Bolshevik versus Orthodox animosity or of national antireligious campaigns, but in the personal negotiations and situational accommodations carried out by individual citizens during the critical communist experiment of 1917–1932.

"Godless Communists"

1 Belief and Nonbelief in Prerevolutionary Russia

"I was baptized and brought up in the Orthodox Christian faith. I was instructed in it both as a child and throughout my boyhood and youth. But when at the age of eighteen I left the university in my second year, I no longer believed in any of the things I had been taught. I did believe in something, without being able to say what it was. I believed in God, or rather I did not deny God, but what kind of God I could not have said; neither did I reject Christ or his teachings, but what I understood by the teachings again I could not have said. "
—Leo Tolstoy, *A Confession*

". . . so much Atheism, Deism, Debauchery, and all kinds of Immorality"—Eighteenth-century description of University College, Oxford, by Thomas Hearne[1]

Militant atheism is more an alternative to religion than its rejection, although neither its supporters nor its opponents in Russia have customarily presented it in this way. In the most frequently cited passage on atheism in all Russian literature, the character Kirilov in Fëdor Dostoevsky's *The Devils* equates disbelief in God with the absence of the possibility of ethics, so that for the atheist suicide becomes the highest expression of self-affirmation and will. Kirilov says, "I cannot understand how an atheist could know that there is no god and not kill himself at once!" But Dostoevsky's literary brilliance notwithstanding, his insistent presentation of religious belief and atheism as a dichotomy does not correspond with Russian historical experience. In practice, the two systems have differed dramatically in their underlying dogmas, to be sure, but both have also persistently claimed to have captured the essence of an ethical and meaningful existence. Each has presented itself as the foundation of a potentially better future for Russia, and in so doing, religion and atheism have more resembled competitors for the same post than practical antitheses.

FROM HERESY TO ATHEISM

In historical time, the conscious and permanent state of nonbelief in the supernatural—the twentieth-century understanding of atheism—is new to the European experience.[2] Atheism in this form was an intellectual impossibility in Europe before the late 1600s, according to an argument Lucien Febvre put forward more than a half century ago. The word *atheist* was in wide use in the late medieval period, but primarily to discredit an opponent who believed differently or to magnify one's outrage toward inimical ideas, not to identify persons who literally denied the existence of deities. The popularity of this insult, he maintained, cannot be taken as evidence of widespread rejection of the supernatural.[3] Febvre's case has stood up well. More recent scholars have pushed the appearance of assertive nonbelief slightly backward in time, but none has gone so far as to contend, for example, that the widespread questioning of the existence of divine spirits predated the Reformation.[4] Thus, whether one sides with Febvre or his critics, until at least the sixteenth century the guardians of faith in Europe concentrated on rooting out heresy, not atheism. The distinction is important. The persecution of religious opinion or practice at variance with accepted doctrine—in a word, heresy—has a long history within Christianity. But despite the appearance of the occasional eccentric or blasphemer, battling premodern heresy involved counteracting rival interpretations of correct worship, not the denial of supernatural control over earthly affairs. Before the Reformation, belief was so thoroughly entrenched in daily life and explanations of nature that rejection of the supernatural would have dictated a complete break with one's surroundings.[5]

The European world of the Middle Ages did not separate church from state or the natural from the religious. However one might feel about a feudal system that failed to distinguish between the worldly and ecclesiastical offices it doled out, this modern distinction would have been all but meaningless to men and women of the period. When popes and emperors clashed, each claimed supreme power in both spiritual and temporal spheres. Kings usurped important church appointments, but without clerics royal administrations could not have functioned. Holy days were holidays, the parish served as the basic administrative unit, and the church dominated education high and low.[6] In explanations of nature and human events, lack of understanding and fear, as David Hume argued in *The Natural History of Religion* (1755), caused most Europeans to attribute to supernatural forces all that they could not otherwise explain.

The universal belief in divine spirits did not translate into high levels of popular piety, though, nor did it lead to centralized church influence over community morals and religious practice. Everyone in the Pyrenees village of Montaillou, to cite one well-documented example from the fourteenth century, subscribed to supernatural explanations of existence, but they lacked even a rudimentary command of church doctrine. None of these mountain people would have denied the sacred, but they were content to leave religious zeal to the urban elite. Residents attended Mass and received the sacraments irregularly, and many defiantly flouted the rules of fasting. Beyond this, sexual permissiveness abounded despite prohibitions by the high church. In this village, the priest deflowered virgins, seduced married women, and rationalized the economic advantages of incestuous marriage without feeling any need for secrecy. As many as 10 percent of the cohabiting couples of the hamlet were unwed, which did not count against the females if they subsequently sought other husbands. Nor did the church have a monopoly on belief in Montaillou. The Cathar heresy made a strong inroad, healing routinely included recourse to magic, and villagers incorporated pagan elements into the ninety holidays they celebrated annually.[7] Montaillou was by no means exceptional in its disparity between church prescriptions and personal behavior. During the medieval period, the combination of virtually unanimous belief with ignorance of doctrine, nonobservance of church moral codes, lax participation in the sacraments, the predominance of local custom in religious ritual, and an ongoing preoccupation with magic and pagan rites were common.[8]

There were, of course, those who attempted to counterpose more stringent interpretations to these situational definitions of religiosity. As early as the year 910, Duke William I of Aquitane so deplored the prevailing level of piety that he could designate no satisfactory place for Masses to be said for his soul after death. He consequently donated land for a monastery at Cluny, which was to be independent of any feudal jurisdiction and subordinate directly to the pope. This new institution would enforce church law strictly, particularly those vows being honored largely in the breach: chastity, celibacy, and the proper selection of church officials. That example spawned additional Cluniac monasteries and far-reaching reformist imitation.

But the high church often inhibited such grassroots spirituality by opposing reformism that it could not control, and it persecuted its critics as heretics. In the fourteenth century, the Oxford theologian John Wycliffe antagonized church authorities when he tried to reconcile the deity in whom he believed with the one represented by the clerical hierarchy. He argued in *On the Church* (1378) that true faith depended on the existence of a community of believers, not the institutional structure of the church. According to Wycliffe, personal conscience and Bible study were the tools of salvation. He subsequently proposed the elimination of the Mass, the priesthood, the doctrine of transubstantiation, confession and other sacraments, penance, pilgrimages, excommunication, holy water, and prayers for intercession to the Virgin Mary and saints. Influential protectors spared Wycliffe the persecution as a heretic that befell the Lollards, as his followers became known. Yet Lollardy, which blended religious with social reformism in a movement dominated by urban artisans and parish priests, survived the fifteenth century underground and resurfaced in the sixteenth. Throughout their existence, Lollards continued to combine advocacy of changes in the church and periodic support for peasant insurrection with steady opposition to bishops and high nobility. Thus, universal belief in the existence of deities did not preclude serious contentiousness over the specifics of religion, nor did it prevent social tensions from being expressed through conflicts over interpretations of faith. Conversely, the church did not limit its repression of heretics to overt public critics and reformers. At the popular level, those who chose to reinterpret belief and practice for themselves, express opinions and perform rituals that contravened church dicta, or simply challenge religiously sanctioned authority could expect persecution. No one can document the degree to which uncertainty and questioning arose in the inner lives of individuals, of course, but all serious public alternatives to the existing church were predicated on belief in some form of deity, not outright rejection.[9] Typically, the premodern impulse in science and philosophy, to cite one example, was not to counterpose reason to faith but to try to reconcile the two,[10] a tendency still strongly in evidence centuries later.

In short, nothing in Europe began to pose a serious threat to general belief in supernatural spirits until the Reformation. On the contrary, the expectancy of a short life and, perhaps more intimidating, the harsh and uncertain fate of the living caused contemporaries to hedge their cosmological bets. People exploited every available option, and those who accepted any new faith did not discard all the instruments of the old. In daily existence, poor diet, worse sanitation, and medical care that was often ineffective when not actually harmful meant that those who survived the actuarial odds would likely live with chronic pain. These circumstances combined with unpredictable and devastating intrusions such as fire, famine, and plague to push people both toward escapism and in the direction of seeking levers of power over their lives. Those who felt overwhelmed found refuge in the drinking, gambling, and fatalism that was everywhere in evidence. But for the more resilient and self-reliant, innumerable combinations of religion and magic held out the prospect of controlling the present and the future.[11]

Religion thus offered, in addition to salvation after death, the potential for access to supernatural intervention in earthly events, the more so if combined with magic. Medical professionals in France and England therefore continued to incorporate charms and amulets into their remedies as late as the seventeenth century. Commoners sought spiritual intercession even more ardently, and they regarded their frequent extra-Christian appeals for help as roughly equivalent to prayer. This obviously blurred the line between religion and magic more than it established a demarcation between them, and the church could not clarify the issue. When it turned serious attention to the matter in the seventeenth century, it did no better than to label practices of which it disapproved "superstitious," though other, similar ones it sanctioned.[12] For the majority of people, of course, this state of affairs reinforced rather than undermined common belief in the supernatural.

Two points need to be made. First, the fact that popular religion placed accepted local practice above knowledge of doctrine and keeping the sacraments in no way meant that customary observances lacked meaning for those who performed them. Within the infinite number of possible combinations of rite and precept, it is altogether possible for a religious life that emphasizes ritual to be as rich or richer in quality for followers than one principally grounded in doctrine. This was, to be sure, not how the leading clergy viewed matters. Elite understandings of religious experience were above all textual and sacramental, and church fathers condescendingly strove to eradicate survivals of "superstition" among the masses. But the non-elite laity did not operate within this dichotomy of "true" religion versus "superstition." Although viewed by their social and intellectual superiors as mere recipients of religious messages that they were prone to subvert with the survivals of paganism and the like, lay men and women were energetic actors in their own religious lives. They blended practices and principles approved by the church with their own innovations as they independently defined new modes of observance, devised alternative understandings of belief, created holidays and religious organizations, and initiated militant actions on behalf of their faith.[13] The very practices most derided by the elite, in which the lay mass combined "true" with "superstitious" or "heretical" elements, were often those most heavily invested with meaning for believers, even though such meanings arose far more from participation than from doctrine.

Second, popular religion was eclectic but by no means random. The accent on practice over text and the retention of pre-Christian customs resulted not from benighted obstinacy but from their importance in the individual and collective experience of worshipers. That is, the laity did not create and alter religious practices gratuitously; they did so in direct relation to the changing demands of their physical, moral, and spiritual environment. Premodern European Christians thus subscribed to a hybrid of divine, magical, and pagan rites for one reason above all: it seemed to work. Popular beliefs demystified nature and made human actions more understandable. They furnished a plausible explanation of observed reality and the unknown, provided a basis for social and familial structure, helped order daily life, and represented access to supernatural assistance.

The explanation lies in the essence of culture itself. Culture consists of sets of strategies through which societies understand their collective experience, and belief systems, including religions, serve this strategic function.[14] In historical terms, it is therefore irrelevant whether the precepts that underlie any given strategy are true, false, or beyond verification. We need not debate, for example, whether the origins of the pueblo-dwelling Anasazi of the American Southwest were in the middle of the earth, as they believed, or lie in some evolutionary, creationist, migratory, or other explanation. The *historical* significance of Anasazi belief derives from the fact of its acceptance by the Anasazi and the ways they employed it to address problems and make sense of their lives.[15] To extend the point, customs and traditions can change, assume new functions in different contexts, or even be invented as required without weakening their ability to inspire loyalty. "Customary" or "traditional" practices whose origins were actually historically recent have frequently ignited tenacious adherence in Europe precisely because of their situational utility, regardless of whether the ideas behind those customs were objectively "true" or not.[16]

· · ·

In this way, the Reformation was a cultural as well as a religious turning point in Europe. As we have seen, pre-Reformation religious canons did not always govern personal, collective, or institutional behavior, even though they largely shaped the environment in which it took place. Popular religion had required that one participate in collective ritual but not necessarily profess any specific doctrine or submit to an imposed moral code. This could no longer be true after the beginning of the sixteenth century. The Reformation affected and was affected by permutations in the social, physical, economic, and moral environment. Challenges and counterchallenges among Protestants and Catholics brought unprecedented scrutiny to the precise expression of belief in every significant realm: theological, ritual, and behavioral.

Conflict initially dominated theology. Irreconcilable differences, such as those over the meaning of transubstantiation that separated Martin Luther from fellow Protestant Ulrich Zwingli and both from Catholic dogma, arose from countless points of explicit doctrinal interpretation. By the beginning of the seventeenth century, religious opponents were devoting so much intellectual energy to the propagation and defense of sectarian positions that the quality of literature and universities, particularly in Germany, experienced temporary decline. Above all, doctrinal differences provided the chief rationale for the persecutions and religious wars in which thousands of Europeans slaughtered one another in the name of their respective beliefs.

Concern over religious practice proved no less intense. The establishment of new denominations created alternative forms of worship that the Catholic Church could no longer repress, despite its protracted efforts. And where empowered, as in the theocracies of Geneva and Zurich, Protestant leaders imposed adherence to their rituals just as determinedly as the Catholic Church protected its own. But the issue transcended simple allegiance to one or another set of regularized observances. As we have seen, grassroots Catholicism depended as much on public perceptions of its utility in facilitating access to the supernatural as it did on formal sacraments and institutions. Protestants therefore undermined the ability of Catholicism to inspire awe when they attacked the appurtenances of "popery"—statuary, stained glass, organs, and ornate vestments—and debunked phenomena like miracles, processions, and the blessing of crops.[17] The well-publicized case of Sister Benedetta Carlini of Pescia in the seventeenth century illustrates how acutely sensitive to its vulnerability the Catholic Church became. When this abbess of the Convent of the Mother of God claimed to have experienced stigmata and direct contacts with Christ, local church officials—perhaps not immune to the advantages of discovering a miracle in their midst—conducted a careful investigation that nevertheless ended in her reinstatement. That did not satisfy Rome. A second and more skeptical team of papal investigators feared a hoax Protestants could exploit, and their tenacity ultimately uncovered Carlini's fabrication.[18]

Yet even this high level of attention to doctrine and practice would not have achieved the same cultural impact had the Reformation not also increased church intervention in the rhythms of daily life. In the battle for the allegiance of the laity, all sides put forward new understandings of faith that included a much stronger emphasis on obedience to church moral codes. And though it can be argued that this created a new consensus on *ideal* behavior as much as it altered actual conduct, it nevertheless served to link personal comportment more directly with perceptions of religiosity in the public consciousness. In enforcing this new morality, the church became a far more regularized presence in both Protestant and Catholic areas.[19] This process was neither rapid nor total, and it failed to eradicate fully pre-Christian survivals and belief in the occult, which exist to this day.[20] But qualifications and disclaimers aside, the evidence is incontrovertible that an ethos of chastity, sobriety, thrift, and responsibility began to compete successfully with preexisting norms and that organized religion assumed a far larger role in day-to-day ministration.

The theological, ritual, and behavioral innovations of the Reformation thus changed not only *what* people believed, but *how* they thought about belief itself, and the ramifications were felt far beyond worship and morality in their narrow sense. In one attempt at comprehensive explanation, Max Weber argued in *The Protestant Ethic and the Spirit of Capitalism* that new values preceded and shaped the Reformation and in due course induced the cultural changes that drove the development of capitalism.[21] Karl Marx, Friedrich Engels, and their popularizers took the opposite view: that an emerging class of capitalists institutionalized their shared ideals in a religion that helped sustain them in power in a newly transformed society.[22] Either way, the Reformation encompassed a new consensus on acceptable behavior and values in Europe after 1500, and once in motion it induced changes in the personal sphere as well: individual public and private conduct, but also the hierarchy of family relationships, conceptions of privacy, and definitions of private and public space.[23]

Where the public and the private intersected, the Reformation also led to greater tolerance. The militant Protestantism of the sixteenth century, which vented activist reformism and resentment that had long been building, matured into a more forbearing form by the eighteenth, when freedom of conscience began to displace a penchant for persecution on sectarian grounds alone. In 1554, Sebastian Castellio had written to John Calvin:

There is almost no sect that does not regard others as heretics; with the result that, if you are thought to be right in one city or region, in the next you will be thought a heretic. So much so that if anyone today wants to live, he must have as many religions as there are cities or sects—just as anyone travelling from one country to another has to change his money from day to day, because what is valid here becomes valueless elsewhere.

Two centuries later, these words no longer described Europe accurately. A recognition of the futility of perpetual religious warfare, the effects of the Catholic Counter-Reformation, and changes in Protestantism itself all led to a coexistence of religions and the replacement of truculent sectarianism with the possibility of open debate over Scripture and dogma.[24]

Such tolerance had limits. Major denominations may have coexisted, but they also continued to countenance each other's persecution of common enemies and minority sects. Furthermore, they displayed little willingness to endure in their midst idiosyncratic formulations of faith or the expression of religious doubt. Carlo Ginzburg's widely read *The Cheese and the Worms* describes how one Menocchio ran seriously afoul of the Inquisition in 1584 for "heretical and most impious" utterances. Arguing energetically but not systematically, this miller from Friuli blended oral traditions and his own deductions with avid but irregular reading, from which he took ideas he frequently misunderstood or distorted. But his conclusions and even the way he reached them are less important for our purposes than Menocchio's considerable confidence in his right to cast public doubt on the divinity of Christ, the virginity of Mary, the usefulness of the sacraments, the sanctity of Scripture, the selflessness of the clergy, and the independence of religious institutions from the interests of the wealthy and powerful.[25] For exhibiting a similar confidence, the nobleman Geoffrey Valée lost his life in Orléans in 1574 for interpreting the Bible and other religious books in a way that repudiated belief in any deity and religion that inculcated fear. And testimony in the controversial case against the student Thomas Aikenhead in Edinburgh in 1697 included his unabashed reference to the New Testament as "'the History of the Imposter Christ'" and his rejection of the Trinity as "'not worth any man's refutation.'" Menocchio thus represented a kind of nonlearned but assertive skepticism facilitated by the Reformation and the spread of literacy. And although Valée and Aikenhead leveled charges against faith that were, by comparison, more articulate, cogent, and internally consistent, their confidence and skepticism had roots identical to Menocchio's.[26]

These individual cases are examples of a broader phenomenon: by encouraging individuals to confront the sacred directly and personally, and by allowing the rank and file to refute the beliefs of others, the Reformation—apart from any reformer's intentions—created an atmosphere in which learned and nonlearned religious doubt could grow.[27] The very elements Protestants used to challenge Catholicism—the ultimate authority of the written word, the direct relationship between each believer and God, justification through faith, a universal priesthood—helped instill in skeptics the confidence to interpret religious matters for themselves. Innovations in the Catholic camp, most notably the *Spiritual Exercises* of Ignatius of Loyola that spurred militant Jesuits, performed a similar function in a different way. Thus, when religious doubts arose, they came not from outside religion but from within, driven strongly by the new reformist influences that dramatically affected both elite and popular conceptions of belief.

No one with strong religious views, therefore, could grow complacent in post-Reformation Europe, and concern about atheism actually preceded its systematic articulation. Certainly not every expression of doubt or dissatisfaction after the sixteenth century constituted a fully conscious and determined repudiation of the supernatural. Contemporaries, as we have already noted, used the term *atheist* with an imprecision that placed personal eccentricity and indifference to collective rites under the same rubric as the actual rejection of revealed religion or the denial of the existence of God.[28] Some varieties of skepticism appeared even before vocabulary could accommodate them, as illustrated by the example of agnosticism, which exercised influence long before Thomas Henry Huxley coined the term in 1869.[29] But this was no mere exercise in semantics. The growing awareness of the possibility of religious doubt by any name caused guardians of faith to find "atheists" everywhere.[30] And although they may have expressed their fears in ways that in retrospect appear exaggerated and alarmist, their anxiety made sense in the context of the time. The issue then was not a philosophical abstraction but a previously unthinkable challenge to the cardinal ideas that underlay their way of life. And the articulate, learned skepticism that has received broad attention from historians of ideas shared the stage with nonlearned variations, which were manifested in ways we can only begin to document.[31]

What happened thereafter touches on much of Western life since the seventeenth century. In terms of the topic of atheism, conscious religious nonbelief took root as an intellectual and personal option in the European world between the seventeenth and the nineteenth centuries. More generally, the careers of David Hume, Thomas Hobbes, Paul Holbach, Paolo Sarpi, Pierre Bayle, and others recast religious and antireligious ideas in new combinations, and the Enlightenment raised further questions about the religious worldview. In conjunction with concomitant changes in popular religious practice, the Reformation and the Enlightenment were therefore instrumental in shaping the complexly entwined processes that we know by the disarmingly simple names of industrialization, secularization, urbanization, the development of new attitudes toward nature, and a modern conception of science and technology.[32] At present, many historians rightly eschew interpretations that see these processes as clean breaks in European history and instead stress the continuities with earlier periods within them. They reemphasize the religious component in the more secularized world after the seventeenth century; devote far greater energy to discerning popular religious practice in society, as opposed to accepting the versions of church officials; and present economic and social factors in a way that has brought new insight to the religious dimension of topics such as witch hunts.[33]

The possibility of religious doubt and nonbelief therefore began to enter the intellectual milieu in Europe during and after the Reformation, but only as one alternative among many. If a myriad of views predicated on belief in the supernatural predominated before 1500, the variety of belief was no less diverse thereafter, even though the range of possibilities was different. The festivals of the French Revolution suggest this new reality. The signals sent by the highly orchestrated Festival of the Supreme Being in the Year II, for example, were not only mixed but intensely so. The occasion lionized neither religiosity nor atheism; it denounced priests for "superstition" while taking pains to exalt the existence of God in terms of arguments from final causes. The burning of Atheism, or of a symbolic atheist, was included, although its role in the proceedings progressively diminished over time. Beyond this, symbols and rites of religiosity did not disappear throughout France despite a revolutionary ban on "external manifestations of worship." They continued to coexist with official efforts to displace religion in favor of a more rationalist worldview.[34]

To recapitulate briefly, the prerequisites for the conscious nonbelief in the supernatural that we know as atheism are historically grounded in the Reformation. Universal spiritual belief was so deeply ingrained in Europe before the sixteenth century that religious skepticism took the form of alternative interpretations of the supernatural, not its disavowal. This began to change as a result of the Reformation, which altered the content and approach to belief for many Europeans. It also enabled religious institutions to assume an unprecedented role in daily ministration, which produced more direct connections between religious precepts and personal behavior. These developments, as historians have rightly noted, were linked to political and socioeconomic processes writ large, such as industrialization, as well as to elements within the personal sphere, such as the development of a concept of privacy. Society could not accommodate all the far-reaching consequences of changes in religion and in the physical, moral, and spiritual environment. On the one hand, the European world about to experience the advent of modern science and technology strove to reconcile its religious faith with the new knowledge of the material world. But on the other hand, it proved less willing to retain other established ideas, such as the religious sanctioning of governments. This was the atmosphere in which thinkers began to raise serious doubt about the religious enterprise as a whole. The processes that had encouraged individual interpretation of Scripture also helped atheism find its voice.

HOLY RUS' AND THE SUPERNATURAL

Separated from Western Christianity by inclination as well as circumstances, Russia encountered atheism from its own direction. Even though Russian religious life mirrored Europe in important aspects (the distinction between official and popular practice is the most obvious), its Eastern Orthodox faith also set it apart. Confessional differences periodically contributed to tensions between Russia and her Western neighbors, but they also saved her from direct involvement in a number of European conflicts, most notably the Reformation itself. And even when influences and innovations did reach Russia via Europe, they were not adopted indiscriminately but were molded to the requirements of Russian experience.

According to a legend recorded long after the fact, the conversion of Russia to Christianity took place quite simply. Emissaries of Prince Vladimir of Kiev summarily rejected Judaism, Islam, and Catholicism in the tenth century but gave a more positive report of their encounter with Eastern Christianity in Constantinople: "'We knew not whether we were in heaven or on earth. For on earth there is no such splendor or such beauty. We know only that God dwells there among men, and their service is fairer than the ceremonies of other nations.'" This splendor, in combination with the politically and militarily advantageous marriage his conversion made possible, influenced Vladimir to remove his pagan gods and order the baptism of the residents of Kiev on a single day in 988. In the words of the Primary Chronicle: "There was joy in heaven and upon earth to behold so many souls saved."[35]

Nonetheless, the conversion of Russia was in actuality not an event but a process. At the time of its religious condominium with Byzantium, the civilization of the Rus' was no tabula rasa. Ancient Slavic tribes had worshiped a pagan pantheon that included deities of the wind, war, wealth, cattle, and even the netherworld. Women once fought beside men in battle, although later the same tribes practiced polygamy and conducted raiding parties to obtain brides.[36] The Kievan Rus' acquired a second pagan pantheon when Varangians from Scandinavia conquered them in the ninth century. And during the eight years of rule that preceded his conversion, the decidedly anti-Christian Vladimir recruited other princes to help him defend both sets of idols from outside assaults. Moreover, certain Christian influences predated the reign of Vladimir. Inconclusive evidence suggests the possibility of a Byzantine Christian diocese in Russia as early as the second half of the ninth century. More concretely, Princess Olga accepted Christianity during her regency for a minor son (945–962), although this personal conversion did not affect the paganism of her subjects.[37] The "baptism of Russia" for which the church ultimately canonized Vladimir therefore did not immediately displace preexisting beliefs as much as it gave significant new impetus to a protracted process of syncretism, not unlike that which existed in the West.

During the centuries that immediately followed the conversion, the Orthodox Church achieved only mixed success in establishing itself in the dominion of the Kievan princes and in its dealings with church hierarchs in Byzantium. Greeks initially acted as church officials and clergy; no Russian reached the rank of Metropolitan until the thirteenth century. Similarly, the artists, architects, and scholars who drove the innovations in high culture that Christianity set in motion came from Byzantium. When Russian bishops were appointed, they too looked to Constantinople for direction. Yet as the administrators of the religion of the realm, church leaders also enjoyed position and influence in Kiev. They occupied a status equal to the military retainers of the prince, presided over ecclesiastical courts, and were heirs to the rich monastic traditions of Byzantium. Moreover, as miracle cults began to be established and Russian martyrs and holy men were canonized, the new religion began to enlarge its place in the popular consciousness.

The chief problem during the Kievan period lay in penetrating the lower classes in rural areas. The general population did not readily discard their pagan idols, customs, symbols, and reliance on shamans after 988. Pre-Christian precepts continued to inform the character of family and social life, and Christian marriage in particular made only slow progress against pagan nuptial festivals and the practice of keeping more than one wife. A preoccupation with the virginity of females at the time of marriage, which had not been a pagan concern, grew only slowly, whereas the use of sympathetic magic—throwing hops on the bride to ensure happiness, keeping sheaves of grain to enhance fertility, presenting a straw rug for easy childbirth—long outlasted the literal beliefs from which it had sprung. As was the case in Europe at the time, the laity continued to turn to pagan priests and charms in times of illness and distress, and the population preferred rites like cremation to the Christian practice of burial.[38]

In promoting its cause, the Kievan church possessed an important asset in the right to dispense justice. Ecclesiastical courts, whose jurisdiction extended to everyone, provided a source of revenue by collecting judicial fees and fines that went to the bishops. The courts also worked to eradicate witches, sorcerers, magicians, and pagan priests, and they tried to impose conformity with Christian norms of behavior. The advent of written law in the eleventh century furthered all these aims. Early codes formalized long-standing custom, articulated shared values, and explained the mechanisms for enforcement. But most significant for the spread of Christianity, laws began to codify the ideals that state and church leaders wished to encourage.

Eleventh-century codes thus combined previous custom with new behavioral models. Kievan society was neither highly institutionalized nor litigious in a modern sense, and recourse to legal redress came only after all direct avenues had been exhausted. In such an environment, it is understandable that the initial *Russkaia Pravda* focused above all on vengeance, personal retribution, theft, property, and commerce. Clerical influences then played a larger role in shaping the expanded Statute of Grand Prince Iaroslav, which moved purposefully into the area of comportment later in the century. The enlarged code outlined explicit penalties for abduction, individual and group rape, abandonment of wives, bigamy, fornication, adultery, incest, and bestiality. The statute prohibited marriage within specified levels of kinship, spelled out insults to honor, and listed the causes for which a man could divorce his wife. It forbade consuming meats considered pagan food, fined husbands for not separating from wives who were witches or makers of potions, barred the faithful from eating or drinking with the unbaptized or foreigners, and punished intercourse with a Muslim or Jewish woman by excommunication. It also admonished priests, monks, and nuns not to get drunk at "an inappropriate time."[39]

Ironically, this church so closely tied to the ruling dynasty actually benefited from the conquest of Kiev by the Mongols in 1240. First, the subjugation of the Rus' to the Golden Horde, the Mongol empire, gave Russian Orthodoxy greater independence from Byzantium. It received its first Patriarch during the Mongol occupation and experienced the Russification of the clergy. Second, the fact that the Mongols concerned themselves with exploiting the resources of the Rus' and exhibited little interest in controlling their subjects' religion helped create a relationship advantageous to the church. Like the Russian princes, church leaders negotiated directly at the court of the Golden Horde, where they won special concessions. By praying for the khan, the church lent legitimacy to his regime, in return for which it enjoyed exemptions from certain taxes and military conscription as well as wide latitude in controlling its own operation. Third, during the occupation the church hierarchs also aligned themselves with the emerging princes of Moscow. They therefore benefited when Moscow replaced Kiev as the preeminent Russian settlement after the overthrow of the Mongols in 1480. From the time when Prince Ivan I persuaded the head of the church to relocate in Moscow in the 1320s, Orthodoxy and the state established a symbiotic relationship, whether in sharing the reflected glory of the construction of new cathedrals or from the territorial and political aggrandizement of the dynasty. Finally, although the Mongol conquest had destroyed many churches, the slow establishment of parishes continued, so that Orthodoxy became a fully national institution in the fourteenth century.

But Russian Orthodoxy was more than an institution; it was also a belief system that found profound ways to express its spirituality. During the Mongol period, those who began to eschew the existing urban monasteries in favor of a life of asceticism spurred an increase in the number of rural cloisters in the sparsely populated north. The example of renowned holy men like Saint Sergei of Radonezh drew monks together in communal monasteries, while others continued their quest individually. In either variation, monks who were "dead to the world" sought an "inner calm" and mystical experiences through modes of prayer and contemplation that kept Russian monasticism essentially the pursuit of a personal union with the divine.[40] Beyond this, veneration of the holy received new momentum from the emergence of an identifiable Russian school of iconography in the thirteenth century, which centered itself in Moscow by the fourteenth. Under the influence of masters such as Andrei Rublëv, a style more economical and more geometrically symmetrical, and with faces less aristocratic than the Byzantine, began to dominate the tiers of icons that decorated Russian churches. The written word was also an instrument for the glorification of God. Hagiography, which predated the Mongol period, continued to provide the faithful with striking examples of the ideal, self-effacing life, while statements of divine pleasure and displeasure dominated reports of actual events as well as legends.[41]

. . .

Thus, from the beginning of the rise of Moscow in the fourteenth century until the reign of Peter the Great in the eighteenth, Orthodoxy touched virtually every area of Russian life. In high politics, it underlay the doctrine of "Moscow, the Third Rome," which has received wide attention from historians. This doctrine interpreted the sacking of Constantinople by Muslim Turks in 1453 as a divine punishment for the sins of the city. Rome had come first, Constantinople was a "second Rome," and now Moscow was the third; according to the doctrine, there would be no fourth. In global terms—Muscovy in the early sixteenth century encompassed forty thousand square miles—the claim was nothing short of preposterous. The doctrine itself appeared only as a secondary theme in a small number of ecclesiastical texts where it expressed an appeal for tsarist justice, not a comprehensive civic ideology.[42] Yet in an era when a succession of church hierarchs inhabited the inner circle of the ruler, it cannot be insignificant that this appeal was couched in terms that not only legitimated the highest ambitions of Moscow's elite but also infused them with a messianic sense of purpose.

The tenets of Orthodoxy also shaped the social environment. This statement requires qualification, since it would be ludicrous to attribute the perpetuation of the social stratification, the patriarchy, and the privileges that dated from Russian prehistory solely to the influence of the Russian Orthodox Church. Moreover, not all scholars agree that the origins of particular Muscovite practices, notably the sequestering of elite females in their homes during the sixteenth and seventeenth centuries, were Christian.[43] In these circumstances, the social utility of religious canon in Muscovy lay not in its universality but in the ways it was invoked to sanction specific continuities and changes. Patriarchal Moscow

did not strive for the legal or personal equality of its inhabitants; it ide-
alized hierarchy and the harmonious complementarity of social roles. In
this system, one derived status both from class membership and from
place within class, the latter determined largely by one's sex, wealth,
and family reputation. Status thus conferred privilege on some but responsibility on all. Order would prevail only if superordinates and sub-
ordinates carried out fully the obligations of their respective positions.

Orthodoxy became a key rationale for this schema. The *Domostroi,* a
sixteenth-century manual addressed to the elite but clearly a prescrip-
tion for all of society, made extensive yet selective use of religious precepts and passages from the Bible. A compendium of practical wisdom,
the *Domostroi* invoked religion only lightly in the space it devoted to
mundane matters: food preservation, garment making, the purchase of
foreign goods, vocational education of offspring, and even wedding
protocol. Its mandates on household and community conduct were another matter. From its opening line, the *Domostroi* required religious
belief and obedience to authority. Power and responsibility extended
from God through the tsar and the clergy to the head of the household,
his wife, the children, and the servants. The family patriarch received
subservience from spouse and underlings, in return for which he answered for their protection and moral education. Through example he
also instructed society at large. His dealings with clerks and traders and
the public deportment of his servants were to illustrate correct behavior
in matters ranging from business practices to the need to shun sorcery,
magic, and gossip. Subordinate to her husband, the mistress provided
the practical supervision of the household and a model of morality, and
she meted out correction to servants as deserved. Children and servants
owed service, obedience, and the responsibility to preserve the honor of
the family in their dealings with outsiders. Substantiated by Scripture
and supported by the authority of religion—it is probable that clergy
wrote all or most of the *Domostroi*—this sense of hierarchy extended
even to the order of food to be consumed at feasts and the ways punishments were administered.[44]

Although Moscow realized in practice only part of the ideals in the
Domostroi, and the work itself reached only a fraction of its intended
audience, religion loomed large. Days were counted by the ecclesiastical calendar, and each was named for a saint. Depending on the year,
fast days numbered around two hundred; religious processions were
frequent. Church officials had a featured place in civil processions, and
their participation in legislation recognized no boundary between the

spiritual and temporal realms. The pealing of church bells punctuated the routine of the city, and residents used religious services (matins and vespers, for example) as a reference for the time of the day. Given the Orthodox belief that philanthropy was not only beneficial to the soul but also essential for salvation, beggars were ubiquitous in Red Square and near the homes of the wealthy. In general, everyone observed the numerous holidays, during which the use of demonic masks, music, games, and other enjoyments withstood condemnation by the church. Christmas was an extended period of street festivals that included minstrels and fortune telling. The population celebrated Easter with a solemn procession to the graves of ancestors; after that all including clergy jubilantly ate and drank to excess.[45]

Understandings of gender were also derived from Orthodoxy. Beyond the requirements of female obedience to fathers and husbands, the intent of additional strictures—such as the law that husbands must punish rather than forgive adulterous wives—cannot be mistaken. The education of every elite male included *The Parable of Feminine Evil,* written by the revered churchman John Chrysostom, and *The Wisdom of Solomon.* Both characterized women as unintelligent but evil and cunning.[46] On a less blatant level, even church-sanctioned safeguards of female honor served as mechanisms of subordination. The very protections that enabled women from a variety of social backgrounds to respond actively to verbal and physical abuse derived from the demands of the patriarchal system and concerns for family and male honor. This was true of the civil laws against spoken insults, removing the head covering of a woman, or pulling her braids, but it also applied to cases of rape, usually adjudicated by ecclesiastical courts. There punishments took into account not only the severity of the attack and local custom, but also the marital status of the victim and her moral reputation.[47]

But although Orthodox society gave men the positions of dominance, its rigid expectations also significantly limited their personal options. Modern sensibilities predispose us to emphasize the repressive aspects of male behavior at all levels of Muscovite society, but we would be historically remiss if we did not also take into account the degree to which such conduct was prescriptive. The point is not to legitimate the behavior of Muscovite men, who as a group did not resist this state of affairs, but to note that society denied them any possibility of renegotiating their obligations. However abhorrent by our own standards, failure to administer discipline, for example, could have had no result other than loss of honor and respect.[48] Nor was personal experience likely to soften such attitudes, since Orthodox society allowed few opportunities for routine contact between the sexes outside the family. Males consequently spent much of their time in the company of other men, where one important measure of their standing among peers was proficiency at drinking and fighting. Adults instructed youths and boys in the art of ritual fighting that took place between villages on Christian holidays, when special intoxicants were prepared and the number of violent acts increased. Not surprisingly, foreign visitors commented on alcohol consumption and fisticuffs that exceeded the levels to which they were accustomed at home. And although we must consider the possibility that European travelers disingenuously exaggerated the level of their outrage, the Russian Orthodox Church Council of 1551 also bemoaned alcohol and its links to "devilish games" and patronizing prostitutes, and it admitted to significant drunkenness in monasteries. A century later, church officials continued to struggle with the same issues: they still railed against the extent of drinking among monks and parish clergy. The church, of course, neither introduced nor encouraged alcohol consumption and fighting in Russia. And, the comments of church hierarchs notwithstanding, the perpetually drunken priest was as much a cultural stereotype as a universal norm. Nevertheless, in the Muscovite period, the church lacked the combination of moral standing and institutional power to combat alcohol and violence effectively, and its holidays gave occasion to the boastfulness and disdain for those who abstained from the rough masculine rites that the dominant, religiously grounded culture promoted.[49]

Popular religion similarly reflected a number of diverse influences, employing various combinations of Christian and pagan elements to make the world more comprehensible. Russian Christians of all classes viewed their environment as inhabited by a combination of benign and evil supernatural forces, who regularly intervened in human affairs and with whom daily negotiation was mandatory. A preoccupation with this *dvoeverie,* a dual faith that mixed Christianity with paganism, has long dominated discussions of popular religion in Russia. The term dates from the medieval period and has fed a belief adopted by modern scholars from nineteenth-century Russian ethnographers: that the world of the Russian peasant changed little between the fifteenth and the nineteenth centuries.[50] More recent studies have rightly called this into question, both because the definition of *dvoeverie* relies on a modern perception of spirituality[51] and because the assumptions of social continuity on which it rests lack evidential substantiation.[52] For our purposes, the concept is descriptive rather than analytical. Given the definition of belief systems employed here—that they are among the cultural strategies every society uses to explain and understand its collective experience[53]—it is not the existence of syncretism in Russia that is illuminating but the variety of situational combinations Russians employed to make sense of their universe. Those who identified themselves as Orthodox—clergy and laity alike—were therefore capable of manifold combinations of "true" attitudes and beliefs within one faith.[54]

As in Western Europe, no single set of beliefs prevailed in a Russian world inclined to see direct supernatural agency in earthly events. Orthodoxy had to compete with belief in good and evil spirits, witchcraft, sorcery, and magic. Its promotion of Christian marriage serves as an illustration. The Muscovite church placed a high priority on increasing the number of sacralized unions, but it ran the risk of alienating the population when it attacked pagan customs. Moreover, Orthodox ceremonies often lacked the vitality to supplant pre-Christian attachments and enjoyments. The church had no choice but to tolerate what it could not eradicate. Consequently, Russians in the fifteenth and sixteenth centuries continued to observe previous celebratory rites of betrothal, for example, even though the marriage contract now became binding only with a second, church ceremony. And the same women who carried out examinations to ensure the virginity of the bride continued the practice of giving the groom the water from her prenuptial bath to drink in order to guarantee the husband's love.[55]

Orthodoxy, in short, did not project a single point of view. There was certainly no resolution to the contradictory position of the church on sexuality: all carnal activities were evil, but procreation was imperative. In practice, church law levied fines on parents for not marrying their offspring in a timely fashion,[56] yet Christianity also placed an unprecedented limitation on the number of spouses a woman could have in her lifetime. The church mandated parenthood, but the absence of Orthodox birthing traditions allowed pagan rituals to predominate by default. Women still turned to charms, amulets, and potions during a difficult birth, even though they likely believed they were actually following Christian procedures. The placenta might be buried beneath the house, according to pre-Christian custom; as an alternative, the mother or even the priest might place it on the altar in order to enhance the fertility of other women; other traditional wisdom held that eating the afterbirth would either cause a woman to conceive or prevent it. A belief in the impurity of females, which exceeded even Judeo-Christian norms, further influenced Russian Orthodox thinking on childbirth. Canon law required a ritual purification before the community could come into contact with either the mother or the place of birth. For forty days no one could eat in the mother's presence; during that time she could not enter the church; nor was postpartum sex allowed.[57]

In addition to these influences from outside the faith, Orthodoxy faced heresies from within. In this regard, surviving records surely reflect only a fraction of the clergy and laity who challenged received religion with ideas they formulated themselves. In 1311, for example, a church council denounced as a heretic a Novgorod priest who criticized monasticism. Later in the fourteenth century, the vigor of the repression of the *strigolniki,* who challenged the validity of the church and its sacraments, led to their eradication. A similar fate befell the Judaizers, who embraced the Old Testament and consequently rejected the church. The Nonpossessors also lost a battle over the correct definition of the monastic spirit. They maintained that ruralization had not led to institutionalized asceticism as intended, but that monasteries had instead acquired significant wealth that they should now divest. During the tenure of Patriarch Nikon in the second half of the seventeenth century, the rejection of the reform of ritual and support for more independence of parishes resulted in the permanent alienation of the Old Believer sect.[58]

The point is not that heresy existed, which is itself unexceptional, but the considerable extent of the latitude Orthodox believers felt they had to define the rudiments of worship on their own. Forms of observance inevitably varied. Furthermore, the persistent propensity to ground spiritual life far more strongly in symbols and rituals than in texts, and to derive religious meaning principally from popular practice, was not confined to any one class or stratum. As an analysis of supplicatory prayers in Muscovite Russia concludes:

> Elements of high culture filtered down even to peasants in isolated localities; members of the elite, including the highest clergy, participated in rituals of popular origin. Boyars consulted folk healers, with their herbs and incantations; peasants reported incidents of sorcery to the authorities. Lay people had no doubt of their Christian identity, but their level of knowledge varied. Some prayers reflected considerable knowledge of Scripture and ecclesiastical literature; others reflected barely a passing acquaintance with a handful of stories and figures. But lay people felt comfortable enough with their Christianity to invent their own prayers and to coin meaningful similes and images. Their prayers intermixed elements from Christian sources and pagan mythologies; they also reflected a basically magical conception of supernatural power.[59]

This applied both to the main church and to derivative sects. The Old Believers, for example, drew members from all social levels and produced, even within their single group, diverse combinations of popularly generated beliefs.[60]

. . .

The pressures on the church multiplied when the state started to impinge seriously on ecclesiastical influence at the beginning of the eighteenth century. Tsar Peter the Great, who considered the clergy parasites and wastrels, inevitably collided with the church as he attempted to modernize Russia. His drunken parodies of Orthodox ceremonies and attacks on religious symbols gave rise to charges that he was the Antichrist, but it was Peter's Spiritual Regulation of 1721 that had the greatest institutional impact. The Regulation replaced the Patriarchate with the Holy Synod, a committee of twelve under a lay Ober-Procurator. The Synod thus became the supreme ecclesiastical organ in Russia, but its establishment fell short of turning the church into a subservient government agency. Rather, in the eighteenth and nineteenth centuries the fortunes of Orthodoxy rose and fell with the talent, agendas, and determination of individual Procurators and Synod members, and because of the character of the church at its intermediate and lower levels. This new arrangement removed religious leaders from direct involvement in many secular functions of the tsarist system, but it by no means neutralized the authority or resilience of the church.[61]

Although deprived of some of its institutional sway, Orthodoxy was able to protect many existing prerogatives and develop new strengths. It remained supreme in the spiritual affairs of the country and did not lose its legal right to state subsidies until 1918. The church contended competently with secular influences in a variety of spheres: education turned out to be a prime example. In addition, at the upper levels of church-state relations a new episcopal elite began to supplement the theological mission of the church with expanded involvement in social issues, and by the end of the nineteenth century a broad range of new attitudes also appeared in the ranks of the faithful. Thus the membership of religious reformers and conservatives, church centralizers as well as proponents of greater parish autonomy, critics and apologists for the tsarist status quo, and political sympathizers of virtually every persuasion made the church that faced the revolution of 1917 spiritually and intellectually diverse.[62]

Yet, during the final two centuries of tsarism, such diversity also bespoke the existence of serious cleavages. Differences over the structure and character of the clergy, for example, gave rise to an emotional public dispute. Divided from the outset into a "black" monastic branch and "white" married parish priests, Orthodox clerics crystallized into a closed caste in the eighteenth and nineteenth centuries. This provided continuity but not solidarity. Differences of education, economic means, and career patterns galvanized the subgroups. Indigent parish priests, who received no salary and survived from receiving emoluments and working a plot of land, became more vocal in their resentment of the way they were treated by the more professional and intellectual black episcopate. White clergy strained to meet the annual and special payments owed to bishops and had to sacrifice greatly to educate their sons at a seminary. But completing a seminary program did not guarantee a church position, because by the mid–nineteenth century, seminary graduates considerably outnumbered the available parishes. Financially vulnerable and therefore dependent on the goodwill of his flock—complaints from parishioners to church officials could result in his removal—the priest could not easily fulfill the role of spiritual leader in the community. Individual circumstances and performance certainly varied, but the priest commonly received little respect, and morale suffered.[63]

Analogous divisions existed between official and popular perceptions of religiosity. When the Synod launched broad attempts to bring popular piety and observance more into line with elite understandings of religious awareness in the eighteenth century, it reflexively concentrated first on state servitors and town dwellers and only later turned its attention to the rural parishes.[64] Lack of respect toward the village also surfaced when church hierarchs attempted once again to control social behavior by regulating marriage. Canon law notwithstanding, before the middle of the eighteenth century the laity and the parish clergy had exploited the institutional weakness of the church to create and dissolve marital unions freely. Between the middle of the eighteenth century and the middle of the nineteenth century, though, religious institutions became strong enough to prevent such light treatment of matrimony. At a time when the state was usurping marital authority elsewhere, church influence made Russian divorce requirements among the most restrictive in Europe.[65] Beyond this, there were also indirect expressions of the tension between the concerns of the elite and parish religiosity, which the example of the founding and the fate of women's religious communities illustrates well. Groups of rural women, with the support of village culture, responded to Catherine the Great's closure of numerous monasteries and convents in the late eighteenth century by establishing

their own self-sufficient religious communes. Opposed to such independence, within a half century the state placed the women's communities
under the authority of the Holy Synod.[66]

None of these frictions and concerns sprang from a perceived lack of
piety. Church leaders did not question the faith and reverence of the
rank and file, but rather their knowledge and understanding of religious
principles. As the twentieth century approached, peasant belief continued to reside far more in symbols and rituals that did not depend on
theology or even clergy, whose perpetual need for emoluments fostered
a kind of elemental anticlericalism. Consequently, despite conspicuous
signs of change—greater church influence over personal behavior, a
better-educated rural priesthood, and a growing preference for professional rather than magical healers among younger and more literate
peasants—most educated Russians could not see past the belief in evil
spirits, sorcerers, and other survivals of paganism when they looked to
the village.[67]

But it would be a mistake to reduce all the salient issues to simple
dichotomies of official and popular religion or, in the civil sphere, theism versus secularism. Although church leaders publicly proceeded as
if elite and popular religion were opposites, textual and practical religion continuously affected one another at all social and educational levels. Church and state tacitly admitted this reality through actions if not
in words. With regard to education and literacy, for example, the same
state that championed the benefits of secular learning in the nineteenth
century clung to the belief that an Orthodox peasantry would be politically quiescent. It therefore required all schools to incorporate religious
instruction even as it expanded the place of nonreligious subjects in the
curriculum. And for its part, the church matched and even exceeded the
state in its sympathies for repressing dissent. Nevertheless, not all
clergy were opponents of science: many welcomed the wide publication of a kind of secular fiction that could be used to fight superstition
and paganism. In this atmosphere, the Holy Synod was able to hold its
own in jurisdictional conflicts against the Ministry of Education and
other agencies at the national level, and every local school board included a representative of the Russian Orthodox Church. Furthermore,
priests entered secular schools formally as religious instructors and informally as supervisors of the lesson content, personal comportment,
and politics of lay instructors. But for all the humiliation, harassment,
and aggravation this caused teachers, such extensive policing was not
necessary. There is little to suggest that the majority of primary school
teachers—offspring of clergy comprised a significant proportion even

after the 1917 revolution—or those who instructed adults harbored determined antireligious sentiments or tried to undermine the faith of their students.[68] On the contrary, after the revolution the experienced teachers turned out to be one of the most significant obstacles to the introduction of a nonreligious Soviet curriculum.

The strength of the church was not as tensile in the realm of public reading, but even there the functions of secular and religious influences overlapped. The appearance of commercial presses in the mid–eighteenth century broke the monopoly previously enjoyed by state and church printing houses, which overwhelmingly published religious titles. In the short term, religious tracts continued to account for half the titles, and by the beginning of the nineteenth century the number of religious publications actually increased, even though the growing popularity of romance and adventure stories reduced their share of the market to two-fifths of the total. The church did not suffer an unmitigated defeat in this sphere even when public preferences turned still more sharply to stories of detectives, bandits, chivalry, morality, and folklore in the second half of the nineteenth century. As already noted, some of these tales provided a counterpoint to superstition, while others carried in secular form the same didactic messages communicated by religious tracts. Moreover, after 1855 the church launched its own proliferation of diocesan gazettes and religious magazines, and itinerant merchants continued to stock lives of the saints and other religious stories.[69]

RUSSIA AND ATHEISM

Whether Russia would be receptive to atheism, however, would depend less on the public face of its religious world than on the influences that most directly affected the experiences of individuals. From the religious perspective, atheism is a rationalist and materialist heresy that nevertheless gained a foothold during the nineteenth century in a country that lacked deep indigenous rationalist or materialist traditions. Unlike Western Christianity, Russian Orthodoxy never emphasized rationalism or empiricism in its educational or homiletic traditions,[70] nor did such impulses emerge in the church from below. There was, to be sure, a multiplication of new heresies in the nineteenth century as the Orthodox faithful continued to indulge their propensity to interpret correct worship for themselves, but the rationalist rejection of the sacred was not among them. Rather, it was the part of educated society who embraced the ideas of the Enlightenment who provided the main constituency for conscious nonbelief in the supernatural. Thus, lying outside the purview of Rome and not having directly participated in the Reformation, Russia did not develop a significant independent interest in conscious nonbelief in the supernatural. It encountered religious doubt among the Western European ideas its intelligentsia engaged during the final centuries of tsarism. Such a beginning, of course, did not augur well for the broad acceptance of atheism, since elite rejections of the supernatural stood no better chance of penetrating the masses than did elite perceptions of piety. Other factors—altered attitudes toward religious observance, generational and experiential changes, apostasy, anticlericalism—combined with the influences of the rationalist rejection of the sacred to determine the extent and limits of the popular audience for atheism in Russia at the beginning of the twentieth century.

Therefore, although the fact that part of the intelligentsia embraced materialism and rationalism in the nineteenth century is an important element in the story of Russian atheism, it is not the story itself. Works of history typically explain the emergence of modern Russian atheism in terms of its philosophical and ideological roots: the influences that shaped Marxist ideas on religion evolved into Marxism-Leninism and ultimately produced Soviet antireligious policies.[71] We should not underestimate this dimension of the process, since ideology far more seriously constrained Bolshevik behavior during the early years of Soviet power than it did later. But still, in light of the many conflicts we have already noted between established authority and popular religion in Russia, it would be fanciful to imagine that any combination of state power and ideology would on its own be sufficient to transform the fundamental beliefs of the population.

There was certainly no single response to Western ideas writ large in late Imperial Russia. One educated segment may have viewed rationalism as the key to the future of their country, but others equally embraced the heroism, subjectivism, and exaltation of the human spirit found in romanticism. Westernizers and Slavophiles who frequented the same salons and shared similar feelings of isolation in their own society disagreed over whether universal education represented an engine of progress or whether education had perhaps already deprived the intelligentsia of a true Russian spirit that now resided only in the peasantry. Differing readings of Hegel led some *intelligenty* to greater inner-directedness, others to the pursuit of small changes, and still others to socialism. A national political awakening in the second half of the nineteenth century gave voice to an even broader range of views. In addition to those who remained apolitical or sought nonpolitical solutions, critically thinking people could be found supporting peasant or proletarian socialism, parliamentary constitutionalism or constitutional monarchy, and reform of the autocratic system from within. Tactics ultimately ranged from preparing for revolution through direct agitation, underground conspiracies, and terrorism to attempting limited consultative politics within a transformed version of tsarism.[72]

In this milieu, religious beliefs inevitably came in for scrutiny and reappraisal. Early in the nineteenth century, radical thinkers among the intelligentsia did not seek to eradicate religion but to harness the passions of discontented religious sects toward revolutionary purposes. The more activist generation (the so-called Sons), however, who entered public life in the 1860s, came to see religion overwhelmingly as an impediment to change, even as these revolutionaries sought to infuse their own movements with a "religious" passion.[73] And though no single movement or thinker was solely responsible, Ludwig Feuerbach's rejection of religion on the basis of philosophical materialism exercised an undeniably broad influence in Russia. Nicholas Chernyshevsky, the seminary graduate and son of a priest who became the most influential political voice of his generation, came to Saint Petersburg in 1846 with his deep religious allegiances intact. Reading Feuerbach's *Essence of Christianity* in 1849 led Chernyshevsky to repudiate religion and inspired him to popularize the ideas of the man to whom he referred at the end of his life as his favorite philosopher. Indeed, the list of those who spread religious doubt under the combined influence of Feuerbach and Chernyshevsky includes many prominent revolutionaries of the second half of the century. Nicholas Dobroliubov, another son of a cleric and Chernyshevsky's collaborator, also credited Feuerbach for the end of his religiosity, whereas Pavel Rybnikov, whose early Slavophile leanings had led him to the study of folklore and religion, similarly adopted Feuerbach's materialist views and became a Populist. The underground Library of Kazan Students included *Essence of Christianity* in the works they published clandestinely at Moscow University in the 1850s, and among the following generation of revolutionaries Peter Lavrov, P. G. Zaichnevsky, and Ivan Krasnoperov listed it as reading that had formed their careers. Still later, Feuerbach helped shape the views toward religion of Anatolii Lunacharsky, the first Soviet Commissar of Enlightenment; the important philosophical journal *Pod znamenem Marksizma* [Under the Banner of Marxism] devoted an entire issue to his work in 1922.[74] But as the revolutionary intelligentsia came to oppose religion politically, nonradical intellectuals engaged the issue from other perspectives. Belles lettres featured the topic prominently. To name only a few well-known examples, Tolstoy's portrayal of the peasantry as the one repository of true Russian faith in *The Death of Ivan Ilyich* carried forward his bald assertion in *A Confession* that "religious doctrine plays no part" in the lifestyle of the privileged in Russia and exists "only as an external phenomenon, disconnected from life."[75] Ivan Turgenev's parody of dogmatic materialism and science in *Fathers and Sons* reduced the younger generation to the level of caricature. And a personal struggle with faith and a condemnation of positivism dominated the latter phase of the career of Dostoevsky.[76]

Thus, everyone had to take Russia's religiosity into account, but no one could take it for granted, and there could be no simplistic identification of religious belief with conservatism or criticism of the church with radicalism. Many who attempted to energize and mobilize spirituality did so in the cause of transforming Russia, not as a prop for the autocracy. In this way, Tolstoy ran afoul of ecclesiastical as well as secular authorities when his midlife reassessment of religious principles took on an air of anarchism. The Christian Socialism of Nicholas Berdiaev mixed materialism with mysticism in its prescriptions for a more moral Russia, whereas that of Sergei Bulgakov gave a central place to the practical failings of the church. Peter Struve, who had collaborated with Lenin in the 1890s, and the liberal activist Semën Frank both emerged in the antirevolutionary but also antitsarist *Vekhi* [Signposts] group that in 1909 urged the intelligentsia to adopt a more cooperative, religious orientation.[77] Reformists within the church pressed for a national *Sobor* [council] to discuss, among other issues, the responsiveness of Orthodoxy to social issues, ways to reinvigorate faith, and a realignment of institutional relationships and the division of authority. Nor was revolutionary Social-Democracy immune to the attractions of religious commitment. Lunacharsky, Alexander Bogdanov, and Maxim Gorky all supported the idea of infusing Bolshevik Marxism and science with elements of religious ecstasy—"God-Building"—until Lenin was able to stifle that movement in the party.[78]

In the short term, neither reactionaries, radicals, nor reformers achieved what they desired. Government officials may have persistently attempted to implant Orthodox messages in education,[79] but the ramifications of urbanization and industrialization ultimately forced all to reconsider their prior assessments of the nature and depth of popular religiosity in the country. The social and political activism in which clergy engaged by the end of the nineteenth century rudely disabused tsarist ministers of their notions of unwavering constancy in the parishes. And at a time when the faltering state overestimated its ability to resacralize its secular foundations,[80] activists of all persuasions outside the government repeatedly found their own ways to misread the range of the possible.

Nonetheless, the strongest impact on popular observance came not from the intelligentsia but from changes at the grass roots. No factor has drawn more attention in this regard than the opportunities for greater numbers of peasants to work in towns and factories after the 1860s. Conventional peasant wisdom already accepted as axiomatic what the educated came to believe: life outside the village corrupted the peasantry.[81] Hence, in the late 1890s one priest from Vladimir province was pronouncing what he believed to be a general truth when he complained: "Migration to the factory exerts a corrupting influence on the workers and their families. . . . a loss of morality, indifference to religion and to the rites of the church. On Good Friday, a worker thinks nothing about duty until [he is] disgracefully drunk, gorging himself with sausage, playing the accordion, dancing, and singing various songs. It's a fact!"[82] The supporting evidence seemed to be everywhere. The factories and towns changed those who went there, the influences they carried back altered the countryside, and the village functioned significantly differently in their absence.[83] Church hierarchs therefore leaned heavily on parish priests through official correspondence and a determined campaign in the ecclesiastical press to battle the ill effects of peasant out-migration from the village. And despite the more concentrated institutional presence of the church in the cities, officials complained that the environment for religion there was even less hospitable than in the scattered hamlets of the countryside.[84]

These concerns did not lack foundation. Many of those who left even temporarily could not, as it turned out, sustain their usual levels of church attendance and attention to the sacraments when separated from familiar village symbols and rituals. A large number of the faithful, as we have seen, viewed these appurtenances not as representations of the sacred, but as its concrete manifestations, and many equated symbols with faith itself. It should therefore not be surprising that the piety of the peasant decontextualized—to use Reginald Zelnik's apt term—could and did weaken when the peasant left the village. And the experience of increased out-migration coincided with a sharp rise in anticlerical attitudes and incidents among the village peasantry between the 1860s and World War I.[85] No one can quantify what took place in individuals' inner lives, but we can state unequivocally that church records of the early twentieth century characterized nonobservance and apostasy among out-migrants as far in excess of the capabilities of priests to react.[86]

Even allowing that alarm and indignation caused the clergy rhetorically to exaggerate the scope of the phenomenon, the large number of public responses to lowered religiosity testify to its frequency and the seriousness with which the issue was treated. In short, during the late nineteenth and early twentieth centuries, the perception that cities corrupted the religious faith of villagers became commonplace in Russia.

But a perception of a decline in piety, however widely held, falls well short of a demise of religion. Indeed, those whose reduced levels of observance caused their personal reputations to suffer left themselves vulnerable to two chief weapons of the village: the tyranny of group opinion and the mechanisms of peasant self-justice. Entire communities stepped forward to battle the neglect and abuse of religious practices; to reintegrate out-migrants into compliance with church rituals of birth, death, marriage, and celebration; and to impose local standards of morality even on villagers away from the countryside. When the worker Semën Kanatchikov reached the point in Saint Petersburg where he "stopped going to the priest for 'confession,' no longer attended church, and began to eat 'forbidden' food during Lenten fast days," a fellow villager caused him trouble by reporting this to his father at home. The experience of Kanatchikov was not unique. Refusal to take the sacraments, apostasy, and flaunting village sexual mores at the factory invited parental and clerical intervention, persecution and shaming rituals by peers, or even the loss of the right to travel.[87]

The evidence thus points in more than one direction. The dramatic drop in religious observance, especially among younger and more literate migrants, cannot be denied, but it had observable limits. The very vigor with which the village faithful responded testifies that a significant majority still considered the loss of religiosity an aberration, not an inevitability. Moreover, far from all abandoned their religion on the road to town. Where factory workers lived in communal barracks, as at many urban textile factories, migrants tended to incorporate religious beliefs into the peasant subculture they re-created in the plants. Through 1917 and later, female laborers as a group were still widely perceived as a pillar of Orthodoxy; experienced workers conducted religious instruction for new arrivals; urban priests enjoyed free access to workers' living spaces; certain factory owners enforced church attendance on Sundays and holidays; and not infrequently workers transferred their full allegiances to urban churches, whose construction and upkeep they supported financially. Production schedules took the workers' religious sensibilities into full account, as evidenced by a universal two-week closure at Easter.[88]

There were additional signs that suggested neither unequivocal support for religion nor its abandonment. Anecdotal evidence, for example, indicates that workers who brooked no insult to sacred symbols might nevertheless tolerate and even indulge in anticlerical remarks.[89] Writers from the working class also took a two-edged position. They employed a distinct religious idiom as they addressed their peers, but their usage—which stressed imagery and terminology above theism—was metaphoric and symbolic rather than being grounded in faith itself.[90] The celebration of holidays sent equally mixed signals. The number of holiday observances among peasants, at least in some rural localities, appears to have increased after the middle of the nineteenth century,[91] and factory workers otherwise assimilated to the city clung tenaciously to their right to observe traditional feasts.[92] But the raucous modes of the celebrations themselves continued to incorporate seemingly secular and even pre-Christian elements.

There is, in short, ample evidence of disunity within Orthodoxy by the beginning of the twentieth century but very little for the existence of atheistic nonbelief on the part of a broad constituency. While one part of the educated society professed conscious atheism, indifference, or apostasy, another manifested a renewed interest in religiosity, and in yet another quarter a faddish revival of interest in the occult penetrated even the court of Tsar Nicholas II. Strong reformist and revivalist movements that arose within and outside (and often in opposition to) the formal church hierarchy prevented Orthodoxy from projecting consensus in virtually any important sphere. In addition, the ongoing close identification of church and state led many critics to extend to Orthodoxy at least part of the blame for the untreated social ills of industrialization and the weakness of the tsarist system, even as others in society countered that the true solution lay in a turn backward to a greater role for the church. And at the bottom level of society, as new influences challenged traditional beliefs, they also spawned a vigorous defense by those who were militantly pious. How did conscious atheism fit into this mix? Among those educated Russians who came to embrace philosophical materialism, positivism, secularism, and science as the keys to Russia's future, atheistic nonbelief was more an element in a broader transformation than a singular goal. Some articulations of antireligious sentiments, such as Mikhail Petrashevsky's sophomoric reference to Jesus as "a well-known demagogue whose career ended somewhat unsuccessfully," can be dismissed as transparently contrived attempts to attract attention to the speaker rather than the issue. Others, notably the rejection of religion in the revolutionary vision of Dobroliubov, displayed greater intellectual rigor. On balance, antireligiosity and anti-clericalism became common among the radical intelligentsia as the twentieth century approached, but no significant broad and sustained effort to promote atheism as an independent goal took shape.

In this environment, the Bolshevik position on atheism developed only gradually and without special urgency. The antireligious leanings of the early Bolsheviks were no more pronounced than those of other Russian radicals, and neither Lenin nor the party devoted significant energy to promoting atheism before 1905. Early in the century, Marxist newspapers periodically called for separating the church from state and school; they explored the possibility of mobilizing persecuted religious denominations and national minorities in the cause of revolution. Nevertheless, the 1903 Bolshevik party program, which Soviet publications later applauded for its militantly atheistic stance, actually went no further than to demand freedom of conscience, secular education, and a division of church and state.[93] During the same year, Lenin's attack on the privileged position of the Russian Orthodox Church and demand for secular education in "To Agrarian Toilers" were couched in terms of promoting religious freedom. The revolution of 1905 changed this, but only relatively. The fact that the Christian Socialist priest Georgii Gapon organized the demonstration in Saint Petersburg that touched off the revolution won Lenin's attention but not his support. Between then and the revolution of 1917, the influence of Lenin bore heavily on the official Bolshevik position: party members were not to be neutral on the issue of religion even though the postrevolutionary state might temporarily have to take such a stand. Nevertheless, the party did not articulate its atheistic sympathies in detail. Whatever specific energy it expended on the issue of religion was devoted largely to fending off rivals, as in counteracting the influence of the radically religious *Vekhi* group on the intelligentsia. Of greatest import, in 1909 Lenin directed his "Materialism and Empiriocriticism" against the "God-Building" attempt by Lunacharsky and Bogdanov to create a proletarian religion without a deity.[94] A victorious Bolshevik revolution would therefore undoubtedly threaten the future of religion in Russia, but before 1917 the party elaborated its atheistic leanings neither in its public propaganda nor in its internal communications.

A CONCLUSION AND A THESIS

Ultimately, the fate of atheism in the early Soviet period depended on unanticipated factors and complexities that the party did not fully appreciate. Having emerged from the radical intelligentsia, Bolshevik leaders understood culture not as something manifested, but as something to be attained. One achieved a level of enlightenment and behavior and tried to impart it to the "dark masses."[95] Moreover, the party unwaveringly defined *consciousness* and *backwardness*—words that dominated its internal and public discussions—in terms of identification with Bolshevik ideals. The degree to which one shared the vision and aspirations of the party, in short, determined consciousness or the lack thereof. What we have defined as traditions and symbols embedded deeply in cultural strategies of understanding social experience were therefore for the majority of Bolshevik leaders nothing more than a misguided worldview to be corrected without great difficulty through education. A demonstration of the advantages of materialism would unseat the "religious superstition" that tsarism and church promoted at the expense of the well-being of the masses. Atheism and belief would thus compete, but party leaders believed the confrontation was strongly weighted in their favor. Consequently, despite the close historical association of the Soviet regime with nonbelief, atheism did not occupy an important place in the Bolsheviks' prerevolutionary message, nor was it a central factor in their rise to power. And because the party gave far greater emphasis to other issues before and during 1917, Bolsheviks easily glossed over whatever differences existed among them on this score.

Bolshevik antireligious positions at the time of the revolution of October 1917 therefore rested more on untested assumptions and facile interpretations of ideology than on clearly articulated plans or experience. The advent of a new society was to make the eradication of religion all but automatic: not an end in itself but a collateral benefit of the creation of a new political and social order. In this belief the party turned out to be greatly mistaken. The Bolsheviks had anticipated postrevolutionary battles involving political parties, classes, nationalities, and interest groups. What they did not foresee was the extent to which competing cultural perceptions and aspirations that emerged around the issue of atheism would bring an important cultural dimension into the equation as well.

2 | Revolution and Antireligious Policy

"There was no cooking at home because today was Good Friday, and he felt famished. Cringing in the cold, he reflected that just such a wind had blown in the days of Riurik, Ivan the Terrible and Peter the Great. Their times had known the same ferocious poverty and hunger. There had been the same thatched roofs with holes in them, the same ignorance and misery, the same desolation on all sides, and the same gloom and sense of oppression. All these horrors had been, still were, and would continue to be, and the passing of another thousand years would make things no better."
—Anton Chekhov, *The Student*

"O patriot of the German mark!
How long will you keep breathing
And instilling Bolshevik ideas in the Russian people?
Your end will come soon, you insolent traitor,
And the tsar will once again gloriously mount
The throne of this great country.
The Rus' will wake up and see
The fruits of your criminal deeds.
They will curse you for posterity,
And misfortune will be your lot.
All your efforts to help troubled Germany are in vain.
Alas, nothing you can do will change her desperate fate.
Wake up while it's still not too late,
Change your criminal ways and get out now,
When there is still some cheap talk of forgiving you.

Greetings to Trotsky, Kollontai, Zinoviev and all the other Russian traitors."
—Monarchists[1]

Seizing political office by force and implementing a thoroughgoing revolution require decidedly different approaches. In the course of every insurrection, those who seek to recast existing institutions, relationships of power, and social values arrive at a pivotal moment when they can no longer exploit the problems of the old regime as their chief lever of public support but must begin providing solutions. This transformation from an insurgent force to a governing party draws to the surface internal differences that the revolutionaries sublimated on the road to rebellion. It tests their commitment to ideals, strains collective resolve, and complicates the task of separating true followers from opportunists ready to advance under the revolution's banner. The Bolsheviks reached this juncture, of course, in October 1917. During the next fifteen years, they would attempt the delicate balance of seeking the loyalty of the population and simultaneously trying to change its mind and heart.

The emergence of Bolshevik antireligious policy captures one important dimension of this complex transformation. Upon coming to power, the party learned that its propensity to project only a nonspecific commitment to eliminating belief in the supernatural, and not to develop a clear plan of action, had led to an erroneous presumption of consensus in the ranks. In reality, there would never be a unified Bolshevik position on religion and atheism, even among the leadership. At least until the Cultural Revolution began in 1928, those who counseled pragmatic restraint generally prevailed over others who favored the rapid repression of religion, but even this required ongoing vigilance. More than one antireligious strategy could be found in every state and party organ, and many were all but evenly divided. The fact that the Bolsheviks consistently expressed themselves publicly in a schematic political idiom only complicated the situation. The party labeled those who identified with its programs and policies as enlightened and conscious; it berated those who did not as backward or, worse still, counterrevolutionary. Terms such as *anti-Soviet, kulak,* and *bourgeois* therefore became self-serving tautologies that linked the perceived enemies of the party to contemporary problems. In practice, since Bolshevik pronouncements associated kulaks with support for the church, any person engaged in proreligious activity might, in a political shorthand, become a "kulak." Similarly, any conversation with an "anti-Soviet element" such as a priest could automatically be considered "anti-Soviet."

The generic inability of the revolutionary regime to establish clear institutional jurisdictions even within its own apparatus complicated the situation further. In theory the Bolsheviks held every association—

party cells, Komsomols, trade unions, factory committees, social organizations—responsible for carrying out antireligious propaganda,[2] but
there was no way to enforce such an imprecise mandate. To exacerbate
matters, lines of actual authority crossed bureaucratic boundaries. The
Central Executive Committee of the All-Russian Congress of Soviets
(VTsIK) created government agencies to oversee religious affairs, but
the party did the same. In addition, important collateral responsibilities devolved upon organs whose raison d'être went well beyond a
concern for the eradication of religious influences: the People's Commissariat of Justice (Narkomiust), the People's Commissariat of Enlightenment (Narkompros), and the secret police (Cheka). Rivalries
over jurisdiction, the shifting of blame for failures, and the duplication
of effort resulted.

Yet the undertaking involved even more than devising guidelines and
delineating authority. Bolsheviks may have referred to their assault on
religion as "storming the heavens," but in this sphere the party reacted
to events as much as it shaped them. As already noted, the Soviet state
of 1917–1932 was not yet a potent dictatorship. Literally every directive from central to lower authorities involved at least a tacit renegotia-
tion of power at this time, and the gap between the intent of directives
and their implementation could be great. In this formative period of the
Soviet state, even local authorities inclined to obey the center could not
simply compel obedience among the rank and file. Every issue of con-
sequence was influenced by the vicissitudes of party power struggles,
factional differences, and various mobilization campaigns. Early Soviet
antireligious policy and practice thus reflected as much a sequence of
reverberations of high and low politics as it did a consistent party line.

RED OCTOBER, NEP SOCIETY, AND THE RISE OF STALINISM

Following the revolution of October 1917, the Bolsheviks intended
their projected journey through socialism to communism to transform
Russia politically, economically, and socially. Bolshevism would, in
short, alter not only the nation's institutions but also its values. To
achieve this, the party would have to begin a social revolution while
still consolidating its hold on power.[3]

Persistent political opposition and the overwhelming pressures of the
Russian civil war of 1918–1921 undermined the Soviet state from the
outset. A strike by railroad workers forced the Bolsheviks into a ruling
coalition with the radical wing of the Socialist-Revolutionary Party

(Left SRs) before the end of 1917, and resistance to the revolution by employees in government offices continued into the following spring. The German army had by that time advanced deep into Soviet territory. The Treaty of Brest-Litovsk resolved this military crisis in March 1918, but at the price of ending SR participation in the government and hurting Lenin's prestige. A civil war against a variety of anti-Bolshevik forces supported by foreign interventionists then began in mid-1918; by 1919 the Soviet Republic appeared on the verge of defeat.

The regime survived all this, but at great cost. By the time the Red Army prevailed in the civil war in 1921, Soviet emergency measures had alienated much of the intended constituency of the revolution. Grain requisitioning pushed the peasantry into open revolt. Cities emptied as destitute inhabitants fled to the countryside in search of food. Seizing the homes of the bourgeoisie for public housing misfired, and as sanitary conditions everywhere deteriorated disease reached epidemic levels. The state nationalized industry by decree in 1918, in part to keep factories open, but at the beginning of the 1920s only a small number were still in operation. Industrial output stood far below pre–World War I levels, and the resultant shortages of manufactured goods led to widespread strikes and other disturbances. The national currency collapsed, and the stillborn government system of production and distribution led to widespread profiteering. In spite of laws against private trade, even state agencies turned to the black market for supplies.[4]

The communists responded in March 1921 by implementing the New Economic Policy (NEP). Nothing foreshadowed this change in course; until the eve of NEP, the party continued to react to crises as it had throughout the civil war: with an increasing centralization of authority. But an anti-Bolshevik uprising at the Kronstadt Naval Base, a former stronghold of party support, influenced Lenin toward more conciliatory measures, and those who supported him pushed through this controversial policy over the objections of other communists who considered it a betrayal. In 1921–1929, NEP thus had backers who felt it was a necessary step toward creating the preconditions for socialism, but there were also those who would never accept it.[5]

The New Economic Policy attempted to restore civil peace while reinvigorating the national economy. Having outlawed rival political parties as well as factions within their own organization, the Bolsheviks reversed some of the measures instituted during the civil war—grain requisitioning and the nationalization of some small-scale enterprises in particular—in the hope of easing public hostility toward Soviet power. NEP's supporters also intended that the restoration of a limited market economy would resuscitate supply and distribution, even though the opponents of NEP in the party and much of the public refused to embrace a policy that allowed entrepreneurs to enrich themselves. Indeed, a significant portion of Russians believed that the financial aggrandizement of one person could come only at the expense of another and especially resented the role of middlemen, whom they viewed as exploitative nonproducers. In the prevailing conditions of shortage, therefore, opponents of NEP easily manipulated public emotions when the more prosperous private traders, known as Nepmen, indulged in conspicuous consumption. As a result, the party reversed itself more than once in implementing the New Economic Policy, and its future place in Bolshevik strategy was never fully secure.[6]

NEP consequently influenced and was influenced by power struggles and factional rivalries within the party; there was no shortage of issues of contention. At the beginning of the 1920s, the party was deeply divided. Influential Bolsheviks criticized the end of independent trade unions, for example, and the decline of democratic procedures in party operations. Others complained that the revolution was progressing too slowly and that by giving preferential treatment to those who possessed much-needed technical expertise (so-called bourgeois specialists), the party was losing its revolutionary ardor. Representing a third position, Lenin decried the burgeoning of bureaucracy and in 1922 launched an attack on it. To this end, the party elected Joseph Stalin as General Secretary, a post with extensive appointment powers that he ultimately used for his own political ends.

When Lenin suffered a cerebral hemorrhage late in 1922, however, the beginnings of a struggle for political succession overshadowed all other issues. His authority, unparalleled if not always unchallenged, derived from his experience, intellect, and political acumen, not any office or title. Replacing him therefore required reconsidering the very concept of leadership in the party, a process Lenin himself complicated when he dictated a "Testament" that criticized all the likely choices. Of his eventual successor he said "Stalin is too rude" and recommended that "the comrades consider removing Stalin from the post" of General Secretary.

The succession struggle proceeded through four distinct stages. Stalin, Grigorii Zinoviev, and Lev Kamenev formed a "triumvirate" against Leon Trotsky in 1923, and by the time of Lenin's death in January 1924 the triumvirs were well on the way to marginalizing their rival. During the second phase, which occurred during 1925, the trio turned against one another. Though behind the scenes General Secretary Stalin proceeded to replace the clients of Zinoviev and Kamenev with his own, publicly NEP was the central issue. Zinoviev attacked what he presented as excessive capitalism in a socialist state, but Nikolai Bukharin, NEP's strongest advocate among the top leadership, joined forces with Stalin in successful counterattack. The third phase produced an unlikely alliance: a united opposition in 1926–1927 consisting of Trotsky, Zinoviev, and Kamenev. When their strategy of carrying the fight directly into the factories failed miserably, they were expelled from the ruling Politburo, then from the Central Committee, and ultimately from the party itself.[7] During the final phase in 1928–1929, Stalin defeated a so-called right opposition headed by Bukharin, head of the Council of People's Commissars (Sovnarkom) Alexei Rykov, and trade unionist Mikhail Tomsky.

The economics of NEP and the dictates of ideology influenced this succession at every turn. The Bolsheviks' survival certainly depended on their ability to revive the national economy, but that could be no simple exercise in expediency. In the 1920s, Marxism had not yet been reduced to the aggregation of pseudo-ideological slogans or the convenient idiom of political discourse it would later become in the Soviet Union. Marxist thought still directly influenced party decisions, its tenets limiting the range of possible courses of action in any situation. And since, according to Marx, socialism could take root only in a fully industrialized economy, all Bolsheviks accepted as axiomatic that Soviet Russia would have to industrialize further. Yet, whether that should be carried out quickly and with the rapid development of heavy industry or gradually and with an emphasis at first on producing consumer goods sparked serious disagreement.

The pressures to find workable solutions quickly were considerable. When the 1921–1922 harvest yielded far less than half the prewar average, famine claimed millions of lives. In industry, runaway inflation and unpaid wages turned factories into battlegrounds. And when, in 1923, industrial prices rose to a level three times as high as those for agriculture,[8] the chronic fear that the kulaks—as the most prosperous peasants were known—would strangle the regime by withholding their grain from the market was deepened. In 1924, industry enjoyed a recovery and the cultivation of arable land approached 1913 levels, but these were gains only in comparison to the hard years that immediately preceded them. The extensive destruction and deterioration of the industrial base that had been occurring since the beginning of World War I dictated that any long-term growth, not to mention socialist industrialization, would require far more capital expenditure than present levels of trade and foreign investment could provide.

At the same time, the village was undergoing its own upheaval. The revolution had brought about the breakup of the landlords' estates but also the reappearance of the peasant commune, which reinstituted collective modes of cultivation. Inefficient strip farming, the outmoded three-field system of crop rotation, and the extensive utilization of non-mechanized implements—the scythe, the sickle, and the wooden plow—signaled a technological regression antithetical to party desiderata. The concomitant low yield per acre increased the long-standing peasant "land hunger," and many of the excess mouths to feed were pushed toward the cities, where unemployment already ran high. In these circumstances, social distinctions among the peasantry narrowed as extremes of income closed. The peasants did not accept their fate (and low grain prices) passively. By the end of 1927, a significant number began to plant more profitable industrial crops, used grain to fatten livestock for slaughter, produced grain alcohol, or fulfilled the worst fears of the leadership by hoarding grain in anticipation of higher prices.

As various party factions debated specific solutions, all agreed on the general principle that the peasantry would absorb the chief cost of industrialization. Agriculture would generate a surplus either through the taxation of profits or by regulating the price the state would pay for grain. This "primitive socialist accumulation" would be "pumped over," as the communists phrased matters, to the industrial sector as investment capital. Economist Evgenii Preobrazhensky, supported by Trotsky and later Zinoviev and Kamenev, called for the rapid development of heavy industry and the substitution of centralized planning for the market. Bukharin, Rykov, and Tomsky championed a gradual tempo, the development of consumer goods manufacturing, and an economic alliance with the peasantry. For the time being, Stalin left the center stage to others.[9]

These uncertainties in politics and economics did not delay the beginning of the social revolution. The Bolsheviks' eagerness to construct a proletarian culture in both the aesthetic and the sociological sense—to create "the new Soviet man"—recognized no limits. Early experiments reconceptualized law and restructured education. Others created party programs specifically for women and youth or tried to alter mass consciousness by eliminating illiteracy and introducing improvements in material existence. Additional government campaigns took aim at alcohol abuse, tried to make justice reflect the social circumstances surrounding crime, and upgraded public health and sanitation. New legislation redefined the family and liberalized strictures against divorce and abortion. And the arts experienced a period of virtually unbridled experimentation.

These abrupt departures led to certain improvements in the quality of life, but they also gave rise to unanticipated and undesired results that reverberated most strongly in towns and cities. The unrestricted dissolution of marriages, for example, produced the highest urban divorce rate in the world and promoted family instability. Homelessness, child abandonment, "hooliganism," and juvenile crime soared beyond already problematic prerevolutionary levels. New standards of sexual conduct and the availability of abortion generated criticism inside as well as outside the party, while teachers and parents resisted the introduction of the new Soviet curriculum in the schools. As artists advanced new modes of expression and in some cases intentionally shocked the public, many citizens reacted with anger and disapproval.

The impact differed in the countryside, where the peasants' identification with their own past far exceeded sentiment in favor of any proposed revolutionary transformation. The state and the party failed to establish more than a minimal institutional presence in the villages; the peasant commune rather than party cells or even rural soviets exercised the principal authority over day-to-day matters. The village thus regained much of its prerevolutionary insularity and control over internal affairs, and the sway of old ways proved strong. The number of church weddings and the birthrate remained high, and divorces did not approach city levels. The reassertion of communal authority once again made the multigenerational peasant household the preeminent social unit, and traditional rather than Soviet law prevailed. But the persistence of the past also meant the perpetuation of cleavages within the village. Friction had long been a dominant internal dynamic in Russian peasant society; the Soviet village was far less unified than its periodic collective resistance to external interference would suggest. Generational, experiential, political, and other differences consequently took on added importance after the revolution, with Red Army veterans, returning factory workers, and the young especially accused of flouting tradition.[10]

Out of these circumstances, Stalin's victory in the succession battle signaled the end of NEP and the beginning of cultural revolution and class warfare. As Stalin solidified his place as party leader, his rhetoric became more confrontational. He exploited the resentment that had resulted from the state's need to retain with privileged rations and other benefits managers and experts from the tsarist era. In early 1928, he began repeatedly blaming greedy kulaks and lenient local officials for the nation's grain procurement problems and Nepmen for generally exploiting the laboring masses, but he also held engineers and technical personnel with unacceptable class backgrounds responsible for industrial shortfalls. His own blueprint called for a more rapid, centrally planned transformation to socialism.

Nonetheless, nothing could have prepared the country for what actually took place. The First Five Year Plan, declared retroactively to have begun in October 1928, went beyond anything that anyone including Stalin had previously proposed for industry. It set output quotas that would have challenged any industrial power, much less a country in the straits of Soviet Russia. And when the party introduced the slogan of fulfilling the five year plan in four, it was tacitly admitting that this was no plan in any conventional sense but a mobilization tool to prod workers and managers to the highest possible levels of effort.[11] Yet party leaders treated it seriously. When shortfalls resulted, they blamed "wreckers" and "saboteurs" and held show trials of engineers.

Stalin's forced collectivization of agriculture and liquidation of the kulaks as a class proved to be, if such were possible, even more chaotic. Begun in 1929 and originally presented as a gradual transformation of the countryside, the campaign quickly assumed the proportions of a civil war between state and village. By March 1930, more than 58 percent of peasant households had been coercively collectivized. Despite a temporary reversal, these proportions grew to higher than 71 percent in 1934 and nearly 90 percent in 1936. This violent upheaval disrupted the agricultural cycle, caused famine, dramatically reduced the number of livestock, pushed millions of rural inhabitants into industrial jobs, and tried to eradicate the traditional peasant lifestyle.[12]

Other Stalinist measures pandered to public resentment and prejudice. Nepmen in particular received short shrift. In 1927–1928, the state increased business taxes exponentially, in some cases retroactively, and those who could not pay lost their apartments, possessions, ration cards, and access to public services. Although this might take as little as three days, their plight aroused scant public sympathy. NEP had not only fostered economic inequity but also had brought back prostitution, gambling houses, drug abuse, and other affronts to public morality for which the Nepmen absorbed much of the blame. Furthermore, in 1928–1931 a cultural revolution against gradualists took place in virtually every Soviet institution as impatient, generally younger radicals attacked their more moderate colleagues and those who remained from the tsarist period. Grim rigidity and proletarian prudishness everywhere displaced the spirit of experimentation that was tolerated before 1928. A new imperiousness reverberated from law, film, and architecture as well as from jazz, literature, history, and education. Literally no sphere of activity was unaffected.[13]

In short, Stalin gained his victory through more than his considerable skill in political infighting. Better than any other high-ranking Bolshevik, Stalin had understood the significance of the changing size and character of the party after 1917. Membership expanded exponentially, with the social and educational background of new candidates differing significantly from that of their predecessors. A decade after the October revolution, young, urban, poorly educated males overwhelmed what in 1917 had been a far smaller party more easily led by the intellectuals who predominated in the leadership. And because of the circumstances it endured during the initial years of Soviet power, the Communist Party of the Soviet Union came to value a different kind of cadre. The ability to complete assignments, even if ruthlessly, now carried more weight than the ideological sophistication that had been critical to pre-revolutionary reputations. Unlike Stalin, whose own credentials as a theorist were not greatly respected, the old guard did not always appreciate this change until it was too late.

Stalin also read the mood of the public correctly. His consistently correct appraisals of popular attitudes enabled early Stalinism to harness not only the cynicism of party and society, but also their idealism. In the late 1920s, the elemental urgency of Stalin's programs captured the revolutionary iconoclasm and renewed socialist radicalism that extended from the party Central Committee to the lower ranks of the Komsomol and into society itself. Outside the party organizations, Stalin especially appealed to the many who resented bourgeois specialists and the new rich created by NEP. Thus, in an environment in which the belief that kulaks were hoarding their grain while others went hungry was not limited to Stalinist henchmen and their dupes, Stalin's policies held out multiple prospects: settling real and imagined scores, satisfying a yearning for stability and tradition, making the revolution fulfill the expectations of 1917. Paradoxically, these options appealed both to those who desired to build socialism in a revolutionary way and to those who sought a reinstitution of the conservative aspects of Russian society. The perspective of historical hindsight, of course, shows that Stalinism ultimately resulted in human and material waste on an unprecedented scale in Russia. This was not evident at the outset, and those who became doubters could not prevent Stalin's programs from running their course.

SEPARATING CHURCH AND STATE

It was in this environment that the church and the revolutionary state pursued their irreconcilable positions. Church hierarchs considered the place of privilege for Orthodoxy in Russia inalienable and any attempt to reduce church prerogatives as sin.[14] Despite serious differences in its ranks,[15] the official church consistently supported the political and military enemies of Bolshevism before and after the revolution, even as clergy and activist laity denounced all measures against Orthodoxy as unprovoked persecution. The state was equally intransigent. Regarding organized religion as a pillar of the old order and an instrument of the class enemy, it refused to differentiate between aggressive and defensive actions by church members, labeling them all "anti-Soviet."

The Bolshevik leadership uncompromisingly held that religious belief should ultimately be eradicated, yet the party failed to make the issue a de facto high priority in the short term. The initial pressures of simple political survival in combination with the conviction that the citizens of the future would ultimately reject religiosity on their own caused the scarce resources and the most talented cadres to be employed somewhere other than in antireligious work. Bolshevism therefore tolerated no ideological neutrality in its own program, but it did not at first implement atheism assertively or consistently in society. Instead, in the early revolutionary period, Soviet power concentrated more on the legal separation of church and state, undermining religious hierarchs and institutions, and destroying the economic base of the church than it did on counteracting religion as a belief system and a cultural strategy.

Party leaders behaved with far greater assurance vis-à-vis the church than their tenuous hold on power warranted. A general land decree published soon after the October revolution nationalized church property along with that of other major holders; the Declaration on the Rights of the Peoples of Russia of 2 November 1917 abolished all religious privileges in the country.[16] A meeting of Sovnarkom on 11 December then transferred all education under church control—from single-class parish schools to seminaries and religious academies—to the jurisdiction of Narkompros.[17] In rapid succession two other decrees deprived the Russian Orthodox Church of the control over marriage and divorce it had pursued for nearly ten centuries. On 16 December 1917, Sovnarkom and the VTsIK empowered local judges to issue divorces to all citizens regardless of their religious affiliation. Two days later they decreed that the state would recognize only civil marriages, which did not outlaw church ceremonies but stripped them of their legal standing. The additional steps of legitimating children born out of wedlock and ordering religious institutions to transfer their registration books of births, marriages, and deaths to civil authorities deepened the affront.[18]

Bravado equally characterized the Russian Orthodox position. The church had convened its long-desired *Sobor* on 15 August 1917 and in

October had reinstated the Patriarchate.[19] It was therefore in no mood to submit passively to Bolshevik rule, the long-term survival of which neither supporters nor opponents took for granted at the time. Furthermore, religious leaders were understandably hostile to the uncoordinated violence that was occurring against clergy, cathedrals, monasteries, and parish churches in the aftermath of the Bolshevik seizure of power.[20] Lacking sufficient material forces, though, on 11 November 1917 the *Sobor* could only label the socialist revolution "descended of the anti-Christ and possessed by atheism" and warn of divine retribution for the blasphemies committed.[21] On 2 December, however, Synod members spoke out more specifically on temporal matters. Their unequivocal—and, in view of what had already transpired, disingenuous—pronouncement on the church as a legal entity included demands that state laws affecting Russian Orthodoxy be issued only with the prior consent of church authorities; that the government recognize church administration, decrees, and courts; that the head of the Russian state, the ministers of religion and enlightenment, and their close associates be Orthodox; that the Orthodox calendar and holidays be observed; that church marriage and birth registries carry legal force; that the religious needs of the Orthodox in the armed forces be administered; and that religious instruction be included in private and secular education at all levels.[22] When the state then released a draft decree on the separation of church and state, Patriarch Tikhon pronounced an anathema on the Bolsheviks.[23]

Sovnarkom exacerbated church-state antagonisms when it issued the Decree on the Separation of Church from State and School from Church—also widely published as the Decree on Freedom of Conscience, Church and Religious Organizations—on 20 January 1918. On the one hand, this act reinforced the unwillingness of the revolutionary leadership to tolerate further any standing the church enjoyed as an institution. Modeled on a similar declaration by the Paris Commune, it ended the use of religious oaths and ceremonies in state institutions and ordered the removal of religious symbols from public buildings. It reaffirmed the separation of school and church, and it forbade religious groups to own property and ordered what they now held to be confiscated. Moreover, the decree stripped religious societies of their rights as a juridical person. On the other hand, by directing its offensive principally against public ceremonies, church organizations, and property, the separation of church and state consciously spared individual observance. "Religion is the private affair of every citizen of the Russian Republic," began the draft version. Although Lenin deleted this sentence from the final redaction,[24]

Soviet publications widely cited the idea during the 1920s and, more to the point, it reflected the dominant spirit of the separation document. Citizens were free to profess any faith or none at all, they could conduct privately the religious education now excluded from the schools, and religious groups were entitled to petition central and local officials for the free use of buildings and objects intended for religious worship.[25] In short, the decree of 20 January 1918 was an act of radical secularization against the church hierarchy and apparatus. It did not, however, mandate the persecution of individual believers or prohibit private worship, and it established entitlements under Soviet law that, as we shall see, believers would pursue to their advantage.

But by leaving religious observance in the sphere of private conscience, the separation decree imposed an unenforceable legalism on the revolution: Soviet society would be *nonreligious* rather than *antireligious* in the immediate future. This distinction between marginalizing religion in order ultimately to render it irrelevant, as opposed to stridently imposing atheism, embodied the Bolshevik conception of freedom of conscience at the time. It also exacerbated cleavages and insecurities within the revolutionary camp, however, and in practice it proved impossible to maintain. If political pragmatism caused the majority of central institutions to attempt to minimize elemental confrontations with the laity, antireligious radicals pushed just as vigorously for the rapid and total eradication of the church. In January 1918, for example, the state tried in vain to contain the negative ramifications of the confiscation of the Alexander Nevskii Monastery in Petrograd, which was ordered independently by People's Commissar of State Welfare Alexandra Kollontai.[26] The leadership subsequently allowed Tikhon to lead peaceful mass demonstrations in Moscow in January and May, limiting Bolshevik actions to publicly questioning the motives of organizers and privately to surveillance by the Cheka.[27] At the local level, many overburdened officials reacted to anti-Soviet outbursts by clergy with nothing stronger than insults and scornful reports in the press, provided that such fulminations failed to incite action.[28] Authorities and the faithful clashed over specific grievances (seizures of church property, the arrest of a village priest) but in routine affairs most rural soviets lacked the capacity even to begin to implement the separation decree, and many could not so much as prevent clergy from continuing to collect emoluments.[29]

Restraint disappeared, however, whenever any component of this weak state felt directly threatened. Where religious demonstrations against the separation decree became riots, as happened in the Vitebsk district, Soviet officials unhesitatingly employed armed force, jailing the leaders. In the Petrozavodsk area of Olonets province, authorities arrested and executed the five organizers of the Union for the Defense of the Alexander Svirskii Monastery, who purportedly gathered as many as one thousand members from surrounding districts and temporarily prevented the nationalization of the cloister. Without the intervention of the Red Army, this kind of direct repression of local religious protests would not have been possible, and nationally the Cheka arrested bishops, priests, and nuns in 1917–1921 in its campaigns against the political and class enemies of the regime.[30] And since lower authorities proved incapable of preventing violence against symbols associated with the old order, and sometimes participated in it themselves, the desecration of the sacred became one indelible early image of communism for a considerable number of Orthodox believers.

In contrast to these inconsistencies in Bolshevik behavior, the Orthodox faced the separation of church and state virtually with a single mind: the distinction between a nonreligious and an antireligious society had for them no meaning whatsoever. The difference between confiscations of church property carried out in accordance with recent Sovnarkom decrees and those conducted without authorization was for Tikhon sophistry that contravened "all right and legality" and "the legal will of the people."[31] In this spirit, on 25 January 1918 the Synod characterized the separation decree as "an open act of persecution" that "was attempting to make the very existence of churches, church institutions and clergy impossible," and it threatened those who attempted to implement it with excommunication.[32] Separating nonreligiosity from antireligiosity resonated even less among parish priests. Their horror at attacks on religious objects, the prospect of loss of income and standing in their communities, and their unshakable equation of Orthodoxy with singular truth obliterated all other considerations. The resistance to the decree that clergy incited, for example, in the factories and villages of Vologda and Tambov provinces as well as in the Klin, Tver', and Kostroma regions paid no heed to legalistic nuance. Priests there represented the separation as a complete ban on prayer and worship and attributed it to demonic forces.[33]

Yet, despite this depth of emotion in religious quarters, the Bolsheviks initially regarded the eradication of religion as essentially an administrative task. The leadership took heart when a national investigation by the secret police reported that resignation was the most frequent public reaction to the separation decree.[34] This encouraged them in their expectation that the VIII (later renamed V) Section of Narkomiust could carry out the routine work associated with the separation of church and state so that the Cheka could concentrate on repressing religiously grounded activism against the regime. But this combination of short-term expediency and long-term overconfidence was flawed. Although led by the militantly antireligious P. A. Krasikov, Narkomiust and its Liquidation Commission (as the VIII Section became known) lacked sufficient apparatus to direct the operation from the center. Apologists lauded this as independence for lower organs, but it left Narkomiust dependent on the assistance and cooperation of the regional and district soviets. These, as we have seen, were only slightly better staffed for the task than the VIII Section itself.[35]

Two specific weaknesses hampered Narkomiust. First, the precise mandate to the VIII Section was to implement and enforce the legal separation of church and state, not to conduct agitation. This consequently fell by default to amateurs, with poor results. When, for example, untrained militants presented only abstract philosophical arguments during disputations (public confrontations between an atheistic militant and a representative of religion common during the first years of Soviet power), they often left audiences confused. Moreover, the disputations, which sometimes drew crowds of more than a thousand, themselves provided a forum in which the public heard not only antireligious ideas, but also religious and sectarian views. And when atheists invoked simplistic ploys, such as demanding that priests produce a miracle on the spot as proof of the existence of God, even Bolshevik sources reported a victory for religion.[36] Furthermore, crude attempts to demystify the remains of saints by opening burial vaults in monasteries and showing crowds the decayed corpses—a tactic that initially had the approval of higher organs if carried out with their prior permission—alienated far more of the population than they impressed.[37] Thus, when the delegate Kobetskii took stock of early rural antireligious work at the Congress of the Friends of the Newspaper *Bezbozhnik* in April 1925, he gave low marks to those who first carried the message to the villages. The hall erupted in laughter when he characterized the common propensity to address peasants with remarks on the class character of religion as a good way to start a counterrevolutionary organization.[38] So disastrous were the consequences of these coarse early tactics that well into the mid-1920s a number of party sources held them up as examples of how not to proceed.[39]

Second, the church possessed resources, infrastructure, and a sense of righteousness that far exceeded anything the Liquidation Commission could marshal. On 19 January 1918, Tikhon mandated a general defense of the church.[40] A letter and a proclamation of 22 and 28 February then went further in specifically ordering resistance to the seizure of ecclesiastical property. He directed the church to become a force against Soviet power.[41] Although the mere existence of such documents can neither confirm nor refute the Bolshevik contention that religious followers actively responded, or prove whether perhaps such pronouncements did not reach all of them and many acted on their own volition, opposition did take root. The faithful were soon found manufacturing delays in surrendering the keys to nationalized church buildings, and parish clergy issued their own proclamations that contradicted official versions of the separation decree.[42]

As intended, such tactics created anger and confusion among the population, and they embroiled the VIII Section in case-by-case wrangling over minute details of the meaning, intent, and legitimacy of Soviet law. In April–May 1918 in Penza, for example, the disorder that reigned as Soviet institutions attempted to divide nationalized property—land to the Land Department, nonmovable property to the Housing Department, monasteries to various public institutions—made it difficult for the Narkomiust organs to sustain their commitment. The provincial commission on the separation of church and state founded there in March 1918 had already disbanded by October. In Nizhnii Novgorod, so successfully did a parish commune confound Narkomiust officials who were attempting to confiscate the profitable diocesan candle factory that the issue had to be referred to Moscow for resolution.[43]

Moreover, the Orthodox had more weapons than obstructionism. Nuns at the Krestodvizhensk Monastery physically blocked the entry of a commissar in April 1918. When they then sounded the alarm that mobilized local believers and the two sides exchanged gunfire, one local man was killed and a Red Guard wounded.[44] As daily reports from state security organs to Lenin during 1919–1923 made clear, this was not an isolated incident. The briefings contained no shortage of frank assessments of the weakness of local support for the regime and the concentrated hostility to Soviet power among the religious faithful.[45]

From these beginnings in 1918 through the end of the civil war in 1921, the conflict between church and state assumed a dual character. First, the two sides uncompromisingly opposed one another in the internecine military conflict in which atrocities and retributions committed by Reds and Whites alike claimed the lives of millions of citizens.[46] As already noted, the Red Army, Cheka, and antireligious militants killed a number of bishops and priests.[47] In the opposite camp, clergy gave active as well as moral assistance to the Whites. The archbishop of Ekaterinburg, for example, organized a pro-tsarist demonstration after the execution of the royal family there in July 1918, and he formally celebrated the entry of anti-Bolshevik forces into the city in February 1919.[48] A pro-Orthodox publication prematurely celebrated the impending "sacred moment" in mid-1919 when "without a doubt" the Whites would defeat the Reds and capture Moscow, according to one Soviet source.[49] Churchmen in Siberia aided Admiral Alexander Kolchak by organizing military "Jesus Brigades" and "Holy Virgin Regiments." High clergy used their considerable influence to support General Anton Denikin on the southern front of the war and in appeals to public opinion in Western Europe. And village priests—by speaking against Bolshevism, spreading rumors, leading White partisan movements, and as martyrs to the cause—made even more diverse contributions.[50]

Second, situational battles continued within territory that the Bolsheviks controlled away from the front. The erratic nationalization campaigns presented a particularly inconsistent picture. Soviet power determinedly seized ecclesiastical buildings for use as schools, workers' clubs, public housing, and the like. But lower party officials and local governing institutions also ignored directives from above and confiscated church property without higher authorization, ostensibly for social welfare purposes but often for their own use.[51] In addition, state and party assaulted the sensibilities of the religious. Some such steps were little more than gratuitous. The Sovnarkom decree that rescinded state financial credits to the church in March 1918, for example, could not have surprised anyone,[52] and there was limited practical impact from decrees of February and April 1919 that disqualified religious believers from serving in the railroad and river police.[53] Other measures, however, had greater substance. On 24 January 1918, the replacement (effective 1 February) of the Julian calendar then in effect in Russia with the Gregorian calendar of the West set off a controversy that continues to this day.[54] The Soviet Constitution adopted in July 1918—although it guaranteed "the freedom for all citizens to conduct religious and antireligious propaganda"—specifically reaffirmed the separation of church and state as the law of the land.[55] And when the first party congress since the revolution met in March 1919, the program it adopted expressed a clear determination to eliminate the "religious prejudices" of the masses.[56]

Even where Soviet power predominated, however, supporters of the church found multiple ways to resist. In decrees of February, April, and July 1918, Tikhon and the church *Sobor* ordered measures that ranged from the militant protection of monasteries to nonparticipation in May Day ceremonies.[57] In September 1918, challenges from the *Sobor* over the right of Narkomiust to seize church buildings for use as educational institutions sapped significant energy and attention of the VIII Department.[58] During the same year, the Cheka in Ufa proved incapable of preventing a local bishop from rallying the population against the Bolsheviks with nationalistic, xenophobic speeches.[59] And a Narkomiust inspection of the village of Staraia Russa in a nonindustrial area of Novgorod province dated 1 December 1918 revealed that clergy had successfully turned the population against virtually every dimension of the separation decree: the confiscation of property, the removal of icons, the introduction of a nonreligious school curriculum.[60]

Orthodox believers, not the Liquidation Commission, came to dictate the terms of the legal battle over the separation of church and state in 1917–1921. The Sovnarkom separation decree of 20 January 1918 had been limited to a confident listing of general principles for secularizing society, a mood that carried over to the formation on 13 April of the Narkomiust Commission on the Application of the Decree on the Separation of Church from State and School from Church. The directives on implementation issued during the spring of 1918 concentrated overwhelmingly on the limited task of providing instructions to the local areas.[61] As reports from the provinces began to reach the center, however, Narkomiust changed its tone dramatically, with defensive language replacing confident assertiveness. Virtually every point of the more detailed Decree on the Implementation of the Separation of Church and State that Narkomiust issued on 24 August 1918 read as a reaction to believers' obstructionism rather than the articulation of a concrete goal. The August decree thus responded to a perceived need to enumerate the religious denominations to whom the separation law applied; to specify the number and destination of required inventories of ecclesiastical property; to devote an entire section to rules on registrations of births, marriages, and deaths that had legally been under civil jurisdiction since December 1917; and to reiterate the previously issued ban on religious ceremonies and symbols in public institutions. The decree of 24 August also attempted to clarify and thereby limit the nature of items believers could petition as necessary for religious worship. Not least important, the decree sought to combat stalling tactics by defining the legal period for compliance with orders of the Soviet of Workers' and Peasants' Deputies, Narkompros, and the VIII Section.[62] The decree failed to produce the desired result. During the following year, Narkomiust and the Cheka found it necessary to issue yet another directive that reaffirmed the August 1918 instructions.[63]

In the end, party and state organs lacked the resources, the training, and ultimately the inclination to pursue secularization systematically during the civil war. When the Narkomiust monthly journal, *Revoliutsiia i tserkov'* [Revolution and the Church], began publication in 1919, it erased whatever doubt might have remained about the nature of the struggle and the limitations of the VIII Section. Its periodic publication of visionary pronouncements notwithstanding, *Revoliutsiia i tserkov'* divided its coverage chiefly between detailed descriptions of the failures of antireligious work in local areas and the publication of new decrees.[64] Most significantly, Cheka reports of 1919–1920 contended that the political police, not Narkomiust or the soviets, assumed most of the responsibility for even the routine implementation of the separation decree in the local areas.[65] The Party Central Committee did not issue its first major circular on strategic antireligious work until 1921.[66]

. . .

In the years immediately following the civil war, Bolshevik policy attempted to deepen and sharpen the attack on the church as an institution, but several factors needed to come together for this to succeed. On the most public level, central organs, no longer preoccupied with the military conflict, would have to do a better job of preventing *uncoordinated* antireligious attacks in the local areas. At the same time, there was growing sentiment among the leadership that centrally directed, *coordinated* repression could overcome resistance and destroy religion, if carried out with minimum offense to public sensibilities. And as a practical matter, success would require organs more capable than those presently in charge of antireligious work.

The Bolsheviks therefore created multiple new state and party agencies to direct the next phase of antireligious activity. Many turned out to be ephemeral commissions that accomplished little, but others played more lasting roles. The creation in 1920 of the Narkompros Central Administration of Political Education, Glavpolitprosvet, gave a single state organ national jurisdiction over all propaganda, including antireligious.[67] But in June of the same year the Party Central Committee formed its own Agitation and Propaganda Department, Agitprop, in which the militantly antireligious Trotsky played a leading role until 1922. In addition to assuming responsibility for all written and oral propaganda, Agitprop was to oversee party training schools, publishing houses, and the work among national minorities as well as a number of its own subordinate commissions, including one for antireligious propaganda.[68] While

Glavpolitprosvet and Agitprop competed, the Moscow Party Committee formed its own special commission for antireligious propaganda. The People's Commissariat of Internal Affairs (NKVD) also then formed an ecclesiastical section in 1922 to deal with religious institutions, even though the Narkomiust Liquidation Commission continued to exist until 1924. This institutional overlap took its most important turn in October 1922, when the Politburo put in place an additional Antireligious Commission (also known as the Commission on Antireligious Propaganda), which was under Agitprop but beyond the influence of Trotsky. The leadership charged this Antireligious Commission with coordinating the efforts of Glavpolitprosvet, Narkomiust, Narkompros, the Moscow Committee of the party, the Komsomol, and the political police.[69]

These new institutions were all variously involved in three major assaults on Orthodoxy: the seizure of church valuables during the famine of 1921–1922; the Renovationist challenge to the main body of the Orthodox Church; and the continued harassment of church hierarchs and lower church organs. With millions perishing in the Volga region in 1921–1922 and thousands of refugees and orphans descending daily on every major city, the issue of famine relief provided Bolshevism a solid opportunity to put Orthodoxy on the defensive. The church donated general property toward aid, but it balked at surrendering its holy vessels. The state portrayed this as insensitivity to the plight of the starving, and when Tikhon's initial attempt to launch an independent Orthodox relief effort in 1921 failed to produce significant results,[70] in early 1922 Soviet propaganda seized the initiative. The initial issue of *Nauka i religiia* [Science and Religion] in 1922, to cite one representative example, included the now-famous poster by Demian Moor—a starving man over the caption "Help!"—and several pages of photographs of famine victims, especially children. Amid descriptions of cannibalism and reports of mothers killing their own offspring, the text attributed to Tikhon a statement of doubt that the famine was as serious as reported. Other entries linked the underlying causes of the disaster to the economic interests of the church as well as to the superstitious, nonscientific approach to agriculture practiced by the peasantry.[71] Narkomiust drew additional attention to the issue when it launched a specialized journal, *Tserkovnoe zoloto golodym* [Church Gold to the Starving], with a press run of fifty thousand.[72]

By the time VTsIK issued its instruction of 23 February 1922 to seize all church valuables within one month, public support for the position of the state reached its peak, while church unity appeared to waver. Public horror at the national tragedy of the famine meshed with the church's own expressions of concern. But the resolutions in favor of relinquishing church property to aid famine victims that believers and priests in some areas began to pass did not always distinguish clearly between general resources and sacred objects. This enabled the Bolshevik press, which only one year earlier had itself been battling rumors that the party was hoarding ample foodstuffs,[73] to paint church hierarchs alone as the villains. And although the VTsIK instruction provided for the preservation of items of historic or artistic significance rather than using all for famine relief, state pronouncements publicly emphasized various meetings where workers and students reacted to the full dimensions of the disaster by calling for seizing church valuables without distinctions.[74]

Although there were cases of compliance—Metropolitan Veniamin of Petrograd agreed to hand over ecclesiastical property on 5 March 1922 rather than endure the sacrilege of forced seizure[75]—Bolshevik strategy was equally served when clergy and laity offered resistance. Fiction could not have created a more patterned confrontation than the one that drew the most attention: the case of Shuia. As a major textile manufacturing center in Ivanovo-Voznesenk province, this town embodied in microcosm the Bolshevik characterization of the "proletarian" and "bourgeois" tensions involved in transforming Russia. Industry dominated the economy, yet the labor force consisted of what the regime called backward and politically suspect "peasant-workers" rather than the true proletariat on whom Bolshevik hopes rode. And the party feared that rural influences, including religion, still exercised sway in the factories, the more so since women—considered by both state and church to be the main repositories of religious piety in the country—predominated numerically in production.[76]

From the Bolshevik perspective, therefore, Shuia was both a problem and an opportunity, with the volatility of religious politics at the center. In terms of the communist categories operative at the time, bourgeois "officials and merchants" could easily excite "the very darkest elements of the population, the elderly, and even children" by spreading one "rumor, among others, that the valuables are not going to feed the starving [as claimed], but as payment to Poland and for the expenses of the Red Army." Thus, when the executive committee of the district soviet believed that it had negotiated the surrender of church property on 9 March 1922, its problems were only beginning. A vocal minority on 12 March, a Sunday, failed to prevent the election of representatives of believers to meet with a commission from the soviet on the following day, so they changed tactics. At the conclusion of the Monday religious service, this group cursed, pushed, punched, and in due course drove away the soviet officials who arrived at the church. By Wednesday, those who favored defending rather than giving up valuables were able to raise a considerable crowd, who drove back the six mounted police sent to disperse them. Revolver shots and a threatening encirclement then greeted reinforcements from the Red Army. The crowd beat four soldiers, one critically, and the troops fired into the crowd, killing an unspecified number of demonstrators. Authorities soon thereafter executed three church activists—other executions later followed—and at the end of the month clergy surrendered the valuables without additional violence.[77]

Lenin believed the potential value of the Shuia incident far exceeded the worth of the property confiscated. By creating a rationale for energetic Bolshevik aggressiveness against the church during the famine, "our opponents have committed a grave strategical error," he wrote to the Politburo. Intending to deliver an object lesson, he directed "that the trial of the Shuia rebels resisting aid to the starving be conducted with maximum speed and that it end in no way other than with the execution by firing squad of a very large number of the most dangerous Black Hundreds in Shuia and, to the extent possible, not only in that city but also in Moscow and several other clerical centers." Lenin ordered the upcoming Eleventh Party Congress to create a secret commission to continue the work of confiscation,[78] which in fact did move resolutely forward after the Shuia incident.[79] This coincided with ongoing attempts by Trotsky to treat the eradication of the church as an exercise in extralegal repression,[80] even as the secret police continued to report significant resistance—crowds of as many as a thousand—to seizures in Novgorod and Moscow provinces.[81]

In addition to this direct assault, Soviet power hoped to undermine Orthodoxy by supporting the Renovationist revolt inside the church in 1922–1923. Building on prerevolutionary discontent and a desire for reform from within,[82] a group of radical priests seized control of the church in May 1922 and temporarily removed Tikhon from leadership. This so-called Living Church, which passed a reformist agenda at the church *Sobor* of April–May 1923, proposed structural and liturgical changes as well as a political rapprochement with the Soviet regime. Their desire for civil peace led the Renovationists to support the adoption of the Gregorian calendar, to advocate the end of resistance to the confiscation of valuables, and to issue a declaration of allegiance to the state.[83] The Living Church cannot be dismissed as a mere pawn of the Soviets. However much the party enjoyed the discomfiture of Tikhon and his supporters, it soon read signs of trouble. Although opposed to Tikhon, the Renovationists energetically protected the independence of the church. This led Bolshevik critics first to question the usefulness of the Living Church and then to become apprehensive that it might itself become viable and therefore problematic. In June 1923, the party reassessed the situation and withdrew its support.[84] Ultimately, Renovationism failed, but not because of the criticism it endured in connection with its willingness to accommodate Bolshevism. Its decline stemmed from something far more basic: the majority of the laity never embraced Living Church clergy or reforms.[85]

The Bolsheviks also continued to assault the church psychologically from top to bottom. After years of threats and surveillance, the state placed Tikhon under house arrest in 1922, and in April 1923 the Antireligious Commission ordered his transfer to prison. During this period, organs of the Party Central Committee prepared to put him on trial for defiance of the separation of church and state, obstruction of the seizure of church property, and systematic anti-Soviet resistance.[86] Negative reactions at home and abroad, however, made such a prosecution highly problematic. In June 1923, the state therefore released the Patriarch without trial after he issued a public statement of loyalty that included ambiguous support for the adoption of the new calendar, but this outcome satisfied no one. The Politburo had granted the release with reluctance, yet the religious community found little cause for celebration. Although Tikhon did as much as he could to back away from the statements that had led to his freedom, church members seriously questioned his act of accommodation. The rank-and-file faithful continued to reject the new calendar and raised a general furor that outlived the Patriarch himself.[87]

There was additional harassment at the grassroots level in 1922–1923, most visibly in the form of Komsomol attacks on religious holidays. The Moscow Communist Youth League carried out the first Komsomol Christmas (it added Komsomol Easter the following spring)[88] from 25 December 1922 through 6 January 1923. Conceptualized initially as a "carnival" and carried out in 417 towns, the campaign sent members of factory Komsomols who had rural ties to the countryside as organizers. Komsomol Christmas began with an afternoon procession that parodied its church counterpart and moved on to didactic activities. House-to-house carolers sang atheistic and antireligious songs, revolutionary films and skits were performed, and lectures presented the Bolshevik understanding of Christmas. In addition, at night there were youth rituals that replicated those associated with religious holidays, with festivities beginning just before midnight and continuing until six o'clock the following morning.[89]

Although much of the press reflexively praised any attempt at antireligious activism, and local officials dutifully filed glowing reports,[90] more circumspect voices within the party criticized Komsomol Christmas and Easter from the outset. The Party Commission on the Separation of Church and State as early as February 1923—that is, following the initial Komsomol Christmas but before its first Easter—specifically objected to the frivolous atmosphere and demanded more ideologically substantial films, songs, reports, and lectures.[91] Carrying satiric "Red Christmas trees" in a mock procession in no way compensated for general poor organization, as when campaign literature appeared only the day before the actual event.[92] And the vandalism into which some of the carnivals degenerated offended not only the tactical proclivities of the Komsomol leadership, but also the religious feelings that persisted in the organization's own ranks.[93] Exercises that merely affronted religious sensibilities and attempted to divide communities along generational lines did not necessarily produce any discernible gain. The angry reactions of the elderly in Kiev, Khar'kov, and Saratov might have inspired humor, but they did not amuse those who were more concerned with winning over the population than insulting it.[94]

PROPAGANDA AND CULTURAL REVOLUTION

With such low returns and a chronic lack of consistency in every sphere of antireligious activity, the party began to alter its course in late 1922 and early 1923. Given the ongoing disagreements over the use of draconian methods and the persistent evidence that repression alone would not eradicate religion, sentiment for a different orientation gained support. In March 1922—the same month that his letter to the Politburo urged harsh measures in the Shuia incident—Lenin pushed the party intelligentsia to improve agitational techniques. His essay "On the Significance of Militant Materialism," which was cited in every subsequent pivotal discussion of antireligious propaganda, pointed particularly to the need to transcend "the boring, dry, non-illustrated expositions of Marxism" generated by "the Russian/Soviet bureaucratism" that presently dominated antireligious fare. He advocated approaching the masses with scientific materials that were intellectually rigorous but accessible.[95] And to improve work in the local areas, *Revoliutsiia i tserkov'* published a call for the creation of a new central organ to settle disputes between the state and religious groups.[96]

Even while controversies surrounding Tikhon, Renovationism, and Komsomol tactics continued to rage in 1923, therefore, the Twelfth Party Congress (17–25 April 1923) sent a clear message that future atheistic work would expand the role of organized agitation and reduce the reliance on repression.[97] The 1919 party program, although radical in intent, had called mass antireligious mobilization and consciousness-raising a task for the future. The priority then was "to avoid any offense to the religious feelings of believers, which leads only to the strengthening of religious fanaticism."[98] But four years later the party had failed even in this. As Zinoviev apprised the 1923 congress on its opening day: "We have gone too far, much too far. . . . We need serious antireligious propaganda."[99] One week later, the delegates passed the most definitive Bolshevik pronouncement on antireligious activism to that time. The use of "deliberately coarse methods . . . does not hasten but instead hampers the liberation of the laboring masses from religious prejudices," the resolution noted. It called for "antireligious mass propaganda in the form of lively and understandable lectures" and approaches "relevant to the social setting." The party would set up special courses to train agitators, develop new techniques, and publish a larger volume of popular and ideological antireligious literature.[100]

To these ends, and within the limits allowed by shortages of paper and printing materials, the state and the party had already begun to expand the body of atheistic literature. Between 1919 and the end of 1922, publications that specialized in antireligious themes—*Revoliutsiia i tserkov'*, *Nauka i religiia*, *Tserkov' i religiia* [The Church and Religion], and *Kommunizm i religiia* [Communism and Religion]—came out sporadically in modest press runs, were often short-lived, and frequently expressed more a philosophical than a mass approach.[101] This changed when Glavpolitprosvet launched the first sustaining mass atheistic newspaper, *Bezbozhnik* [The Godless], on 21 December 1922.[102] *Bezbozhnik u stanka* [The Godless at the Workbench], a militant monthly directed specifically at workers, emerged early the next year, as did a journal also entitled *Bezbozhnik*. The activist but by no means mass journal *Ateist* [The Atheist] appeared on 1 May 1925 with an array of philosophical and historical attacks on religion, and in January 1926 the self-proclaimed "scientific-methodological" monthly journal for agitators, *Antireligioznik* [The Antireligious], joined the fray.[103] Furthermore, the Krasnaia nov' and Bezbozhnik publishing houses led the way in turning out a variety of books, pamphlets, and texts for propagandists and mass consumption[104]—a million and a half such items by

1927[105]—and regional and specialized antireligious periodicals such as *Derevenskii bezbozhnik* [Village Godless] came into existence either independently or as supplements to existing publications. The newspaper *Bezbozhnik* undoubtedly played the most important role. This organ, above all others, was designed to compensate for the shortfalls in antireligious work by cadres. Intended to be passed from one reader to another, read aloud for groups of illiterates, or shared in village and factory reading rooms, each issue combined illustrations in color with simply written articles on topics ranging from the class essence of religion to popularized science to the need for improved agronomy. Ideally, its network of regional correspondents provided news from the local areas and linked the center with the periphery.[106]

Given such a strategy, maintaining a high circulation was crucial but not always possible. In 1925, material shortages led the Central Council of Trade Unions to order reduced press runs for all newspapers, including the party daily *Pravda*. Circulation figures for *Bezbozhnik,* which stood at 15,000 in 1923, 100,000 in July 1924, and 210,000 on 1 July 1925, fell to 114,000 in October 1925 and 90,000 one year later. From October 1926 through early 1928, individual issues temporarily ceased including information on press runs,[107] although the beginning of the Cultural Revolution again boosted the press run from a nadir of 60,000 to 400,000 by 1930.[108] But Emelian Iaroslavskii, the most influential antireligious activist in the country, held that shortages alone did not fully explain poor circulation. Noting that reduced printings were not limited to *Bezbozhnik* and other atheistic publications, he complained that the party made antireligious work too low a priority. And his criticism of the paper's inability to generate revenue through subscriptions even from atheistic activists intimated a lack of public interest.[109]

Indeed, neither the number of antireligious materials nor the quality of those that did appear satisfied Bolshevik leaders. Despite repeated party instructions and the entreaties of the antireligious press,[110] a sustained atheistic campaign involving all mass publications never took shape. General periodicals failed to give systematic attention to antireligious themes, instead usually addressing them only in response to some major party pronouncement or just before Christmas and Easter. Even *Bezbozhnik* had trouble fulfilling its ideals. Though its "living newspaper" propaganda troupe successfully reached a significant number of workers in large-scale factories,[111] and a rural correspondent described the impatience with which each issue of the "invigorating radiant sunlight" that was *Bezbozhnik* was awaited,[112] the paper far more frequently manifested the weaknesses of the movement. In addition to their consistently negative assessments of antireligious propaganda in general, the editors revealed their opinion of the audience in the instructions they gave to correspondents: write briefly and in language that "a dark peasant in a remote village" could understand; raise only a single issue in each article; do not rebut religion but demonstrate your argument through science; and provide an accompanying photograph or hand-drawn picture. Writings should concentrate on successes, such as peasants who had lost trust in their priest, and on methods to liberate the countryside from the influence of religion.[113] A dearth of submissions to the antireligious press led the 1925 national congress to listen seriously to a proposal by Mikhail V. Gorev, on behalf of the editorship of *Bezbozhnik*, to compel every antireligious activist to contribute one article per month. In the same report, Gorev questioned whether even contributors read the paper. And although the number of correspondents expanded in 1926, the editors repeated this charge in print.[114]

But if *Bezbozhnik* failed to achieve all it desired in the realm of propaganda, its very existence provided the foundation for organized antireligious work. Activists established the first provincial antireligious bodies in Voronezh and Moscow in 1921, and others followed elsewhere. The following year Krasikov organized the Atheist Society to publish antireligious classics of the past, but there was no viable framework for a national organization until the Society of the Friends of the Newspaper *Bezbozhnik* first met in August 1924.[115] Following several postponements, about one hundred members of the society and the paper's correspondents opened a week-long first congress on Good Friday in April 1925 to discuss organization and related tasks. Delegates from Nizhnii Novgorod and Ukraine resisted establishing a centralized national body, but the more hierarchically minded at the meeting prevailed. In June, the fledgling organization changed its name to the League of Godless [*Soiuz Bezbozhnikov*] and began operations at 35 Tverskaia Street in central Moscow, sharing space with the editorship of *Bezbozhnik*. Divided into five departments—organization, agitation, scientific-methodology, nationalities, foreign affairs—under a Central Council, the League of Godless began to set up a hierarchy of provincial, *oblast'*, district, and *volost'* organizations.[116] The league's approximately 87,000 members in 2,420 cells in 1926 expanded the following year to 138,402 members in 3,121 cells. Thirty-one provincial organizations grew to forty-five in 1927, with 40 percent of the membership coming from outside the party. The quality of this cadre, nevertheless, did not impress the leadership, who carried out a reregistration of members in early 1928 that reduced membership in Leningrad from

30,000 to 11,000 and nationally to 123,000. But growth resumed later in the year, and in 1929 approximately 9,000 cells encompassed 465,498 followers.[117]

The periodic rhetorical excess notwithstanding, no one seriously claimed that the League of Godless carried on antireligious work very effectively during its early years. Technically a voluntary social organization, it nevertheless experienced early internal differences over whether nonparty elements should be eligible for membership. In April 1926, the Party Central Committee issued a major general pronouncement on antireligious work intended to clear up misunderstandings everywhere in society, to give such agitation greater emphasis, and to make it more systematic. In response, by July 1926 a league directive opened membership to any Soviet citizen. The leadership also, however, publicly acknowledged other problems—primarily its conflicts with other organizations such as party, Komsomol, soviets, trade unions—and its own subordinate cells. The Central Council of the League of Godless hoped to redress these by announcing a relaxation of centralization and declaring itself a body for ideological and methodological leadership, not an administrative center.[118] Meanwhile, at the grass roots, groups of dedicated readers continued to hold regional, city, and even neighborhood conferences as an organizational and instructional device.[119] But this only underscored the widespread perception of poor organization—the prominent atheist I. I. Stepanov-Skvortsov later denigrated the antireligious propaganda of this period as a "cottage industry"—and that reliable activists constituted but a small fraction of the total membership of the League of Godless.[120]

Criticisms of antireligious work became a leitmotif in party discourse. As the eleventh anniversary of the revolution approached, *Rabochaia gazeta* [Workers' Newspaper] collected in a single article many of the prevailing reproofs of atheistic activism. Despite public declarations by the leadership, excessive centralization even within the Central Council of the league continued, and there were no viable links with local organizations. Individual cells performed no better—"in almost no region of the USSR does there exist an active struggle against religion"—and they still relied on administrative closures of churches rather than propaganda to accomplish their aims. Nor were other institutions obeying the party mandate to assist the League of Godless. Although the Komsomol was "worst of all," no party organ was performing antireligious work adequately, which allowed the Orthodox and sectarians actually to gain supporters.[121]

This disarray in the antireligious movement mirrored a deep lack of constancy in party behavior and tactics. Trotsky, the champion of the extralegal tactics euphemistically called administrative measures, still played a large role in the Thirteenth Party Congress of May 1924, but other voices dominated the discussion of religion. Foremost was VTsIK chairman Mikhail Kalinin, who spoke at length on the need to maintain a radical spirit in antireligious work while lessening reliance on administrative measures. The party, he emphasized, could not be neutral; it sought not simply to limit religiosity but to combat it. To do so effectively, it needed neither violence nor "professorial" tactics, but "political" approaches that would demonstrate the superiority of the materialist worldview: scientific explanations of the weather, for example, and a leading role for agronomists in rural antireligious instruction. The congress passed resolutions that reflected Kalinin's position: administrative measures against churches, synagogues, and prayer houses must be eliminated; propaganda in the village would concentrate on a materialist explanation of nature and society; reading rooms and schools were to be the foci of activism; and caution was to be used not to offend the religious feelings of believers.[122] After the congress, the party circulated to lower bodies a compendium of its antireligious declarations to date, which prominently featured the decisions taken at the Thirteenth Congress and pointed out that the deliberate work of "enlightenment" would take years and even decades.[123] In October 1924, the Party Central Committee once again instructed subordinate bodies to follow revolutionary legality and categorically to end reliance on repressive, administrative approaches in the realm of antireligious work.[124]

The new strategy did reduce the number of excesses against religious institutions, but in the process it also introduced new rifts. The emergence of Kalinin as a major spokesman on atheistic activism before and during the congress challenged Iaroslavskii's preeminent position. Iaroslavskii reacted by lamely defending the antireligious movement from criticisms similar to those he had himself leveled in the past, and he created small ways to distance himself from suggestions by Kalinin with which he generally agreed.[125] The new orientation also raised antagonisms among Soviet institutions, where the Komsomol came in for particular scrutiny. Charges of Komsomol frivolousness, similar to those the Party Commission on the Separation of Church and State raised in February 1923,[126] led the League of Godless to assume the leading voice regarding rural agitation. The league instructed local atheistic and Komsomol cells not to concentrate on narrowly conceived Christmas and Easter campaigns but to conduct cultural-enlightenment work continuously. They were to devise tactics for the city different from those used in the countryside,[127] and the general tenor of the propaganda needed to change everywhere. The leadership felt that any similarity to previous Komsomol holidays—they suspended Komsomol Christmas and Easter in 1924 and did not observe them again until 1928—would cause peasants to dismiss the event as "new" or "Soviet."[128] In this spirit, the 1928 and 1929 anti-Easter campaigns provided separate urban and rural strategies, and they promoted May Day as an alternative to Easter as the featured spring holiday.[129]

But the Thirteenth Congress also unintentionally undermined the intensity of the movement as a whole. Many grassroots organizations interpreted the resolutions of the congress as a signal to relax or even end the antireligious effort.[130] In Voronezh and Saratov provinces as well as in Ukraine, locals claimed to understand that the party and Komsomol would no longer be involved and that only teachers would conduct future antireligious work. Higher officials complained that lower organs in practice equated the word "caution" [ostorozhnost'] in the party resolution with "retreat" [otsutplenie], and both in villages and towns they dissolved atheistic cells and antireligious circles.[131] In Samara, where the Society of the Friends of the Newspaper Bezbozhnik numbered fifteen hundred members, church bells had already been seized and tractors purchased with the proceeds. Apparently concerned that central authorities would view this ex post facto as a violation of the caution and patience counseled by the Thirteenth Congress, the organization disbanded.[132] One expedition of ethnographers who surveyed twenty-eight volosti of Penza province commented on pronounced passivity on antireligious issues following the Thirteenth Congress,[133] and even writers of texts for agitators felt it necessary to explain that by curbing excesses the party congress did not mean the full abandonment of antireligious propaganda. The directive on antireligious propaganda that the Party Central Committee issued in April 1926 was designed to reverse the trend. The party position was not to end such work, it explained, but to improve organization and systematic implementation.[134]

Meanwhile, the framework of church-state rivalries changed. The proportions of the religious feeling that poured forth from all social classes following the death of Patriarch Tikhon on 7 April 1925 disquieted the revolutionary government, the more so when his funeral became a major public event. Nevertheless, two days after his death the Politburo published Tikhon's declaration of loyalty to Soviet power, a position that his eventual successor Metropolitan Sergei reiterated in May 1927.[135] The public statements of loyalty that had led to the end of Tikhon's imprisonment in 1923 constituted the beginning of a shift in the tactics of church hierarchs. Defiant opposition changed to accommodation and circumvention as Orthodox leaders began to protect the church by working within Soviet law, a strategy Sergei carried forward. In June 1926, he thus petitioned for the legal registration of the Patriarchate and for full legal rights for the church; other petitions for subordinate Orthodox bodies followed.[136] In sum, the party now relied more strongly on agitation than in the past, and by the mid-1920s the main tactics of the hierarchs of the Orthodox Church began to concentrate on working within the Soviet system.

. . .

The radicalization of all spheres of endeavor that began with the Cultural Revolution upset this relative lessening of direct confrontation in 1928. As aggressive tactics everywhere displaced restraint, atheistic propaganda was subsumed under the general party aims of rooting out deviationists of the right and left and mobilizing the fulfillment of the First Five Year Plan and collectivization of agriculture.[137] Consistent with this strategy, in 1929 the state seriously limited remaining religious freedoms, and the forces of repression that led the virtual civil war against the peasantry that was collectivization now became the leading instrument of eradicating religion. In the process, the membership numbers of the League of Godless grew dramatically on paper during these years, but the organization itself was effectively marginalized.

The renewed radicalism and impatience with gradualism that had aided the rise of Stalin and had driven the Cultural Revolution[138] did not spare the church or the League of Godless. On 8 April 1929, the VTsIK and Sovnarkom declaration "On Religious Associations" largely superseded the 1918 separation of church and state and redefined freedom of conscience. Though reiterating central aspects of the 1918 separation decree, the new law introduced important limitations. Religious associations of twenty or more adults were allowed, but only if registered and approved in advance by government authorities. They retained their previous right to the free use of buildings for worship but still could not exist as a juridical person. Most important, the new regulations rescinded the previously guaranteed right to conduct religious propaganda, and it reaffirmed the ban on religious instruction in state educational institutions. In effect, proselytizing and instruction outside the home were illegal except in officially sanctioned classes, and religious rights of assembly and property were now more circumscribed.[139] Not everyone grasped the full implications immediately. When the League of Godless held its second congress in June 1929, Iaroslavskii and others who understood antireligious agitation as a task of cultural conversion still prevailed over the champions of the interventionist tactics that would be the hallmark of the Cultural Revolution. With unintended irony, the group renamed itself the League of Militant Godless, but it was soon to be shunted aside in practical antireligious work.[140]

The tactics of 1929–1932 increasingly incorporated coercion. The military, the police, and the worker brigades who closed churches by force and exiled priests during dekulakization rendered the victory of gradualism at the League of Godless congress null. In practice, collectivization campaigns regularly included an assault on churches and local priests as part of the class war against kulaks. Millions of urban and rural dwellers were automatically enrolled in atheistic organizations, and antireligious work in general meshed with national politics and attempts to root out the real and imagined enemies of the emerging party leadership.[141]

Forces of restraint did not disappear, but the new circumstances limited their influence. At the time the state published "On Religious Associations" in 1929, it also created a permanent VTsIK Commission on Religious Issues, which still worked successfully beyond 1932 to enforce conformity with Soviet law and acted on petitions of complaint from legally constituted religious bodies. At the same time, membership in the League of Militant Godless grew to two million in 1930, three million at the beginning of 1931, and five million a mere four months later,[142] but in private the leadership did not rejoice. At one meeting of the Central Council in June 1932, the atheist Sorokoumovskaia maintained that, if even half the number of official members were reliable followers, the situation would be far better than what actually existed. Cadres were of poor quality, she continued, since anyone who proved capable in antireligious work was immediately transferred to ostensibly more important duties. In reality, the number of the true activists rose and ebbed in an ironic rhythm: "The mass is born at Christmas, dies at Easter, and is resurrected by May 1."[143] Thus, although the party continued to be far from unified on antireligious issues by 1932, the number of churches closed, local priests arrested or executed, and individual worshipers intimidated presented a different challenge to the survival of Orthodoxy, and church-state relations entered a new, more fully Stalinist phase.

STORMING THE HEAVENS

Behind Bolshevik antireligious slogans such as "storming the heavens" lay a complicated story of determination meshed with disunity and lack of preparation. The very inability of state organs to compel obedience among the population in 1917–1932 was exacerbated by a lack of consensus in the party at central and local levels on how best to eradicate religion. The Bolsheviks' unwavering allegiance to Marxist ideology mandated a long-term commitment to atheism, but the political and economic realities of the moment dictated cautious pragmatism. The struggles between and among institutions of the revolutionary regime resulted in instability at virtually every turn, and the antireligious policy of the moment was hostage to the political fates of its champions in the party. Moreover, the Russian Orthodox Church did not submit easily, forcing Soviet power to react to events in society as much as it imposed its will.

In the larger sense, though, the use of official policy and institutional power was for the Bolsheviks a means, not an end. Whether they would succeed was not a function of politics writ large or their ability to counter Russian Orthodox institutions, but how successfully they could inculcate a new worldview among the population. The battle for the hearts and minds of the people could therefore not be waged only by force or instruments of repression, and it would be in the personal sphere that Bolshevik antireligious aspirations were to face the greater test.

3

Materialism and the Secularization of Society

Bor'ba za Novyi Byt

"There's far too much of this science nowadays—there should be less of it! People believe in science, but they don't believe in God. Why even the peasants want to be scholars."
—M. E. Saltykov-Shchedrin, *The Golovlevs*

"'What we have here is not a village, but a *kolkhoz,'* a young village fellow told me with pride. A few days ago there was a holiday in this *kolkhoz:* in the afternoon on the square next to the soviet they demonstrated how the newly purchased tractor works. In the evening they showed a film in the reading room. During the intermissions the loudspeaker played [the radio]. Radio has firmly entered the *byt* of the new village. They have grown used to radio, [and] the radio broadcast is used productively; they talk about radio with enthusiasm."
—*Radio v derevne,* 1927[1]

As much as it was a political, institutional, and economic battle for the Bolsheviks, the period 1917–1932 was, to employ the party's own terminology, *"bor'ba za novyi byt"* or a "struggle for a new lifestyle." But ultimate victory or defeat depended on transforming more than "lifestyle," "way of life," "daily life," or the other common dictionary definitions of the elastic word *byt.* Rather, it demanded recasting the predominant worldview, consensual cosmology, and quality of existence that constituted the full essence of *byt.*[2] Citizens of the future were to interact differently in the spheres of politics and economics, to be sure, but real success in the *bor'ba za novyi byt,* the argument ran, would come only when they reached more enlightened understandings of their physical, ideological, and ethical environment. As the Soviet population learned to replace received practices with new ones grounded in philosophical materialism, their political consciousness would rise, they would exhibit greater mutual cooperation and honesty, the ordering of daily life and labor would improve, society and the family would be fully reconstituted, and all remaining spheres of activity could be made more rational. In this schema, religion impeded the liberation of the "new Soviet man" from the expectation of spiritual intercession in worldly affairs, and in so doing it lowered the prevailing levels of ethics and material life.

In pursuing the overarching goal unrelentingly if indeterminately defined as building socialism, party strategy called for extensive cultural-enlightenment work to instill new values and deliver important object lessons. In theory, the advent of socialism would end nonscientific thinking and with it a myriad of social ills: alcoholism, prostitution, juvenile crime, the subjugation of women, and anti-Semitism. As this transformation was taking place, materialist beliefs were to displace faith in the supernatural. In practice, Bolshevik pronouncements put forward two distinct understandings of materialism. It was, for one thing, a tenet of state *ideology,* and discussions by and for the party intelligentsia therefore promoted the term in its philosophical and Marxist sense: all existence derives from matter and conforms to the physical laws that govern it. But there was also an issue of *tactics.* Party officials understood well that they would not win over a mass audience with philosophical abstractions; peasants and workers required some demonstration of a positive impact on their well-being. Bolshevik declarations therefore also employed the word *materialism* in a second variation that closely parallels its American vernacular usage: acquisitiveness, especially of devices that reduce physical labor, and an appreciation of science largely dependent on its potential as applied technology. In other words—and this point deserves emphasis—the party actively promoted philosophical materialism in the realm of ideology, but demonstrations of the practical utilizations of science and technology were to be the principal vehicle of mass acceptance. It was in this manner that the message of materialism in both its senses broadly penetrated general discourse, education, and rituals.

BOLSHEVIK MATERIALISM

In its report on the first year of Soviet rule, Narkompros stressed that the revolution was not just a struggle between the proletariat and the bourgeoisie, but between two irreconcilable ideologies and worldviews. The initial steps of every revolution inevitably involve the use of force, the document noted, but final victory in Russia could result only from the widespread application of judicious reason.[3] Coming at a time when the survival of the regime was in serious doubt, this observation reaffirmed the cardinal Bolshevik belief that "culture"—and lack thereof [*nekul'turnost'*]—was a level of consciousness attained through education and enlightenment. Since one could achieve "culture" and impart it to others, Russia's "dark masses" would need to imbibe strong measures of more elevated thinking if the revolution was ever to progress beyond a transfer of political power and of the ownership of economic means.[4] But this party axiom did not give rise to any single mode of implementation. As in other spheres, Bolshevik attempts to inculcate a materialist ideology and worldview rested on a unified ideal, but they expressed themselves in permutations as diverse as the movement itself.

In the broad terms that characterized the majority of party declarations on the subject, tsarist society had been not only backward but insidiously so. Those who controlled the economic and political environment had manipulated mass ignorance and fears to enrich themselves and ensure the political malleability of workers and peasants. Relying on social relations and economic techniques characteristic of a much earlier age, the system had consciously perpetuated low levels of literacy in order to stunt mass consciousness, and it had counted on the poor health and physical exhaustion of the population to stifle initiative and unrest. According to this explanation, religious institutions served the interests of the beneficiaries of the old regime and enabled them to exploit prevalent beliefs—read superstitions—to keep society quiescent.[5] Economic hardship, a poor understanding of technology and science, and religiosity were therefore not only inextricably joined but also self-perpetuating. In Bolshevik parlance, the dependence of peasant agriculture on nature, and a paucity of knowledge about nature's functions, gave rise to the self-formed logic that supernatural forces were in control. Peasants felt helpless before illness and the elements and viewed a poor harvest as a punishment for sins. Belief in God, the party argued, mitigated these fears, even giving peasants a sense of empowerment, although they were just as likely to consult the village sorcerer as the priest for assistance in avoiding such catastrophes.[6] One should therefore study the forces of nature in order to conquer them, communist pronouncements maintained, since each demonstrable victory over famine by technology would drive religion back.[7]

The process of constructing the new order in Russia would consequently have to extend far beyond politics and economics and the battle between church and state institutions. The tasks of addressing contemporary political concerns, advancing a materialist worldview, and promoting antireligious ideas would require simultaneous attention.[8] The undermining of church institutions in early Bolshevik antireligious policy was thus a necessary revolutionary step, but it was not sufficient to alter views that most Russians accepted as natural. Hence, despite its early attacks on the church, the party did not pursue the elimination of religion as a separate objective; it was considered to be one facet of a broader campaign to improve *byt*. Antireligious propaganda would succeed only if

> tied to an improvement of the material condition, with a betterment of every mode of the economy; to the restructuring of daily life [and] the dissemination of natural-scientific knowledge; to the struggle against sorcery, backward forms of agriculture, and non-sanitary and non-hygienic conditions of life; and for electrification, a higher level technology, and science.[9]

Variations on this theme included the elimination of illiteracy and anti-Semitism as well as the promotion of the benefits of personal hygiene and regular exercise.[10]

For the Bolsheviks, therefore, promoting atheism included fostering social attitudes that would also raise labor productivity and improve the quality of life. Different party factions might debate the respective ideological merits of NEP and industrialization, but creating a new mass consciousness, although contentious in its own way, did not give rise to the same breadth and depth of disagreement. Proceeding from the conviction that *nekul'turnost'* and technological backwardness were always causally linked,[11] the majority of Bolsheviks counted on the mechanization of industry to transform the urban economy, whereas electrification and the use of tractors would end the impoverishment of the village.[12] In this quest, the party regarded mass literacy as a partisan, revolutionary weapon. The eradication of illiteracy was inseparable from efforts to inculcate initiative, enthusiasm, consciousness, and creativity among the urban proletariat and to end the psychological alienation of the worker from labor. By extension, "the liquidation of illiteracy is the path to godlessness" joined the arsenal of party slogans. And despite serious economic and organizational problems that limited instruction, literacy did reach more than 56 percent nationally by the end of the first decade of Soviet rule (over 80% in the cities). In industry, Bolshevik campaigns introduced technical training to counteract the dearth of skilled workers and strove to strengthen discipline in the factories. Transforming peasant labor presented a different challenge. Though party leaders claimed a share of success, they blamed illiteracy—which remained a serious problem among rural adults after a full decade of Soviet rule—for undermining attempts to replace manual labor with mechanization, to promote agricultural cooperatives over individual cultivation, and to provide instruction on agronomy and livestock.[13]

Proceeding a priori that Marxism was objective and scientific and that "science and religion are incompatible,"[14] the state worked to create a national scientific establishment that represented the class interests of the revolution. Soviet science made no claims to neutrality. The First Party Conference on Public Education, held December 1920–January 1921, specifically addressed the training of scientists and scholars in a new ideological tradition. The Institute of Red Professors, the Communist Academy, the Marx-Engels Institute, the Party Commission on the Training of Scientific Cadres, and other organs began to teach a Marxist-Leninist approach to the physical sciences. Creating this new cadre was not an end in itself, but a way to link science to immediate concerns. Narkompros, the Supreme Council of the National Economy, the Academy of Sciences, and the Communist Academy—although competitive with one another and riddled by internal factionalism—thus managed to create institutional networks to address large-scale projects such as the electrification of the country and the national coordination of science.[15]

Since the objective was to inculcate new attitudes among the rank and file, there was equally important work to be done in the social sciences, where ideological goals also informed short- and long-term agendas. The field of ethnography received special attention. State and party institutions sponsored extensive research during the mid-1920s despite the general scarcity of resources. In 1925 alone, the Central State Museum of Popular Customs in Moscow carried out more than twenty expeditions to study the Russian and Ukranian rural population and the various nationalities of the former empire.[16] This involved more than disinterested scholarly investigation. Academic research and even gathering data on the human and material resources of the country for use by state social organs were inseparable from constructing a socialist society and culture.[17] "Comrades! The goal of our expedition is antireligious propaganda," began the methodological instructions for one expedition from Leningrad.[18] As they set out to study marriage customs, living conditions, the influence of religion on the local economy, witchcraft and sorcery, popular tales of the occult, and other so-called superstitions,[19] Soviet ethnographers were eager to criticize vestiges of "backwardness" and uncover evidence of Soviet "enlightenment." Leading researchers consciously evaluated observed practices and traditions in terms of their potential to help the party achieve its aspirations,[20] and most expedition members embraced with conviction the dual role of scholar and social worker. They did not regard it a contradiction to include instruction with their research or to work as teachers, feldshers, and employees of the local soviet, but rather viewed these activities as a natural benefit to their subjects and society.[21] Only a minority of researchers disagreed, and even those who criticized combining fieldwork with agitation, rejected predetermined political goals as valid evaluative criteria, and stressed the need for scholars to confront mass culture on its own terms often linked their objections to the regime's priorities. They argued that antireligious propaganda, for example, could be effective only when—contrary to the present practice—activists understood the religious worldview and did not dismiss it out of hand.[22] Agitation against religion, they contended, should not continue the existing reliance on cheerleading [ura-podkhod], meetings, and planned campaigns but instead should engage citizens in their normal spheres of activity.[23] For the most influential ethnographers of the period, however, even in this limited form "such scholarly purism is misplaced";[24] in most cases, then, the study of the population included attempts to convert it to new values and to improve its lot.

State and party organs thus began to popularize science in society; they attempted to use the techniques of social science in doing so. When the Propaganda Department of the Party Central Committee turned its attention to a strategy for mass antireligious work in late 1921 through early 1922, it emphasized the role that popularized science must play.[25] Thereafter agitators generally incorporated science into their curricula of lectures, and elementary explanations of meteorology, electricity, and common scientific principles became a regular feature in periodicals.[26] As one Soviet newspaper summarized matters in 1923, to teach the scientific history of humanity was, by definition, to conduct antireligious propaganda.[27] Party publications repeatedly asserted that illustrated articles on evolution, human gestation, geology, and the similarities of Orthodox beliefs to those found in other cultures conveyed basic information that challenged Christian faith.[28] A new planetarium in Samara, for example, would show the workings of the universe, and this in itself would help counteract descriptions of the heavens by the clergy.[29]

. . .

By presenting science and technology in this manner, materialist propaganda merged medium with message. "Radio is not only a measure of cultural enlightenment, but also serves as a weapon in our socialist construction on all fronts," wrote *Radio v derevne* [Radio in the Village], "and in the hands of the proletariat it is a long-range weapon which helps the *bedniak-seredniak* masses in the class struggle."[30] Consistent with such thinking, the ability of the Kremlin to broadcast to London, Paris, and Berlin would further the cause of world revolution, the argument ran, whereas internally this "newspaper without paper" made possible direct contacts with the population "without bureaucratism." Establishing radio connections to the village of Pokrovskoe, located a hundred versts from the nearest railroad station, could have no effect other than the political and cultural betterment of the inhabitants. According to this opinion, the very act of demonstrating how to install radio equipment and having peasants listen to national programs such as "Peasant Newspaper" using headsets—a stock photographic pose in journalism—impressed them with the accomplishments of the revolution, provided political instruction, and disseminated advice on practical questions of agriculture. Advocates of this approach maintained that listeners who initially attended amplified broadcasts out of curiosity or to dance would enjoy themselves and thereby lower their resistance to the verbal content. Special programs directed to different segments of the population were to open new areas of cultural experience and deliver a unified message; radio technology itself would demonstrate the benefits of materialist-scientific thinking to the audience. In the Bolshevik view, the forces of religion recognized all this and reflexively opposed radio.[31]

Writings on health and sanitation conveyed the same point. In the most extreme variation, overtly antagonistic writers employed virtually any available ploy to discredit religion. For example, the hundreds who used the same communion spoon, exchanged ritual kisses, or touched some venerated cross were said to spread "tuberculosis, and syphilis, and scarlet fever, and diphtheria."[32] The idea that reading party newspapers, having a clean apartment, and rejecting religion all went together was treated as self-evident.[33] And in the hospital at the Likino Textile Mill in Moscow, where both clergy and doctors tended the patients, the burning of incense by a priest fouled the air to the extent that he—ignoring protests—opened all the doors. In this account, presented in a format that suggested it demonstrated a universal point, every patient in the room caught cold.[34] Other offerings relied less on emotion. There were modest articles that took the prior knowledge of the audience into account and wrote simply, for example, that children need sufficient quantities of high-quality food and that everyone requires clean, fresh air.[35] Teachers were advised to inculcate basic sanitary principles such as to avoid polluted water, not to share a cup with a sick person, and to maintain a sanitary living space.[36] Doctors discussed alternatives to sorcery and conventional wisdom in prenatal care, women whose workday caused them to neglect breast-feeding their infants, the deleterious effects of frequent and protracted fasting, and the need to study more closely the link between religion and alcohol abuse. Accordingly, they maintained, an understanding of medicine might counteract peasant fatalism in the face of illness and, by extension, improve the emotional state of the patient.[37]

The call for responsible health care and sanitation also emerged in descriptions that contradicted party stereotypes and ideals. Official publications reflected the overarching intelligentsia bias that the village had not changed appreciably in centuries, but evidence that the Soviet state itself gathered made this position difficult to uphold in all cases. For example, despite frequently repeated tales of peasant hostility toward outsiders and unthinking allegiance to sorcerers, one ethnographic study reported that the inhabitants of Goritsa *volost'* took a decidedly practical approach toward medicine in 1917–1924. After a shaky beginning, two female doctors working at half salary in difficult times revived confidence in the local hospital. When they left for personal reasons in 1922, their replacement Ignat'ev rapidly destroyed the goodwill they had built. His uncooperative attitude and a series of unsuccessful operations, especially in the area of gynecology, sent patients back to popular healers forty-five *versts* away in Kimry. In the fall of 1924, a competent new doctor, Uspenskii, once again restored trust in professional medicine, but when he departed a year later both Ignat'ev and the village healers were back in business.[38]

Facile assumptions about workers and the factories also faced challenges. Although the future was said to be bright, living conditions in many enterprises were now worse than they had been under tsarism. Ten or more people inhabited family apartments that measured two and one-half by four meters in the Moscow Trekhgornaia textile mill. Conditions outside the plant in apartments expropriated from the bourgeoisie were no better, a three-shift work schedule prevented privacy and order in the factory barracks at any time of day, and children had to be left unattended while parents worked.[39] At the former Tornton Factory, standard Bolshevik expectations were inverted. It was the "October Youth" who lived in filth in one dormitory, where drunken fights broke out nightly. Order, cleanliness, and sobriety prevailed only in the barracks of the older workers, who were predominantly religious and had served the former masters "like slaves."[40]

And one classified report by the Information Department of the party of 6 April 1929 directly contradicted the official attempt to equate religion with attitudes toward health and sanitation antithetical to those of the revolution. Some churches maintained their own clubs and in one case even medical facilities, the document noted, and a disquieting number of religious groups promoted goals similar to those of the party. Like the Bolsheviks, they stressed the basics of health: the need to wash hands before meals, the importance of cleanliness of children, and the usefulness of agronomy manuals. They decried smoking, drinking, and the health risks of a promiscuous sex life.[41]

No issue surpassed agriculture in exciting the expectations and frustrations of Soviet materialism. In the broadest terms, the party ideal from the outset was to mechanize agriculture and organize it as a large-scale industrial enterprise, the path it ultimately pursued through forced collectivization. Historians have well documented how the peasantry, who had exhibited scant interest in the party's encouragement of voluntary collectivization in the early and middle 1920s, actively resisted the uprooting of their lives and existing patterns of labor by the coercive campaigns that began in 1929. What must be emphasized, though, is that this entailed more than elemental resistance to outside compulsion. It also embodied a pivotal conflict of cultures between the state and the peasantry that surfaced during the implementation of specific initiatives, such as the introduction of tractors.[42] Soviet writings of the period did not approach the issue in this way, however, but concentrated on presenting frictions and inherited problems as vestiges of the interests of the class enemy. Those who publicized the party position continued to blame chronic poor harvests, recurring famines, and the devastating effects of drought on the primitiveness of agricultural technique, but they took the additional step of attributing backwardness in agronomy to the influence of the predominant spiritual beliefs.

In this interpretation, the class orientation of organized religion and the self-interest of the clergy worked together to perpetuate the idea that successful agriculture depended on benign supernatural intervention. Priests who received emoluments for purifying fields and blessing seed rejected innovations that would improve yield, and they promoted ineffective alternatives that left the population vulnerable to disaster. The antireligious press exulted in chronicling these practices in detail. Peasant wisdom passed from one generation to another held that a bright moon on Christmas Eve was a good sign for crops and that Monday and Thursday were the best days for sowing. Fields everywhere had to be cleared of evil spirits before plowing and planting, and seeds were blessed at Easter. Among the Russian population of Ukraine, religious ceremonies called for sprinkling both seed and fields with holy water before spring and fall sowing. On Iur'ev Day in Arkhangel'sk province, peasants carrying icons and candles circumnavigated the area to be cultivated in the belief that this would both cleanse it and improve fertilization. On the morning of Egor'ev Day in Vologda province, every homemaker burned a candle before an icon of Saint George placed in a cup of rye, then carried the cup three times around the home and ultimately presented the rye to the parish clergy in church. And in a number of regions, villagers sought to improve fertilization by burying an effigy of a penis. Other forms of sympathetic magic included trying to control rain by submerging a clergyman in a river in full vestments. An alternative subject for the dunking was a dummy in women's clothing. Additional popular ceremonies existed for cattle breeding, beekeeping, fishing, choosing sites for new houses, and constructing homes.[43]

For much of the 1920s, the party did not make counteracting such perceptions of cause and effect its first priority. References to mechanization, the promotion of agronomy, and the like were staples of antireligious writings on agriculture from the outset,[44] to be sure, but it was not until the eve of collectivization that they became the predominant foci. In March 1926, the Central Council of the League of Godless heard a report that criticized the past tendency to focus antireligious work against Orthodox priests, which provided opportunities for sectarians to increase their influence significantly.[45] Similarly, a number of speakers at an Agitprop meeting devoted to antireligious issues in 1926 complained that the initial orientation of propaganda had been to concentrate on the church as a tool of capitalism rather than on its relationship to believers. This resulted in antireligious work that was narrowly focused on the bourgeois origins of religion and not linked to issues, such as knowledge of nature, that would actually help people lead more productive lives.[46] Party agitators therefore received new instructions in 1926 to increase the emphasis on nature in agricultural propaganda and to avoid directly confronting the clergy in doing so.[47]

The propaganda of the second half of the decade specifically linked antireligious attitudes to immediate, practical concerns. *Bezbozhnik* forcefully maintained that the battle for the countryside was above all a conflict between the poorest peasants and the kulaks for the loyalty of the middle peasant [*seredniak*]. And since the kulak was the ally of the church, the battle for the *seredniak* was also one against religion, which would not be won without agricultural cooperatives, tractors, and the elimination of illiteracy.[48] Still more specifically: "The success of antireligious propaganda during the spring sowing campaign depends in significant measure on how closely it will be tied to the concrete tasks of a given agricultural region."[49] In practice, Bolshevik organs in the early 1920s had gleefully reported when priests tried to produce rain and failed or when an unmarried female bore a clergyman a son after he "stared into her eyes." More soberly they pointed out that peasants regularly went hungry several months a year but still contributed bread to the church, or they noted that the pay of the priest for one year was equal to the cost of a tractor.[50] This kind of coverage continued after 1926, of course, but it was increasingly overshadowed by reports of peasants rescued from the brink of starvation by the realization that their hard work and not God was the engine of a better life.[51] *Derevenskii bezbozhnik* used simple language and multiple illustrations in antireligious messages, and in 1928 it published an agricultural calendar that included advice on cleaning and sorting seeds, the repair of machinery, and the like.[52] There were even articles in antireligious publications, such as one that appeared in *Bezbozhnik u stanka* in 1929, that discussed topics such as the mechanization of agriculture without direct reference to atheism.[53]

In sum, as Bolshevik propaganda tailored its materialist message for mass dissemination, it subordinated ideological nuance to directness of expression. Public statements might carefully distinguish between the spheres of material life and spiritual faith when defining the problems the party faced, but the proposed solutions were far less precise. Thus, although the Marxist tenet that existence determines consciousness informed the broad lines of argument, in specific statements it appeared largely in caricature—as an exaggerated confidence that alterations of economic life would automatically affect personal belief.

NONRELIGIOUS AND ANTIRELIGIOUS SCHOOLS

"To the teacher's question: 'why do you make noise in school, but behave yourself quietly at home?' they answer, 'because here we can—there are no icons.'"[54] Whether such a contrived conversation ever took place verbatim, or merely reflected one ethnographer's effort to communicate accumulated experiences, it captured the Soviet dilemma of attempting to use public education as a conduit of cultural values. On the one hand, the party relied strongly on the potential of schools to inculcate norms and mores that would supplant religious beliefs. On the other, institutions of learning did not yet teach unalloyed Bolshevik positions in the 1920s, and the decidedly different ideas that students encountered at home and in the community persistently found their way into the Soviet classroom.[55]

From the outset, the party expected the educational system to act as a significant revolutionary force. On 28 October 1917, Narkompros announced ambitious goals: mandatory free schooling, the creation of "an army of people's pedagogues," increased public involvement through the decentralization of authority, and the elimination of illiteracy in "the shortest possible time." Above all, Soviet schools would move beyond instruction to education, that is, transcend the simple transfer of information in favor of inculcating the creativity and enlightenment that make learning a lifelong endeavor.[56] To achieve this, the curriculum would include socially useful labor, shop crafts, and a practicum in an industrial enterprise, and it would eliminate homework, promotion examinations, and assigning grades. The party program adopted in March 1919 gamely expressed the intention to establish proletarian schools free of religious influences. Two years later, Narkompros began to promote its Complex Method, which was to replace traditional academic subjects with integrated modules in which students learned about labor, nature, and society through direct involvement.[57] Religion, with its dogma and claims to the possession of absolute truth, was deemed inimical to the freedom of criticism and analytical thinking on which this new curriculum depended.[58]

But Narkompros and other Soviet agencies initially attempted the secularization of schools rather than vigorous atheistic instruction. Minister of Enlightenment Lunacharsky and his deputy Nadezhda Krupskaya believed that nonreligious, scientific lesson content—not antireligious activism—would inculcate the desired materialist beliefs among students as it prepared them for new modes of labor and social behavior. When Narkompros addressed the issue definitively for the first time on 18 February 1918, it declared religion a matter of individual conscience that state schools would neither promote nor repress.[59] In keeping with the law on the separation of church and state, the Commissariat forbade teachers to engage in religious instruction and mandated the removal of religious objects from classrooms,[60] but it did not replace Orthodox with atheistic proselytizing. Yet even these steps disrupted instruction. The new nonreligious orientation made inherited tsarist textbooks and curricula obsolete,[61] although nothing existed to replace them. And the removal of icons and religious instruction from the school system, which had previously devoted as many as twelve of twenty-seven instruction hours per week to religion,[62] generated far more public opposition than support.

Orthodox officials, clergy, and laity offered variegated resistance both to nonreligious education and to the Commissariat's experimental teaching methods. Following the separation of church and school in January 1918, the Patriarch and the Holy Synod issued protests as Narkompros attempted to take control of the more than forty-two thousand church schools.[63] Parish clergy presented a more palpable problem, although hardly more of a surprise, when they used local demonstrations against the separation of church and state to protect their influence in the schools.[64] But the parents who directly battled the new changes had the greatest impact. In cities as well as villages, as a result of the cessation of teaching religion, the removal of icons, and the introduction of pedagogical experimentation, some parents withdrew their children from school and even attacked teachers.[65] A larger number pursued more pragmatic alternatives. When the end of central funding of schools in 1921 transferred financial responsibility to local areas, national institutions surrendered significant control over the curriculum in the process. Parents, such as those in Moscow who tried to bring monks and priests into schools to carry out religious instruction,[66] began to assert direct influence over lesson content. Moreover, the majority of teachers either shared the parents' religious concerns—Lunacharsky probably erred on the side of conservatism when he estimated that 30 to 40 percent of teachers were still religious believers in 1929[67]—or at least opposed direct affronts to Orthodoxy. And like parents, the more experienced pedagogues preferred traditional academic approaches to educational experiments and activities, which they viewed as wasting time.[68]

What the Bolsheviks needed in order to pursue a consistent and systematic educational policy did not exist: a corps of classroom instructors who actively supported the revolution. The state expected teachers, like scientists and social scientists, to carry out cultural missions while they performed their regular duties. Ideally, the party would enlist them to the cause through their union and professional organizations, and later in the cities through the League of Godless. The rural instructor was to assess and address the local level of religiosity, the observance of holidays, the extent and effectiveness of antireligious propaganda, and the role of the Komsomol. And as members of the "village intelligentsia," underpaid and already overworked teachers were expected to perform adult literacy instruction and participate in the numerous party campaigns as they arose.[69] But the first steps were inauspicious. Teachers went on strike in Moscow and other towns to protest the Bolshevik seizure of power, and during the civil war they predominantly supported the Whites. The Third Congress of Soviets made note of how rarely one encountered a socialist teacher and that the pedagogues frequently considered religious instruction a regular duty.[70] The Society of the Friends of the Newspaper *Bezbozhnik* reported in early 1925 that throughout Saratov province teachers rejected the godless and their teacher-training courses.[71] Moreover, throughout NEP experienced teachers—in 1926 no fewer than 40 percent in the Russian Republic had been on the job ten or more years—also distinguished themselves by their opposition to changes in the curriculum by Narkompros, and it was difficult to find competent replacements. Half of the young teachers trained after the revolution received only one to three months' preparation, and in one survey conducted in 1922 five out of eight had not read a journal, a newspaper, or a brochure in the past six months.[72]

It proved even harder to dislodge the influence of the clergy. As in the prerevolutionary period, daughters and sons of priests constituted a significant part of the teaching profession.[73] The Thirteenth Party Congress in 1924 placed the proportion at 50 percent,[74] and stories of their misconduct abounded. In Iaroslavl' province, where the thirty offspring of clergy who worked in the twenty-seven schools of a single *volost'* ignored directives to halt religious instruction, religiosity among students approached 100 percent. The son and two daughters of a deacon who ran the village school in Kresty observed even minor religious holidays and lost half the academic year in the process. In Zakharovo, the teacher constantly sang religious hymns and declared that all good derived from religion; rapporteurs in Nizhnii Novgorod and Tomsk provinces filed descriptions of teachers who led children to church during instruction periods, kept icons at home, baptized their infants, and invoked devils when they wanted to frighten the students. The anti-Semitism of the teacher Vishniakova in Khristopol included tales of the ritual murder of children and drinking of Christian blood. And even amid the burning of icons that took place in Velikie Luki during the Cultural Revolution, not all teachers agreed to join the League of Militant Godless. One made a point of using only capital letters to write the words "god" and "church." Nor could the Bolsheviks expect much improvement in the short term. Pedagogical institutes, where half the students continued to come from clerical families, provided little antireligious training by the beginning of the Cultural Revolution. Even those teachers sympathetic to antireligious work were ill prepared to carry it out,[75] and to the end of the 1920s party documents assessed levels of religious belief among the young near or above 50 percent.[76]

These realities sobered and intimidated local and national officials, who routinely made extensive concessions to religious sensibilities. Soviet periodicals eagerly seized opportunities to publish reports, such as one from Novgorod province in 1918, that claimed no negative ramifications of eliminating religious training from the curriculum.[77] Nevertheless, fanciful communiqués such as these did not reflect the true perspective of any operative institution. Local soviets—not only in remote villages but throughout urban and rural sectors of Tver' province, for example, and in Moscow itself—continued to allow religious instruction during the civil war. In the 1920s, educational directives to local areas advised against overt antireligious agitation, which could be counterproductive, in favor of incorporating such material into lessons on natural science, literature, and history. Radical atheists, especially in Moscow, periodically questioned the science-versus-religion approach, but for much of the decade school councils took religious holidays into account in academic scheduling and canceled instruction for major feasts. In so doing, they were actually following an official Narkompros policy that lasted until the beginning of the Cultural Revolution.[78] Local conditions dictated such flexibility. In fifteen schools in Voronezh, only 37 percent (1,328 of 3,605) of pupils attended on Orthodox Christmas. One rural teacher estimated a usual rate of 75 percent absenteeism on church holidays. The Korchezhinskaia school in Smolensk province lost thirty-five of seventy-five instruction days to weddings, holidays, and other religious observances. One atheistic teacher complained in 1928 that, despite a curriculum that encouraged secularism, the "percentage of nonbelievers is becoming smaller and smaller."[79]

. . .

Prevailing Bolshevik opinion presented the situation as just one more manifestation of "backwardness" to be corrected. Nonetheless, the financial problems of education placed serious limits on what even those who cooperated with the revolution could accomplish. In one area where teachers had lived in one or possibly two rooms before the revolution and received a monthly salary of thirty rubles, in 1921–1922 they were given a half month's pay only twice in eight months, and during the next two years nothing more was done to aid them.[80] One expedition of ethnographers to Kursk province developed their own technique for identifying the school as they entered a new area: look for the building that lacked a door and windows.[81] Soviet power could not provide much relief. Even as the Sixteenth Party Congress confidently mandated universal elementary education in late 1931, it tempered its self-congratulation with observations on the poor material condition of teachers and facilities.[82]

Many private citizens understood more than the party's repetitive recitations of grievance would suggest. They instinctively recognized schools as a crucial venue of cultural conflict between state and society, and they quickly learned to turn economic scarcity into a weapon. For example, material conditions within Andreev *volost'* of Kostroma province did not vary widely in 1925, yet public attitudes toward teachers and the condition of facilities were diverse. For example, in Nuksho, where parents approved of the local curriculum, all children of school age attended, and in the Andreev school the teacher similarly enjoyed full public cooperation. By contrast, peasants in nearby Sandogor withheld support from a school "where there is no Law of God." And in the same *volost'* the school in Gul'nev, which only one-fourth of the children attended, was allowed to fall into disrepair for the same reason. Nor could one miss the point made by the occupants of neighboring Fefelovo. Parents there declared their preference for the moral lessons of the priest over academic learning, and their children attended church faithfully. Although the school building was unusable, school was open all year; yet villagers built the priest a new house.[83] During the same period in Zuevko (Kursk province), peasants failed to collect the several wagons of firewood necessary to heat the school, and in December 1924 it closed. But in the same *volost'* in Nikolsk, where the public school had not been open for four years, peasants paid the deacon's wife one and a half poods of grain per month for each child in the large group she taught.[84] Furthermore, young teachers who arrived in a village often had no place to live; when only the priest offered shelter, they became dependent on him and useless as purveyors of materialist lessons.[85] Those not co-opted could be driven out. When schools closed, only the teachers with local ties stayed.[86]

Economics also had other effects. During a decade when as many as half of the school-age children in the Russian Republic did not attend at all,[87] family finances largely determined which stratum could afford schooling. Even if parents were willing and able to pay for instruction, children of the most impoverished often lacked the proper coats and shoes for winter. A 1924 report to the Party Central Committee noted that if the *bedniak* lacked a horse to transport his children to a distant school, local clergy exploited the opportunity to intervene. As parents acted on their own priorities, the number of girls attending in some areas fell to practically zero; that hampered them in the present and left them unprepared to attend a factory school if they later entered the industrial labor force.[88] By contrast, schools under Orthodox and sectarian control provided the textbooks, notebooks, and hot breakfasts that their state counterparts could not.[89]

The militant godless were first frustrated, then emboldened. Orthodox priests worked extensively among the young, and foreign and indigenous sectarians were accomplishing even more. Indeed, the activist proselytizing carried on by Old Believers and evangelicals in their own communal schools produced the kind of results that Bolsheviks openly envied. Jewish clergy also provided instruction, and in Islamic areas enrollments in religious schools were higher than in state institutions. The Central Council of the League of Godless blamed these circumstances on the Narkompros policy of nonreligious education, which they felt did more to eliminate antireligious work among children in public schools than it did to eradicate religion. The "mistakes" of Krupskaia and other leading Narkompros officials had left atheism defenseless against sectarian aggressiveness and largely accounted for the increase in religious belief among the young.[90] *Bezbozhnik* called for greater militance in teaching materialism,[91] and when Iaroslavskii addressed the Organizational Bureau of the Party Central Committee on 10 December 1928, he held a variety of institutions responsible for what he characterized as "pacifist and neutral" positions. It was impossible to raise even four hundred to six hundred rubles a year to support an atheist university in Moscow, he charged, and neither the Central Council of Trade Unions nor any other organization would help. The Presidium of VTsIK allowed believers to construct a church at the Communist Avant-Garde Factory, Iaroslavskii complained, and Evangelicals were permitted to hold national congresses. In his view, policies such as these tied the hands of the League of Godless.[92] "Neutrality" in the classroom would have to end; religious teachers could no longer be tolerated.[93]

The deepening of the Cultural Revolution of 1928–1931 brought antireligious messages forcefully, albeit temporarily, into the classroom and increased the criticism of Narkompros. At the second plenum of the Central Council of the League of Militant Godless in March 1930, to cite one gathering characteristic of the period, speaker after speaker heaped abuse on the nonreligious position Narkompros had previously taken. Not only had the party found the orientation itself faulty, but the antireligious movement now had to deal with its legacy: textbooks in need of revision, a paucity of antireligious films, and teachers improperly trained for an atheistic curriculum. Nor had Narkompros yet done enough to eradicate the idea that religion was a personal decision.[94]

Religious celebrations lost their standing as school holidays in 1929,[95] the political police closed religious schools made illegal by the 1929 decree on religious associations,[96] and in the spirit of the period the journal *Bezbozhnik* went so far as to print a photograph of an anti-Christmas "demonstration" at a Moscow nursery school.[97] But other educational objectives of the Cultural Revolution soon overtook this emphasis on intensifying antireligious measures. At the beginning of the 1930s, restoring academic rigor became the paramount educational issue in the country. By 1932, a concern with the reinstitution of homework, grades, and high standards pushed antireligious militancy in the classroom to the margins, and Narkompros reinstated its policy of tolerating religious holidays.[98]

In the end, Soviet power extensively succeeded in removing Orthodox instruction from the curriculum of the public schools, but this did not eliminate religion as intended. It proved far easier to take away icons and prohibit catechism than to convince teachers to adopt a materialist approach in the classroom with conviction and enthusiasm. Moreover, emotional confrontations notwithstanding, not all parental and community concerns could be reduced to the issue of religion. Simple capriciousness governed certain episodes. In Lenino (Penza province), children attended classes on the feast of Pokrov because the school was heated but the church was not.[99] Conversely, peasants in Petrovskoe (Moscow *oblast'*) said they went to church because, unlike other village facilities, it was clean and warm.[100] And *Bezbozhnik* reported that several locales attempted to implement the separation of church from school simply by locating the two structures further apart.[101] But there were also deeper issues. Even parents who were resigned to the elimination of religion from lessons found other fault with the new curriculum: a ubiquitous decline in discipline, second-year students unable to recite the entire alphabet, and third-year students who could not multiply two times two. Adults blamed the time the new Complex Method curriculum spent on excursions, painting, and sculpture.[102]

Nonetheless, scientific, nonreligious pedagogy also claimed a share of limited but real victories. In some areas where local populations had noisily protested the removal of religion and icons from the schools and later resisted the seizure of church valuables, Narkompros reported that over time students and teachers came to accept some of the practical applications of materialist views. A sizable segment reacted positively to sex education classes that encouraged abstinence for adolescents fourteen to seventeen years of age "in the interest of their offspring," lectured on the evils of smoking and drinking, and dispensed information about venereal diseases and general health. In due course, "questions of religion [came to] occupy almost no place among our children." With the exception of one daughter of a priest who influenced a circle around her, the older children in this particular school were said to have no knowledge of the Bible, catechism, or prayers.[103] At the Chertovsk school in Penza province, the efforts of one antireligious teacher brought the level of reported atheism among students to 75 percent. In nearby Kochetov *volost'* there were only five or six student atheists in the full sense of the word, but interest in religion had fallen so much that the priest could not fill his Easter choir.[104] On balance, materialism became the official ideal of the national curriculum. But as the party moved at the beginning of the 1930s to reinvigorate discipline in the schools, extend access to education, and raise the quality of teaching,[105] its full acceptance was still being contested case by case.

HOLIDAYS AND RITUALS

Soviet power also promoted materialism through the creation of public and personal rituals, where the appeal was as much emotional and psychological as intellectual. The regime desired that the population come to associate the symbols and ideals of Bolshevism with public ceremonies as well as with key episodes of personal celebration and solemnity. Thus, the leaders worked from ideological motivations to replace religiously grounded holidays and rites of passage with secular observances, but they hoped at the same time to harness the social and ethical potential of ceremonial occasions.[106]

As in other undertakings of this type, gaps immediately developed between conceptualization and execution. One contingent of propagandists writing in *Rabochaia Moskva* [Working Class Moscow] and *Krasnaia nov'* [Red Virgin Soil] proceeded as if denunciations of existing practices alone would achieve their objective. When *Krasnaia nov'* devoted significant space to the subject in 1923–1925, the paper glibly dismissed traditional observances by noting their magical and mystical elements or citing the need to replace "church theatricality" with a "theatricality of *byt* [*bytovaia teatral'nost'*]."[107] Other propagandists relentlessly belabored the link between emoluments and the performance of Orthodox religious rites. Typical of this genre, one account published a simple recitation of the religious expenses for the year 1924 in Medveditsa as a seemingly self-evident indictment. The village priest collected a half-pood of rye for each of 441 christenings and 234 funerals, and he charged seven poods for each of the 104 weddings in the *volost'*. In this instance, the cleric also refused to baptize the child of Elizaveta Barykina, who was herself without bread and could not pay.[108] More insightful Bolshevik commentators did not limit themselves to simple denunciations of existing practices: they also weighed public willingness to observe Soviet rituals as a significant barometer of acceptance of the new order. In this view, a rejection of Soviet observances might signify a conscious renunciation of the regime and its appurtenances on spiritual grounds, but the retention of old traditions could also rest on an impulse even more basic: a desire simply to enjoy oneself in familiar ways.

In practical terms, undermining church holidays and rituals was no trivial matter for a state hoping to improve labor productivity and alter social consciousness. Orthodox holidays numbered between 150 and 200 per year, and Russians generally observed about 50, in addition to Sundays, as days free from labor. Beyond Christmas and Easter, there were eight major feasts and a half dozen other special observances. Moreover, according to the inclinations and especially the means of individual parishes, there might be one or more additional celebrations associated with the Virgin Mary; feasts of Michael, Nicholas (in May as well as December), and other saints; in addition, various days venerated miracle-working icons or commemorated past military victories. Every locality also observed from one to four regional patrons' [*prestol'nyi*] holidays,[109] as well as weddings and baptisms. Pre-Christian survivals such as Paraskeva Fridays and the day of Ivan Kupalo pushed the total even higher.[110] And to repeat an earlier point for emphasis, these were not anachronisms. In some rural localities the number of observances increased in the second half of the nineteenth century.[111]

Ideally, establishing Soviet holidays would not only reduce the number of labor-free days but also eliminate modes of celebration that cut into productivity prior to and following the observance itself. Party officials mounted strident criticism against the fasting and ritual drunkenness associated with Orthodox religious feasts. Six-week fasts occurred during Lent and before Christmas, a four-week Fast of the Holy Apostles took place during the summer, and two weeks of fasting preceded the Dormition. Whole-week fasts were associated with Shrovetide, Easter, Pentecost, Christmas Tide, and the feast of the Publican and Pharisees. A one-day fast was to take place every Wednesday and Friday and also at the Epiphany, the Beheading of John the Baptist, and the Exaltation of the Holy Cross.[112] The Bolsheviks articulated their opposition to such protracted periods of minimal sustenance principally in terms of public health. Among an already poorly nourished population, they argued, the diet of those observing the fasts resulted in chronic anemia, malnutrition, digestive problems, and night blindness.[113]

Bolshevism also gave significant attention to ritualized drunkenness. When the state lost its battle against illegal distillation and in the mid-1920s retreated to a pragmatic reimposition of the state liquor monopoly that existed under tsarism, individual Komsomol and party organizations campaigned to ban the sale of vodka at least during Christmas and New Year's celebrations and called for sterner administrative measures against bootlegging.[114] *Bezbozhnik* mixed its numerous reports on "drunken holidays" in various regions with didactic cartoons, such as one of a man drowning in a bucket of *samogon* [home brew].[115] One teacher complained: "In the villages we cannot afford books or primers or pencils, not to speak of paints and other teaching materials. But the peasants spend hundreds of rubles on God's drunken holidays." According to this account, each household laid out a minimum of five rubles on a *prestol'nyi* holiday and larger sums for major celebrations. A rural correspondent in Riazan province wrote that households would leave themselves destitute rather than scrimp on hospitality. One family of eight who lived in a filthy space measuring eight by eight arshins entertained twenty to thirty guests so lavishly on the Feast of Pokrov that they were reduced to eating black bread, cucumbers, and potatoes the rest of the year. The gathering consumed 36 liters of vodka, 180 of home-brewed beer [*braga*], a sheep, and a thirty-six-pound pig. At a Pokrov celebration in Chelatny, home brew and vodka "flowed like a river." Young and elderly men and women, boys and girls as young as five years of age, and even the officials of the rural soviet became drunk, swore, argued, and fought. During a typical Easter period in Omsk *okrug,* violence related to alcohol consumption resulted in four deaths and forty-four serious injuries. One doctor estimated that 56 to 80 percent of all children drank vodka in earnest on holidays, and 90 percent had at least tasted it.[116]

The antireligious press persistently focused on the link of holiday "drunkenness, hooliganism, [and] fights" to lost productivity.[117] Officials in Borovich *raion* (Leningrad *oblast'*) calculated that the six hundred labor days lost during the three-day winter feast of Saint Nicholas cost eleven thousand tons of output. That figure was undoubtedly exaggerated, but the noticeable interruption of labor was nonetheless real.[118] Observing a large number of religious holidays caused the Path of Socialism Collective Farm in Orenberg *okrug* to fall so short of its quota that it had to give up a significant part of its land to a neighboring collective.[119] And spring holidays, especially the Purification, annually brought forth a plethora of reports of disrupted sowing in outlying regions.[120] Nor were industrial workers immune to the lure of customary enjoyments and traditional observances. During the civil war, even factory administrators sympathetic to the revolution felt it necessary to continue the practice of closing textile mills for two weeks at Easter.[121] When officials promoted the worker Iurova to an administrative post at the Red October Factory (Saratov province) in the mid-1920s, she used her new power to press for a four-day closure at Easter.[122] At Easter in 1928, notwithstanding claims that attendance at work was generally better than in the previous year, the Voznesensk Factory in Moscow experienced six times its usual absenteeism and the AMO Factory reported truancy in excess of 10 percent of the workforce. Only eighty of six hundred students of the Industrial-Economics Technicum reported for classes. In Leningrad, the Elektrosila Factory recorded 125 absentees, 100 more than normal.[123] Outside the major cities, workers stayed away in even greater proportions. At the Krasnyi Perekop Factory in Iaroslavl', 548 machines stood idle while 1,101 workers observed Easter. In the Tver' Wagon Works, 25 percent of the force failed to appear; 30 and 50 percent chose celebration over labor at the Trud Factory and the Vitebsk Bread Bakery.[124]

But the reluctance of workers and peasants to give up time off from work, an opportunity to eat gluttonously, the prospect of community dancing and singing, rituals of courtship, and a socially sanctioned excuse to get drunk depended on more than their level of religiosity. Leaders of the League of Militant Godless readily admitted the folly of simply asking the population to surrender holidays with nothing more than slogans in return, but they also resolutely maintained that the observance of feasts did not necessarily involve an active religious commitment for all. The party consensus was that most celebrated unconsciously, that is, they performed both religious and pagan rites as symbolic reenactments rather than manifestations of literal belief.[125] Hence, advocates of atheism took encouragement from the fact that village youth in particular—regarded as less educated, sophisticated, and organized than their counterparts in the factory towns—eagerly anticipated religious holidays but observed them largely as days of recreation. Even though the event began with attending church, the young exhibited far more interest in dressing up in holiday finery, flirting, music, and drinking. In many areas youth placed pre-Christian survivals such as the day of Ivan Kupalo, with its games that invoked the occult, on the same plane as church holidays.[126] Between designated celebrations, as one peasant in Petrovskoe (Moscow *oblast'*) informed an antireligious agitator from VTsIK, "there is nowhere else to go" than to church for entertainment. It was clean, warm, and—unlike the monthly movie at the club—free.[127] The phenomenon was not only rural. Moscow workers who had long ceased actively practicing religion also turned up at church on a major holiday before celebrating.[128]

The revolutionary state tried to counterpose its own holidays to long-standing observances. In 1918, the regime instituted International Labor Day (1 May), the Day of 9 January 1905 (22 January), the Day of the Fall of the Autocracy (12 March), the Day of the Paris Commune (18 March), and the anniversary of the October revolution (7 November). Soviet New Year's, which later included decorated trees and the exchange of gifts, was to displace Orthodox Christmas (7 January). In due course, May Day also took on the function of a Soviet surrogate for Easter, and at the end of the 1920s the Bolsheviks created additional spring celebrations of full collectivization and agricultural labor. Harvest Day (begun in 1923) and the Day of the Tractor were designed to replace traditional late summer and fall festivals with instructive observances that included lectures by agronomists and demonstrations of farming equipment. Later in the decade, International Women's Day, the International Day of Youth, and International Cooperation Day also became part of the calendar.[129] In keeping with the operative principle that the dialogue between state and society was not between equals but was didactic, the mass festivals that marked these occasions were designed as political and technical education. Organizers intended their sumptuous theatrical spectacles, like religion, to create an atmosphere of group identification and community. They thus appropriated the symbolism of religious life in order to combat it and deliver other political messages, and they created new Soviet symbols for a kind of secular veneration.[130]

All this proved difficult to implement in the villages, and only relatively less so in factories. To lessen the regime's embarrassment during the transition, therefore, Article 112 of the Codex of Soviet Laws allowed for as many as ten additional labor-free days based on local conditions and traditions, and in the early 1920s local officials had wide discretion in using these to accommodate different religions even within the same region. Nevertheless, these extra days did not cover all eventualities. Even those Bolshevik sources that regularly put the best face on party antireligious efforts conceded that absenteeism plagued industry at the times of religious feasts.[131] And regardless of whether the rank and file observed church holidays out of a deep sense of religious feeling or not, most did not transfer their loyalty to Soviet

creations. There were, of course, bold public claims that Soviet observances were taking root while churches emptied and that on state holidays "one rarely meets a drunken person." But candid party reports presented a different picture: peasants either ignored Soviet holidays
altogether or observed both religious and secular feasts, thereby increasing still further the total of work-free occasions.[132]

Official pronouncements routinely blamed this lack of success on
poor planning and organization, but the root cause was even more basic: the population simply did not enjoy Soviet holidays as much as
those they were being asked to discontinue. People came from as far as
thirty versts away at the feast of the patron of the village of Vyemkovo,
for example, to put their offspring of marriageable age on display and
to examine prospects from other villages. Youth began a flirtation and
courtship promenade [gulian'e] at dusk that lasted until sunrise while
their elders socialized. To counteract this, a newly formed Komsomol
cell built a stage on the path to church and regaled those returning from
services with the performance of a living newspaper. Members delivered reports on the international situation, science, and the essence of
religion, and as the final church bell pealed they sang "The Internationale."[133] Harvest Day celebrations elsewhere included mock trials of
the wooden plow and the three-field system of crop rotation.[134] Such
ritualized stiffness, which relied strongly on lectures and equated antireligious didacticism with entertainment, typified Bolshevik celebrations. Special variations might appear—the Day of the Harvest would
feature "games 'of a harvest character'"—but in general the format
(lectures such as "Primitive Man and the Conception of Religious Belief" and the performance of an antireligious play) did not deviate far
from the norm. And when the party was not wearying its intended audience, it talked past them. Responses, as when a lecture in Tambov
province generated about thirty questions, concentrated on issues both
more specific and more mundane—"was God on earth?" "will our
church soon be turned into a club?"—than the prepared themes of the
event.[135] Moreover, by the late 1920s the party encountered new rivals.
Singing, dancing, and musical circles organized by sectarian proselytizers also proved more interesting than atheistic festivities,[136] which
bored even those responsible for organizing them. When reproached in
1930 for the shortfalls of antireligious work in the Middle Volga, the
head of the agitation-propaganda section of one Komsomol cell replied
unabashedly that he "did not find it interesting."[137] Similarly, the Komsomol in Syzran' considered organizing an anti-Easter observance simply not worth the effort.[138]

Beyond its attempts to subvert holidays, the party attacked Sunday as the designated day of rest, and in the process it launched an attendant offensive against church bells. Historians have customarily presented these as parts of a single strategy of repression, but the essence of what occurred at the beginning of the Soviet period differed markedly from what took place later during the Cultural Revolution. Immediately following the revolution and during the early 1920s, the principal concern of the party with regard to the day of rest was to avoid exacerbating further the relations between state and society. The Soviet Codex of Laws guaranteed every worker forty uninterrupted hours of leisure per week, which usually encompassed Sunday. As was the case with holiday celebrations, though, state authorities could and did shift to another day to accommodate local non-Orthodox religious customs.[139] By contrast, the initial motivation to confiscate church bells was baldly confrontational. The prevailing representation in party propaganda was that factory workers resented the bells and whole neighborhoods demanded they be melted for needed industrial materials. In actual fact, antireligious militants targeted bells as noxious religious symbols from the beginning of the civil war, and when the climate surrounding the confiscation of church valuables in 1921–1922 presented the opportunity, they needed no further rationale to remove them.[140]

Both the motivation and the implementation changed in 1929, however, when VTsIK tied the silencing and seizure of bells to its inauguration of the so-called uninterrupted work week. The uninterrupted week was designed to raise productivity by keeping the factories in continual operation. Workers would alternate their days off, and Sunday would lose its privileged status. The regime anticipated multiple benefits from this change. First, industrial output was expected to rise. Second, religious observances would no longer be accommodated, but exacerbated. And finally, bells that disturbed either work or laborers' rest could be melted down for industry at the discretion of city soviets and *raion* executive committees. VTsIK added a further economic incentive when it decreed that only half the proceeds from confiscated bells would go to the People's Commissariat of Finance; the executive committee of the local soviet would retain the rest. This was more than sufficient to spur many soviets to action, yet Sovnarkom subsequently set a quota. Between October 1930 and June 1931, twenty-five thousand tons of scrap from bells were ordered collected in the Soviet Union, of which twenty thousand tons would come from the Russian Republic. Consequently, all bells were to be seized in areas where local authorities forbade their ringing; and where the ringing was not prohibited, soviets should confiscate the "extras."[141] The results disappointed the architects of this campaign. The issue of bells spurred parishes to direct resistance—an episode in the village of Sentianino, where believers nearly beat the organizer of a bell seizure to death, was representative of many.[142] Furthermore, the uninterrupted work week failed to stimulate productivity. The rotation of leisure days in the factories meant, for example, that key supervisory personnel might be absent when needed.[143] And in newly formed collective farms, it was not the uninterrupted week that established the schedule of work, but religious tradition: plow by the feast of Petrov; harrow by Il'in; and seed before the Day of the Savior.[144]

. . .

In addition to secularizing collective observances, the Bolsheviks sought to infuse private rituals with revolutionary meaning. This created a challenge different from merely co-opting old forms and incorporating an imposing symbolism—the red star and banner, the hammer and sickle, "The Internationale"—into public spectacles. Penetrating the family sphere required appurtenances and symbols that revolutionaries could counterpose to icons and church accoutrements to recognize birth, marriage, and death and introduce into daily home life. The task was formidable. Even in areas where church attendance fell significantly after 1917, the population continued to perform traditional baptisms and funerals in large numbers and to indulge in drunkenness and fights on holidays. The task of the revolution, therefore, was to create rites that would be sufficiently attractive but would not simply replicate religious regalia.[145]

As we have seen, both church and party coveted hegemony over marriage. The state had reduced religious nuptials from legal to symbolic observances by decree on 20 December 1917, but it could by no means mandate public acceptance of the civic rites in the same way. The new Red Wedding had to displace what we have already noted as one of the country's most entrenched customs, since marriage in Russia was a community as well as a personal event. Before the revolution, bride and groom both underwent a significant change in status under intense public scrutiny. The young woman experienced an abrupt personal displacement in joining the household of her spouse. She also altered her circle of activity, signified in an elaborate sociology of dress that the whole community enforced, and once married she could no longer associate with unmarried friends at work or play. Through marriage the groom achieved the status of an adult, which he could not attain through any other mechanism of village life. Prescribed rituals governed every stage of this process. Once matchmakers concluded the preliminaries, the families of the prospective bride and groom exchanged exploratory visits on successive days. Neighbors might actually stand outside the house during negotiations to discuss the bride's capacity for work and speculate on the economic arrangements. The betrothal then became formal with a ritualized meal and a church ceremony. Throughout the following weeks, bride and groom exchanged gifts, women prepared special food, men distilled holiday intoxicants, and the bride took leave of her female friends of youth at a series of highly orchestrated parties. On the wedding day, the procession to the church and the dinner that followed the marriage ceremony were both replete with symbols of transition and sympathetic magic, while all closely watched the behavior of bride and groom for harbingers of the future course of their married life. Even the poorest peasant spent lavishly beyond his true means to provide guests with food, drink, and merriment.[146]

How could the Red Wedding offer a ceremony that citizens would want to link to such a significant personal occasion? *Pravda* provided an answer with its approving account of December 1924 nuptials in the Tanners' Club of the Kineshma Leather Factory. In the small but brightly lit room, the young couple sat at a head table covered with a red cloth. Also in a place of honor was the chief clerk of the departments of civic registration of birth, marriage, and death. Members of the party cell sat on the side, and directly in front of the guests hung a portrait of Lenin. After the singing of "The Internationale," the couple turned to the messages of congratulation they had received from various organizations; there were so many that they could not look at them all during the ceremony. During testimonials to the couple, one speaker said: "You are showing the way to others who are not party members. I am certain that the time is not far off when people will be happy and without priests!" The groom responded, after the applause ended: "We understood the priestly addiction. . . . We did not want to go to church. . . . We decided it would be better to go to this very club." Once again there was lengthy applause. The guests then heard a report on the new Soviet *byt,* the couple signed the marriage registry, and there were additional speeches and a final singing of "The Internationale."[147]

Beyond the differences in tone and intent of the respective ceremonies, there were other considerations that impeded the acceptance of Soviet personal rites. Rural women were especially negative toward civil marriage, which they feared was less legitimate.[148] Rather than approaching it as an alternative, they applied the rules and strictures for church proceedings to state ceremonies. One Soviet source reported that in the first years of Bolshevik rule there was not a single marriage registered in Petrograd province during the "fasting" month of March, when church weddings were forbidden.[149] In the rural north, Soviet researchers reported at least as late as 1926 that new, outside influences had absolutely no effect on marriage traditions.[150] In comparison, city dwellers more readily embraced Soviet marriage *and* divorce. This led by the end of the decade to unanticipated negative consequences, most notably family instability and the highest urban divorce rate in the world.[151] The attempt to alter marriage by fiat also created administrative problems. For example, since the Central Department for the Registration of Acts of Civil Status [*Tsentral'nyi otdel zapisei aktov grazhdanskogo sostoianiia*] did not exist until 1920, and since Siberia had been under the control of the Whites for much of the civil war, local officials there complained of confusion regarding the enforcement of the December 1917 decree on marriage and the validity of church unions concluded in the period 1917–1920.[152] In other cases, interest in Soviet marriage extended no further than transparent attempts to manipulate Soviet law to circumvent canon law. In 1919, the peasant I. V. Abramov sought state permission for his underage son to marry because the household needed the labor of the prospective wife. In the city of Ivanovo-Voznesensk, one man petitioned for permission to marry the sister of his deceased spouse; A. I. Ianovich brazenly asked Sovnarkom to order the Patriarch to allow him a second Orthodox wedding to the niece of his first wife.[153] To complicate the issue further for both state and church, even from the most pious came pressure on the Bolsheviks to recognize both church marriage and divorce, and at the same time the church was urged to adopt the more liberal Soviet norms for divorce.[154]

Revolutionary funerals fared comparatively better in execution if not in number, perhaps because the solemnity of the occasion lent itself to the Bolshevik penchant for delivering speeches and in part because the party borrowed Orthodox symbolism heavily. On the level most obvious, Lenin received quasi-religious veneration. His body was not cremated in the revolutionary fashion but embalmed, displayed for forty days (the Orthodox period of prayers for the deceased), and ultimately housed in a mausoleum.[155] Even earlier, the funeral "without a priest" that Glavpolitprosvet counterposed to Orthodox services beginning in 1921 retained the choir; and subsequent instructions, especially if people who were not party members were to be present, stressed that "the very most important thing is the organization of the procession, music and speeches." Although the number of nonreligious funerals was small, revolutionary publications rationalized by noting that the majority of those who died were old and therefore less receptive to new ways. They reviewed those that did take place as the rare nonreligious event that actually achieved its aims. The Komsomol funeral of the wife of the communist Vaganov, herself an agitator, drew a crowd larger than Easter rites in Bolychevo in 1925. Even the elderly attended the first such funeral in the area out of curiosity, and the personalized eulogies delivered by communists and the loud music that followed made a strongly positive impression. The musicians then led the procession to the cemetery, the red coffin followed, and Komsomol and party members carried an array of flags. Following the burial, mourners of all ages reportedly discussed the music in particular as they walked the five versts back to town; many expressed a desire for such a ceremony when their own time came.[156] During the second half of the decade, the party continued to champion secular observances and also began to push cremation over burial. Officials thus had to take care not to rob the occasion of its personal dimension, even as they cast the issue in terms of health and sanitation. Urns containing ashes could therefore not be stored in living spaces, although they could be displayed as appropriate in state and public institutions, buried, or disposed of ceremonially by such means as dropping them from an airplane or scattering them on a river or a sea.[157]

The revolution enjoyed a significant opportunity to invest a personal event with revolutionary significance when it undertook to replace Orthodox baptism with a newly devised Red Christening. This provided officials an occasion to reiterate publicly their customary faith in the future and at the same time attempt to convert rank-and-file adults to Bolshevik practices. These Octoberings, as they became known, combined elements of an atheistic rally with ersatz religiosity. There were local variations, but in general the ceremony included some invocation of proletarian myth, a replication of the functions of godparents, and bestowing a name with revolutionary significance. Self-evident symbolism emerged in one factory ceremony as the child passed from the hands of a party member to a Komsomol to a Pioneer to the parents. Another in the village of Kobeliak featured the civil war hero Grigorii Kotovskii, who stood on a rostrum and raised each newborn above his head, pronounced its name, and returned the child to the parents with the admonition that it be educated to struggle for Soviet power. In the town of Serov in the Urals: "We make a sign over you not with a cross, not with water or a prayer, the legacy of slavery and ignorance, but with our Red Banner of struggle and labor." The Komsomol or in some cases a factory official rather than the parents might decide the name of the child: Oktiabrina (for girls; Oktiabrin for a son), May, Klara (for revolutionary Clara Zetkin), Zvezdina (in honor of the Red Star, *krasnaia zvezda*), Ninel (Lenin spelled backward), Vladilen (acronym for Vladimir Il'ich Lenin), Rem (the first initials of the Russian words for revolution, electrification, and peace), Kim (the first initials of the Russian words for Communist International of Youth), Proletarka, Diamat (dialectical materialism), and others. Reports from rural areas communicated that many peasants approved of the order of the ceremony but not the revolutionary names. One declared them fit only for a dog. Officials suggested using names such as Vladimir in honor of Lenin rather than alienating the population with idiosyncratic constructions. When mobilized as campaigns, the first Octoberings drew substantial crowds. Hundreds of workers came to the initial Red Christening in Kiev; three thousand attended the Octoberings of eight workers' children at the Krasnyi Treugol'nik Factory in Moscow in December 1923 and January 1924.[158]

IDEOLOGY AND *BYT*

In terms of implementing ideology and philosophy, party policy rested on a paradox for most of 1917–1932. The Bolsheviks could successfully inculcate the materialist philosophy that would shape the revolutionary *byt* only if a significant portion of society were already receptive to the basic message. Scientific thinking and the utilization of technology could take root only among those predisposed to appreciate their merits and willing to place them above existing beliefs and practices. Schools could not instill materialist and secular values unless instructors taught them with conviction, the community tolerated them, and students attended in the first place. Similarly, only those who had hitherto understood and accepted the new order would be willing to associate significant personal celebrations and rites of passage with revolutionary symbols and ideas. None of these requirements, of course, were fully satisfied in Russia during this period. Soviet power perpetually found itself in the untenable position of trying simultaneously to create the prerequisites for its programs and implement the programs themselves. Thus, for example, many of the same activists who worked for the eradication of illiteracy were responsible for carrying out other projects that depended on the prior existence of a broadly literate population. Demonstrations of science were to establish a sense of the need for science in Soviet Russia. Those who studied social conditions were expected to furnish correctives to problems and teach new values. Proletarian schools of the future would reflect the basic principles of the future proletarian society, but in the present a secular curriculum was to change rather than manifest the status quo. And Soviet holidays and rites would simultaneously win over the population and cement the loyalty citizens supposedly already felt. In short, the Bolshevik strategy in the "struggle for a new *byt*" was largely circular.

Bolshevik materialism, both as an ideology and as a tactic, nevertheless made progress. The pace of change was slower than expected and comprehensive results fell short of party desiderata, but individual campaigns recorded victories in every sphere of operation. Moreover, the leadership—however sincere and spirited their attempts to impress a new philosophy on the Russian masses—never intended to rely on intellectual and symbolic approaches alone. So in addition to having confronted the church as an institution and having promoted a philosophically materialist, secular *byt* as a goal for all society, the party also set out to carry its antireligious message vigorously and directly to individuals.

4 Soviet Family Values
Antireligious Ideals and the Individual

"You've been filling his head with all sorts of beautiful language, but what have you done to make him a class-conscious proletarian instead of a cheese-paring haggler? That's the way you have to put the question, my dear Comrades."
—Fëdor Gladkov, *Cement*

"The egg doesn't teach the chicken."
—Russian Proverb

No dimension of promoting Soviet values ultimately proved more important than attempting to alter the rhythms of the lives of individuals. Campaigns to reconfigure institutional, economic, philosophical, and symbolic relationships would succeed only to the degree that party ideals penetrated public consciousness. Yet the attempt to do so gave rise to exactly the kind of challenge with which Soviet power was least equipped to cope. The problem was twofold. We have already seen that citizens were loath to part with the familiar in favor of innovations whose worth and utility had yet to be demonstrated. Second, as this chapter will show, many of the Bolsheviks' operative assumptions about their intended constituency proved to be faulty. The party consequently misinterpreted not only the reasons why part of the population clung to religion but also the reasons why others ceased practicing it.

The Bolsheviks proceeded more frequently from imprecise ideological assumptions than from closely observed reality. In the complex negotiation among Soviet power, society, and the individual—in which persons or groups might accept parts of the new order but reject what was anathema, distasteful, against their perceived interests, or simply inconvenient—simplistic, bifurcated categories dominated party discourse, propaganda, and the work of cultural enlightenment. Thus, the city, workers, industry, males, Red Army veterans, youth, and the impoverished were regularly equated with the "new," whereas the village,

peasants, agriculture, women, the clergy, the elderly, and those economically better off than their peers consistently represented the "old."[1] In
an environment in which the party regarded all who identified with its
agenda to be politically conscious and labeled those who did not as
backward, "new" science and reading rooms directly benefited the harvest and industrial production, whereas the "old" church promoted
vodka and hooliganism. In this formula, kulaks, Nepmen, and the elite
of the former regime [*byvshie liudi*] exploited religion as a weapon to
protect their interests; believers joined these and other class enemies in
attempting to thwart innovations in industry, agriculture, and social
welfare.[2]

The party leadership, of course, had access to better information
than this approach would suggest. The political police filed daily reports from around the country that reflected significant regional differences and described problems of security and instability that defied
easy categorization or generalization.[3] Soviet ethnographers also stead-
fastly reported striking variations even within the same region, and the
evidence they collected provided a valuable corrective to the prejudices
of the prerevolutionary radical intelligentsia that informed official
proclamations.[4] In addition, the predominant leitmotifs in the leadership's own apologetics—justifications for the continued reliance on
bourgeois specialists, evaluations of the peasant characteristics of the
"proletariat," complaints about the physical mobility of the population
during the unstable 1920s, and the like—testified to a profound appreciation of the situation, even when delivered in communications generally
framed in much less sophisticated terms. This was certainly the case
with antireligious policy. At the highest level and at intermediate state
and party levels, a frank and nuanced understanding of the problems of
promoting atheism competed directly with oversimplified maxims. But
in the end, a combination of glib overconfidence in the potential of didacticism and a perceived lack of viable alternatives reduced public
messages to an ideological lowest common denominator. Most often,
then, it was an explanation that relied on a formulaic, bifurcated version
of the situation that reached the party at large and the public.[5] And although this possessed the advantage of directness of expression for propaganda purposes, it ultimately placed the revolutionary state at a critical disadvantage as it tried to reconfigure beliefs as intensely personal
as constructions of gender, generational biases, accepted practices in
living and working spaces, the retention of religion in the party, and
nonreligious appeals to the supernatural. In practice, both supporters
and opponents of the revolution exhibited combinations of beliefs and

behaviors that reflected their individual circumstances and predilections more than they demonstrated a militant allegiance to any religious or antireligious cosmology writ large.

GENDER AND GENERATION

As the party strove to recast public consciousness at the level of the individual citizen, the topics of gender and generation received special attention. Neither church nor state challenged the assumption that females were the most pious segment of the population; the revolutionaries expressed a special need to convert them to new ideas. Youth were the object of a different kind of consideration, since all sides viewed them as the generation who would disseminate the values of the future but whose present loyalty neither state nor church could take for granted. And Bolshevik pronouncements consistently presented the elderly as the element most resistant to change, but because of their age they were seen as only a temporary impediment to building socialism.[6]

The northern village of Vyemko seemingly represented a living embodiment of prevailing Bolshevik assumptions about society. From this hamlet of 675, half the men served at the front during the civil war, and those who returned brought new opinions home with them. When the Komsomol cell founded in 1920 began an education circle at the village club, it was mostly veterans and other young males who attended. Women did not enter this particular Komsomol until 1922; beginning with those whose fathers and brothers worked there, younger rather than older females started appearing at the club, but only gradually. In 1923–1924, the club expanded, becoming a venue where no topic was excluded from the lively and undisciplined discussions that took place on winter evenings. On the night when "Religion, the Opium of the People" was the announced topic, all seats were filled; because the priest agreed to participate, the middle-aged and elderly men—but few such women—attended. The priest, however, almost immediately walked out of a debate that began at ten and raged until five the following morning. That left the proceedings in the hands of his designated opponent, an antireligious recent graduate of an urban pedagogical technicum. Passions flared, and several elderly men came forward to defend Orthodoxy, including one who announced his intention to be shot in defense of his faith if necessary. From this experience, the local Komsomol drew up a plan for antireligious propaganda for the next ten years, by which time all youth were to be won over and children would have grown up as atheists. The sole remaining habitués of the church were to be the old men and women. By mid-decade, the able-bodied men of Vyemko seldom attended church, and then only the church lodge, which had become a kind of second male club for the discussion of politics, taxes, and—not infrequently—religion.[7] A story from Voznesensk *volost'* (Leningrad province) produced a similar impression. There a mother engaged the young chairman of the rural soviet in a spontaneous public disputation over religion. Her two daughters looked on intently, but her son, himself a candidate member of the Komsomol, tugged at her sleeve throughout and tried to silence her.[8]

Tidy descriptions such as these notwithstanding, the complicating factor in practice was that although behavior conforming to the prevalent social stereotypes seemed to be everywhere in evidence, as in Vyemko and Voznesensk, it did not represent the complete cultural experience. Consistent with the party's version, on the one hand, it was not only the Bolsheviks but young as well as established male and female urban workers who considered the peasants newly arrived in the city to be backward. Their work habits and their propensity to set up "urban villages," re-create a rural subculture in factory barracks, or mix vestiges of urban with village religious culture attracted censure outside as well as within party ranks. Moreover, by the mid-1920s young people in the cities and factories did lead the way in abandoning church marriage and driving the divorce rate upward, and we have already seen that rural women were far less enthusiastic about these newly liberalized and secularized procedures. And in keeping with characterizations that surfaced frequently in antireligious propaganda, differences of experience and generation outweighed even economic issues in abetting stratification and ferment in the villages. In short—and the point deserves emphasis—we should not underestimate the degree to which observation and experience seemed to lie at the root of the prevailing stereotypes for those who propagated them.[9]

On the other hand, some behavior ran counter to party formulations and conventional prejudices, and other developments that appeared to confirm Bolshevik social stereotypes often had causes different from the explanations the party offered. For example, during the 1920s relocation to urban factories did not, contrary to the logic of party resolutions, necessarily increase the peasants' identification with plans for building socialism. Instead, they brought with them collective, task-oriented work traditions that impeded the goals of industrial rationalization and individualized production. And peasants required something more substantial than an appeal to build socialism to persuade them to alter their behavior in the interest of raising productivity. Employing the village tactic of framing their objections to unwanted pressure in religious terms, peasants in the factories labeled shock workers as the Antichrist, to whom they also attributed the idea of the uninterrupted work week.[10] Critics characterized all such conduct as backwardness, but more was involved than benighted obstinacy. Whether consciously calculated or simply a reflexive response, these were among the strategies peasants employed to ease their transition to unfamiliar surroundings and to new modes of life and work. To cite a second case in point, the reasons underlying the hesitation of rural women to reject church nuptials on the same level as their urban counterparts did not lie solely in religion or prejudice. Indeed, peasant women who took up work in urban textile factories showed little reluctance to enter common law unions in significant numbers even before the Soviet marriage decree. The lack of enthusiasm for such options by those who stayed in the village was embedded not in spiritual and moral issues so much as in factors specific to their immediate environment: patterns of customary law, issues of agricultural land usage and redistribution, distrust of civil institutions, and the fear of abandonment and concomitant loss of financial support.[11] Finally, living conditions in both village and town might simultaneously bear out Bolshevik categories and render them effectively useless, as when competing attitudes toward religion—between husbands and wives, parents and offspring—coexisted within the same household, thereby forcing the party repeatedly to clarify its position.[12]

Proceeding from a constellation of schematic assumptions consistent with the descriptions of Vyemko and Voznesensk, campaigns to eradicate female religiosity were fraught with inconsistencies. The party declared the liberation of women a programmatic priority, but the leadership viewed with suspicion any practical attempt to separate issues of special concern to women from the general task of building socialism. The *Zhenotdel* [Women's Section] consequently experienced a combination of neglect and animosity from male officials, the more so at local levels, and in late 1929 the party announced its dissolution. In the specific work of promoting atheism, the eradication of religion among females was similarly an announced goal, but the behavior of antireligious activists unintentionally replicated many of the assumptions about gender the *bezbozhniki* were ostensibly setting out to change. Beyond this, the supporters of atheism expressed frustration that although the church played an instrumental role in creating and maintaining the secondary status of women, when women rejected the party message they regularly expressed their opposition in terms of religious piety.[13] In these circumstances, antireligious propaganda unwaveringly presented the role of Russian Orthodoxy in the subjugation of females as a proposition beyond debate. Publications quoted Gorky that the church encouraged men to regard women as their inferiors. Other sources attributed the global repression of women since ancient times to religion without apparent need for substantiation, and a national women's congress in 1927 singled out the Orthodox Church as responsible for a system that repressed village females in particular. Yet cultural-enlightenment efforts directed at rural women could disintegrate quickly if activists criticized God or the church. Frequently *Zhenotdel* as well as Komsomol agitators declined to conduct antireligious propaganda for fear of losing their audience.[14]

Antireligious literature on the liberation of women consequently expressed both concern and condescension. Bolsheviks emphasized the importance of winning mothers away from the church, the priest, and the evangelist and toward social work, the factory committee, and scientific reading materials both out of the belief that worker and peasant women were more religious than their male counterparts and because of their influence over children.[15] More than a decade after the separation of church and state, many mothers observed all holidays and taught their offspring how to pray and follow church services, kiss the hand of the priest, and cross themselves before and after meals. They brought children to Orthodox services of five or six hours' duration, and the party publicized reports of women who beat their children for attending school rather than church on holidays. The mother of one Elena Banina in the village of Rozhok (Nizhnii Novgorod province) became concerned when her daughter attended church less frequently after entering literacy school. Under questioning, Elena reported that school had taught her religion was a narcotic, whereupon the mother shredded the daughter's primer and copybook and ordered her at once to church.[16] Consistent with such beliefs about women, when the League of Godless circulated a list of theses for antireligious reports to be delivered on International Women's Day (8 March) in 1928, it first stressed the link between economics and religion in capitalist countries. Religion defined females as second-class citizens, the instructions argued. As such they received lower pay and, by extension, their presence in the workforce drove all wages downward, a circumstance that in turn reinforced both capitalism and religion. Conditions were only relatively better in tsarist Russia, the report continued, and at present Orthodox and sectarian groups were still successfully organizing the most backward women—defined as the wives most dependent on their husbands and the daughters most dependent on their parents—with a special eye toward spreading their message from mother to child. The document also dealt with practical concerns. Female religiosity supports *nekul'turnost'*, the directive held, and it impedes the creation of a new *byt*. By way of illustration, the directive contended that not only did the Bible consider the pregnant woman unclean, but religious females also sought prenatal advice from old women, sorcerers, and other charlatans. These combined factors were said to have a deleterious effect on public health, especially when mothers later allowed sorcerers to treat their "defenseless children."[17]

In this spirit, the work of promoting an antireligious worldview among females often mixed repetitive calls to action with simplistic propaganda materials. In one popular variation, the problem was circular. The heavy domestic responsibilities of the woman prevented her from participating in activities in society that would raise her level of consciousness, and cultural-enlightenment activists were not providing an adequate corrective. Indeed, among the delegates to the First All-Union Congress of Female Collective Farmers [*kolkhoznitsy*] who identified themselves as atheists, as many claimed to have become antireligious independently as there were those influenced by the party and Komsomol.[18] Newspapers such as *Rabotnitsa* [The Woman Worker], *Krest'ianka* [The Peasant Woman], and *Golos Tekstilei* [The Voice of Textiles] that were directed toward women neglected atheistic propaganda all but completely, and a 190-page handbook published under the auspices of the party Central Committee in July 1928 for those about to conduct propaganda among women did not include a single word on the topic of religion.[19] The Bauman *raion* party committee might therefore include the need to step up antireligious work among young girls in its 1928–1929 objectives,[20] and the League of Militant Godless announced as a goal a 40 percent female membership by the time of its third all-union congress.[21] These ideas were virtually lost, however, among the redundant general appeals in periodicals and conference resolutions for the cells of the League of Militant Godless to increase the involvement of women in antireligious work.[22] When propaganda materials did reach women, they addressed even such well-known topics as the revolution in terms so elementary that it would be hard to imagine much real political education taking place.[23]

Many who engaged in cultural-enlightenment work, moreover, not only subscribed to the party's partisan definitions of consciousness and backwardness, but even hardened their opinions in light of personal experience. In the Moscow Krasnyi Treugol'nik factory, political activists knew well that most workers did not come randomly to the city looking for work but were aided by long-standing networks that linked established urban workers with relatives and other neophytes from their native villages. This informal but deeply rooted system, known as *zemliachestvo*, provided living arrangements for new arrivals from the countryside, surrounded them with familiar persons in an otherwise faceless metropolis, helped secure employment, and in general smoothed the transition from village to city and from agricultural labor to work in the urban industrial, domestic, or service sectors. In 1922–1923, activists at the Krasnyi Treugol'nik decided to use *zemliachestvo* in reverse in conducting cultural-enlightenment work, that is, to send agitators specifically to the villages that provided the workforce for the plant and that might therefore exhibit greater receptiveness toward city workers. For this purpose, some fifty-five hundred Komsomol members set out to conduct lectures and organize conferences in the countryside. But as a letter of one Maria Ivanova indicated, what they encountered only reinforced their sense of the superiority of the city and the primitiveness of the village. She found Bel'skaia *volost'* (Leningrad *oblast'*) "very poor, dark, drab, and backward." Most women were illiterate; and to Ivanova's consternation, few had ever seen a railroad, even though they were but fifteen versts from the rail stop. The one feldsher among the eleven thousand inhabitants of the *volost'* treated not only old and young people, but also horses and cows. Youths still engaged in ritual fisticuffs on holidays, a circumstance that during the last Shrovetide had resulted in five severe injuries and recently had even cost a young girl her life. Women were excluded from holding offices in the rural soviet, but the instructors from the city concluded that the village females, although "dark," considered themselves happy. The campaign seemingly had less effect on the population of Bel'skaia than on the activists themselves. These young urbanites had set out with positive expectations, but both women and men returned with more strongly held opinions of the "backwardness" of rural life and the "darkness" of rural females in particular.[24] The view that village women lagged in the spheres of political and social consciousness was not only a male bias, but one that experienced female party activists also commonly expressed.[25]

Young girls appeared in this schema as both the hope for the future and a cause for concern in the present. In keeping with the general content of party propaganda, the Komsomol in Tambov province reported that a generation gap and a gender gap inhibited its work. It was therefore problematic but by no means unexpected that married peasant women played a conservative role in the family and were regarded as the chief enemy of the Komsomol. There were so few adult female peasant communists in the province that their number was reported as zero. What greatly concerned organizers, though, was their perception that the daughter was following the example of the mother and that the new ideology did not penetrate her worldview. Prior to the revolution, the girls of Tambov attended school only until Christmas, when the head of the school distributed gifts around the tree and, having received some calico or chintz, they "considered their education complete." As a result of even this amount of schooling, the young women of the 1920s were slightly more literate than their parents, but this was not translating into the anticipated higher levels of consciousness; that is, they were not discarding traditional activities in favor of Bolshevik values. Thus, although there were two thousand on the rolls of the Komsomol, "we can count on our fingers the number of Komsomol girls," and village youth considered the absence of female Komsomol members "normal." Instead, young girls reportedly concentrated on social life and the anticipation of betrothal. The flirtation and courtship promenade known as *gulian'e* became their chief preoccupation beginning at the age of fifteen or sixteen; the *chastushki* that girls sang expressed their strong preoccupation with marriage.[26] There were, of course, young women and men who managed to break with village culture, but this did not advance the Bolshevik cause as expected. Rather than remaining in the countryside as purveyors of Soviet values, a large number in this category exercised a different option: they left for the city and factory work.[27]

Other observers tried to look beyond making judgments based on categories like "conscious" and "backward"—which, even had they been accurate, were symptoms rather than causes—and to address specific practical problems. The leadership of the League of Militant Godless singled out the issue of organization. The league could not overcome the problem that antireligious activists conducted their work sporadically in the so-called campaign style, whereas Orthodox believers and sectarians proselytized continuously and systematically. During 1929, antireligious agitation in the town of Vologda, for example, was largely unplanned. More than one *zhenotdel* separately promoted atheism, as did various uncoordinated women's commissions, delegate conferences, and ad hoc special meetings for housewives married to workers. By contrast, prior to the International Women's Day in Petropavlovsk, the bishop himself conducted a weekly Wednesday meeting for adult females, and the clergy counterposed their own women's holiday to the celebration sponsored by the state. Priests in a number of regions also maintained networks of organizers for women [*zhenorganizatory*] as rivals to the Women's Sections of the party. In the village of Viazentsy (Arkhangel'sk province), the wife of the former deacon gathered local women every evening to discuss an agenda that included eliminating atheists from the village. This group tore down antireligious posters and impeded the work of the atheistic schoolteacher at every turn. And in a development reminiscent of the eighteenth century, when the state closed their convent, nuns near the Parofomensk Barracks transformed their "sisterhood in God" into a legal *artel'* that sold needlework and knitted goods to workers, in addition to holding discussion groups and distributing religious objects.[28] No one denied that atheists failed to match religious believers at organization. Although the Russian Orthodox Church had not attempted extensive proselytizing among women before World War I, it made this a priority during the war and reaped dividends thereafter. Relying heavily on the wives of clergy to create organizations for women—a single diocese in Saratov set up 406 such groups by 1916—former female monasteries throughout Viatka, Perm, and Moscow provinces, and individual parishes virtually everywhere, became the sites of religious-political discussion circles for women after the revolution.[29] Moreover, Russian and foreign sectarians significantly increased their work among women by the end of the 1920s as well.

Emotional issues such as abortion involved even more complex combinations of loyalties. On 20 November 1920, the People's Commissariats of Health and Justice jointly decreed the availability of abortion on demand and without charge in state hospitals, if performed by a doctor. Implemented as a temporary corrective to the large number of illegal abortions and related medical complications, the directive was also certain to undermine midwives and other village healers. Those who framed the decree took pains to condone neither abortion nor the rights of the individual over the collective; in the future—with the availability of a universal child care system and when better-educated women achieved a higher socialist consciousness—Soviet female citizens were to recognize the social obligation of childbearing. In addition to being a concession to pragmatism over the ideology of building socialism, however, the abortion decree gave rise to other problems. Medical professionals who shared the party's vision of promoting a scientific-hygienic lifestyle expressed concern that the decree might in fact undermine the influence of doctors at a time when it should be increasing. This was the position of Obstetric-Gynecological Society No. 259 in Petrograd, the oldest in Russia, which in 1921 also raised concerns about health risks attendant on abortion that were known "not only to the doctor, but to every currently enrolled medical student." Their communication questioned whether abortion was to be granted for "medical, social, or eugenic [*sic*] reasons" or merely the unilateral desire of the woman to terminate the pregnancy. Leaving no doubt of its own position, the society endorsed the provision of the decree that only doctors perform abortions but strongly opposed any removal of the physician from the decision-making process, advocated agitation against abortion among the laboring masses, and called for promoting broadly the defense of maternity.[30]

In contrast to this tendency to concentrate on single issues, a minority looked for more integrated solutions. As the correspondent Niurina argued in *Revoliutsiia i kul'tura* [Revolution and Culture], a whole complex of barriers rooted in traditional attitudes and culture stood between women and the party's vision of cultural enlightenment.[31] Soviet society could therefore not count only on education, literacy training, or a combination of lectures and meetings to solve the problems presently facing women. Even the party's own ideal of the socialist future held that liberation would have to be grounded in a comprehensive reconfiguration of daily life, including the establishment of communal dining facilities, expansion of family support services, access to more meaningful labor, and a redefinition of roles within the family. As *Voprosy truda* [Problems of Labor] noted in 1925, though, the woman who presently stayed home could not participate in society, whereas the employed female carried a double burden that lowered her performance both domestically and at work. Everywhere the new Soviet woman faced higher expectations of her, yet the cultural remnants of the old *byt*—past legal and economic inequalities that combined with "a whole series of complicated reasons of a social character"—held her back. The prejudices of the former order persisted even within the working-class family, *Voprosy truda* argued, where above all socialism needed to liberate the wife from housework. Society had yet to determine how to measure the worth of labor in the family; the conclusion of this article introduced time budgets that suggested using the principles of industrial organization in the home.[32] In the short term, however, discussions of single issues far outnumbered more comprehensive proposals, which, in turn, produced an unbroken litany of failure to attract women to revolutionary and antireligious ideals.

General characterizations of youth and the older generation projected a similar congeries of conflicting impressions invoked in the name of Bolshevism. Conventional party wisdom held that the young did not need to follow their parents in all things since the latter could be conveying incorrect, "anti-Soviet" attitudes. Friction between the generations therefore might be necessary.[33] Ethnographers in Kostroma province certainly approved when impassioned arguments over the functions of nature broke out between youth and "the bearded ones" [*borodachi*] in Andreev *volost'*, especially when the old men contended that the earth did not rotate and that the image of Cain killing Abel was visible on the lunar surface during a full moon. These outside observers interpreted the smirks and grins of the young as an indication that both the ideas and those who expressed them had lost credence, and they attached even greater significance to the strong interest in science among the peasantry that the debates suggested: questions about the origins of fire and of life, about whether the earth was eternal, and about the nature of the sun.[34] When other ethnographers working in rural parts of Vladimir province encountered similar frictions between generations, especially within families in which the offspring belonged to the Communist Youth League, they attributed them to a combination of the parents' ideological opposition to the Komsomol program and the influences of an agricultural lifestyle.[35]

Consistent with this approach, writers predisposed to discover an identification with party ideals among adolescents seized upon virtually every manifestation of perceived pro-Soviet behavior and presented sanitized versions of problems. This propensity came to dominate one mode of antireligious Soviet writing,[36] as when students of village life generalized from disconnected instances in which young women rejected religion.[37] In their eagerness to find merit, some correspondents carried the commonplace to the level of the absurd. When four hundred delegates convened in late 1929 for the first conference of atheistic youth in the Zamoskvoreche *raion* of the city of Moscow, *Antireligioznik* made a point of the fact that all were in their places punctually and that proceedings opened "without the slightest delay."[38] And when a small group at the Renaissance Youth House in Moscow passed high-sounding resolutions before Komsomol Christmas in 1923 and prepared a special issue of their *Young Atheist* newspaper, *Bezbozhnik* deemed it worthy of the attention of its national audience.[39]

This tendency to maximize the significance of the mundane or to interpret every act of youthful independence and lack of interest in church as a turn toward atheism was, of course, not a sign of the strength of the antireligious movement but an indication of its weakness. The antagonism between the League of Godless and Komsomol that overflowed into the national press at the time of the second congress of the league in June 1929 was simply one highly visible and acrimonious episode among ongoing mutual recriminations.[40] Typically, reports lamented youth who still attended church, were married by a priest, and remained under their parents' influence, as well as adolescent males whose idea of antireligious agitation was to drink heavily, play the accordion, and sing rollicking songs before setting fire to the nearby church, thereby angering the general population.[41] But when Bolshevik pronouncements persistently evaluated public behavior in terms of either the complete acceptance or the complete rejection of antireligious values, they failed to appreciate the extent to which individuals were bringing together their own combinations of attitude and behavior from across the political and social spectrum in ways that made sense to them, regardless of the preferences of state or church.

THE VILLAGE IN THE FACTORY

Antireligious messages also strained to reconcile Bolshevik ideas concerning class and the influence of social environment with observed behavior. The revolution inevitably added to the socioeconomic displacement that began seriously to disrupt the traditional rhythms of Russian society long before 1917, but the process was not unilateral. What the party considered "old" did not merely resist the "new"; to a significant degree, the "old" penetrated the "new" and shaped its implementation. Nowhere was this more true than in the factories that experienced an influx of peasant workers during 1917–1932. As already noted, these arrivals did not automatically change their beliefs and predilections when they took a job in industry, but they did alter the plants and cities with their presence. In this regard, the correspondent A. Nukhrat expressed in a 1926 article buried in the back pages of *Bezbozhnik* what everyone in the factories already knew: many workers did not differ greatly in habits and outlook from their peasant counterparts.[42]

In the nineteenth century, life in the factory shops, dormitories, and barracks had substantially replicated village existence, with religion in a prominent place. Workers adorned their living spaces with icon lamps at the massive Prokhorov factory in Moscow, and in the women's quarters most kept five such icons at the head of their bed. To the consternation of the factory hospital staff, females turned to fortune-tellers during illness and consulted sorcerers to determine the sex of an unborn child. A "new *gulian'e*" dominated the nearby square on holidays, and, as in the village, a festive air prevailed when a young bride, bedecked in flowers and ribbons, set off for her prenuptial bath. The peasants also brought with them the less humanitarian elements of the village. The familiar ritual village fistfights now took place between different crafts and against neighboring plants in vacant lots on holidays; these so-called walls battled on the frozen Moscow River in winter. A pervasive lack of privacy "led to an abnormal sex life" in the small rooms in which two or even three families lived and the more so beneath the plank beds in the open dormitories at night. Women received scant respect—men referred to the female barracks as the "mares' yard"—and did not feel safe passing through the square late at night. The neighborhood surrounding the plant resembled a caricature of a village: three churches, four taverns, five additional beer halls, two state wine shops, and an undetermined number of brothels.[43]

Factory owners, motivated by a combination of personal piety and opinions that linked religiosity to docility in the workforce, abetted this situation. The prosperous Prokhorovs woke workers for church, joined them in the virtually continuous Orthodox fasts, and spared no expense in decorating the nearby Nikolo-Vagan'kov church. Similarly, the proprietress of the Ustinskaia Silk Mill, one Nyrnova, imposed a strict religious regimen on her nine hundred laborers, personally leading them the few steps from the workers' barracks to church on Sundays and holidays. In addition, the Prokhorovs provided instruction on the lives of the saints, organized a factory choir, and operated a religious Sunday school. They observed the reopening of the factory after vacations as an ersatz religious holiday, with singing, the presence of clergy, and blessings of machines and workers with holy water to mark the occasion. Workers consequently counted on spending the first day following the Easter and Christmas break in wild drunkenness. And like the village, the Prokhorov celebrated its own *prestol'nyi* holiday in August, in this case to honor an icon believed to perform miracles.[44]

After the revolution, such factories experienced serious discord, with religion providing a highly charged symbol of the internal divisions. During the civil war, the large number of believers at the Red Army and Navy munitions plant in Moscow province, formerly owned by the Krupp family, quashed every attempt to close churches there.[45] And at the beginning of the 1920s, religious activity in the former Prokhorov factory remained vigorous. Priests retained full access to workers' barracks. Despite a directive by the factory party cell, several old iconostases continued to be displayed. Senior skilled workers persisted in conducting religious instruction among the unskilled, and they collected donations for the support of the priest and construction of a new church. This exacerbated the animosity between those who had fought on the Soviet side during the civil war and others who had spent it in the countryside; supporters of Bolshevism could not gain the advantage. The party began publishing a factory newspaper, *Without God and Boss*, in 1923. It came out irregularly beginning that year, and it took until 1925 for the factory committee to succeed in closing one of the three churches and to launch a campaign to remove icons from the factory. Ultimately, the issue was not so much settled as neutralized through a combination of the increased cultural influence of the city and the fact that a larger number of workers moved out of factory quarters and into the surrounding neighborhood. In short, the direct sway of the subculture of the barracks lessened both as the proportion of the labor force living there diminished and as workers began to avail themselves of museums, movies, and theater tickets distributed at the plant rather than to attend church functions.[46]

Other enterprises experienced much greater acrimony. A general factory meeting at the former Putilov (later Kirov) factory in Leningrad in December 1924 produced a resolution to close the church, but priests and believers fought back. Clergy and religious women canvassed workers' apartments with a petition, and believers gathered at the factory committee office "from morning until late at night" with a variety of appeals and documents obtained from superordinate institutions. These, in combination with the fact that a gathering of seventy-eight office workers on 3 January 1925 produced only nine votes for closure, forced a new meeting, which religious supporters disrupted so effectively that the issue could not be resolved. The antireligious faction then enlisted reinforcements from the Egorov, Goznak, and V. I. Lenin Nevskii factories and five hundred supporters from the Volodarsk typography plant for a meeting attended by two thousand on 25 January 1925. But when religious sympathizers carried their protest to the streets, into the market, and back to the provincial soviet, they managed to delay the church closing until 5 February. Eight thousand then watched as the worker Smoliak cut down the crosses amid cries of "Antichrist."[47] Similarly, in Moscow, the funeral of the pious Nyrnova disrupted production at the plant she formerly owned when mourners led their large procession onto the factory grounds during working hours. Elsewhere in the capital, the size of the Palm Sunday observance at the Red Rosa factory caught the attention of high party officials, as did the scope of the resistance to closing the church at the Leader of the Proletariat [*Vozhd' proletariata*] factory.[48]

Believers showed as much energy in building new churches as they did in battling closures. In this connection, the Agitation and Propaganda Department of the party singled out the peasants who streamed to the urban plants and new Soviet construction sites during the 1920s as the most difficult stratum among whom to conduct antireligious work. As the Agitprop activist Kostelovskaia reported, throughout Moscow province factories that had previously eradicated religion and rejected priests experienced the reappearance of religious sentiments and the reopening of churches when new laborers from the villages arrived in mid-decade.[49] As these newcomers established their communities, especially at large enterprises, they incorporated Orthodoxy. Officials at the Dneprostroi construction site complained that a majority of the fifty-five thousand who came there brought a combination of religious attachments, low literacy, and poor labor skills.[50] Elsewhere, women played a large role in financing a church built during the construction of a workers' settlement at Sobink (Vladimir province), and in Kuznets *okrug* workers collected the money to build a church at the Red October factory. The same happened at the Okulov, Iartsev, and Communist Avant-Garde factories; in the main workers' center at Molotovk (Nizhnii Novgorod province); at the Proletarian factory in Novorossiisk; and in the industrial regions of Murmansk. When officials nationalized the church at the massive Glukhov factory and converted it into a club, workers there paid for the construction of a new church.[51]

Furthermore, religious observances in factories reportedly rose during the second half of the decade. *Antireligioznik* noted with concern the increase in the percentage of personal occasions that were accompanied by religious rites in Moscow between 1925 and 1928. And though we must treat the motivations behind this kind of reporting circumspectly—formulaic self-criticism and publicizing the negative were common Bolshevik mobilization devices in the late 1920s—the numbers nevertheless caused concern among those expecting progress on the antireligious front. Figures fluctuated, but the number of births free of religious ceremonies was 3.5 percent lower in 1928 than in 1925. In the same period, the extent of the decline of civil funerals and of the increase in religious ones in the city was close to 8 percent. Only in the realm of marriage did the proportion of civil ceremonies increase during these three years, but even then the paper hinted that the unavailability of church weddings during Lent affected the count.[52] At the end of the decade, two-thirds of the workers' marriages at the Serp i Molot factory in Moscow took place in church; in other words, the percentage of religious weddings actually exceeded the reported level of religious belief in the plant.[53]

In a related sphere, the church joined the state in its opposition to so-called superstitions, that is, non-Christian and pre-Christian appeals to the supernatural. The beliefs of a significant number of citizens transcended the tenets of organized religion, and well-entrenched herbalists, midwives of various levels of skill, faith healers, shamans, witches, sorcerers, and fortune-tellers posed a threat to both Soviet and Orthodox teachings. To exacerbate matters, these practitioners often had to hide such activities from the priest before the revolution, but now the reduction of the formal power of the church allowed them to operate in the open.[54] By mid-decade, one Agitprop report from the field went so far as to rank the sorcerer higher in local importance than the priest and to equate all peasant religiosity with the popular superstitions concerning agriculture, nature, and illness.[55] Although this certainly overstated the case, experience in the countryside led even the seasoned ethnographer V. G. Tan-Bogoraz to include the local sorcerer among the four significant personages in every settlement. He noted further that though one or more of the other three—priest, teacher, and feldsher—might often be missing, there was always a sorcerer.[56] The phenomenon was not limited to villages. Every provincial town had a celebrated folk healer (and imitators) that medical doctors could not displace, magical healers were tolerated by local officials even in religiously significant towns such as Kolomna, and nonmedical practitioners served a clientele from every social class in the large cities. The Urikov brothers of Leningrad, for example, enjoyed a wide reputation.[57] Related beliefs included the rites of fertilization, modes of sympathetic magic, and celebrations discussed in the previous chapter. In addition, harbingers of personal fate were seen in the behavior of cats, chickens, dogs, and other animals. Midwives employed techniques—the transfer of water from mouth to mouth, for example, or the custom of spitting on the newborn baby—during childbirth that sometimes harmed both infant and mother, especially in a difficult delivery. And healers continued in the twentieth century to draw upon a full arsenal of traditional medicine that encompassed phenomena such as mystical associations with the family stove (which led to putting an ill infant inside it) and the strategic placement of water within the dwelling for certain maladies.[58]

As happened in other circumstances, revolutionary responses to these phenomena exhibited more than one level of sophistication. Simple dismissals, usually written in a declarative tone and with a procliv-

ity to contrast popular beliefs with science and professional medicine—
and cast in favor of the latter—certainly appeared regularly.[59] But these
amounted more to catharsis for readers predisposed to share the view of
the author than persuasion for the unconvinced. The failure of such materials to treat seriously the reasons behind the continued attractiveness
of such beliefs in society significantly limited their potential to make
new converts. By contrast, the journal *Bezbozhnik* offered comparatively
more effective fare with its simply written and strikingly illustrated attacks that took the existence of differences of opinion within the community into account. These explanations, in which elementary language
typically captioned didactic cartoons, equated the blessing of fields by
clergy with the work of devils, house spirits, and sorcerers, and they
linked all invocations of the supernatural to emoluments.[60] P. A.
Krasikov demonstrated a third approach at the first congress of the Society of the Friends of the Newspaper *Bezbozhnik* in April 1925. Since the
peasant was a realist, he argued, antireligious work would not succeed
in the form of propaganda alone or even as instruction in spheres such
as agronomy. Success would derive only from explanations and demonstrations that were integrated with all facets of *byt* by an activist permanently resident in the village.[61] Taking the matter a step further, Nikolai
Semashko, People's Commissar of Health, offered an understanding of
belief at the All-Union Congress of Women in 1927 that went beyond
economic self-interest and widespread ignorance. In an era when doctors commonly refused to take up a practice in remote areas and rural
citizens might live sixty to eighty versts from a hospital, he argued, recourse to a faith healer was a rational step. The new society would not
eradicate belief in the supernatural until it could provide a demonstrably
viable and universally available medical alternative.[62]

Nor did results among established, politically conscious, skilled
workers satisfy the leadership. As a secret report by the party Information Department noted in April 1929, "even among the workers' van-
guard religious traditions are still very strong." The levels of belief uncovered in Tula and Moscow by surveys of religion in metal and
instrument shops—that is, the kind of worker regularly represented as
the foundation of the proletariat—alarmed the Information Department.
The communication lamented how the influx of new arrivals raised the
number of believers and altered the character of the cities, instead of urban and modernizing influences enlightening the countryside. And with
undisguised concern, the report estimated the level of belief among
Moscow children to be as much as 40 percent in the lower grades and

higher in the upper forms.[63] Materials for public consumption concluded that the new *byt* as well as socialist cities and factories were not
a present reality, only an ideal for the future.[64]

HEDGING COSMOLOGICAL BETS

The Bolsheviks faced still different combinations of belief and personal predilection as they battled religion among party members and
their families. Those who hedged their cosmological bets by accepting
the general Bolshevik line but also retaining their religious attachments
presented the revolutionary leadership with a predicament that was as
complex as it was galling. First, the continued existence of spiritual belief within the ranks affronted the party program. Second, among the
Bolsheviks could be found those who, though they did not literally believe in religious observances, found them too deeply ingrained in their
social experience to reject. These cadres therefore took part as a kind of
symbolic reenactment in rites—holidays were the foremost example—
that were grounded either in Christian or even pre-Christian practices.
Finally, there were members who accepted atheism for themselves but
desired greater latitude and understanding in dealing with religiosity
among their immediate families, where the party position on religion
could threaten the survival of a marriage. These individuals often underwent both Christian and civil ceremonies in the interest of preserv-
ing family harmony. As the party attempted to transform itself from a
small group dominated by intellectuals into a mass organization in the
first half of the 1920s, the situation only worsened. New recruits did not
hesitate to make their religious preferences known, and a significant
proportion expected to be accommodated. Challenges from the ranks
increased, both in the form of questioning the party position and as direct disobedience.

Because the existence of this phenomenon embarrassed the party
leadership, they hesitated to identify its scope. Given the Bolshevik
penchant for quantification, it is noteworthy that, unlike the census of
1937, the 1926 census did not include a question on religious identification.[65] Questionnaires distributed in schools and at places of employment often included an attempt to discern the level of local religious belief, but neither state nor party made a concerted effort—beyond the
occasional unsubstantiated rhetorical estimate—to synthesize the data
and, more to the point, publicize the findings on a national scale. If sophisticated compilations were ever attempted, they have been far over-

shadowed by the frequent and repetitive complaints that testified to the persistence of religiosity in the party but gave only an impressionistic sense of its full proportions. Yet despite the lack of any reliable, comprehensive public declaration, complaints about remnants of religion were a leitmotif in internal party documents, which often relied on fragmented statistics on belief among specific segments of the population (such as school children, university students, teachers) for substantiation.[66]

The most striking aspect of the professed confusion within the ranks regarding the tolerance of religion by the party is that it existed at all. From the outset Bolshevik resolutions took an unequivocal and detailed position that was widely disseminated. When in 1919 *Krasnaia volia* [Red Will] incorrectly printed a statement that church weddings were completely permissible for party members since "there is not a single decree of the Soviet state that says Communists absolutely must be atheists," *Voenmor* [Naval Power] led a number of other periodicals in setting the record straight. It explained that, regardless of the religious choices guaranteed to the general public by the January 1918 Decree on the Separation of Church and State, party members could not be indifferent or neutral on the issue. Twice during 1919 *Revoliutsiia i tserkov'* carried an approving account of the same general party meeting in Maloarkhangel'sk, which expelled five leading members for their church weddings and continued attachment to religion. The paper furnished additional examples.[67] And when the Plenum of the Central Committee issued its major circular on antireligious work in 1921, it specified that persons with religious ties could not be admitted even to party candidate status. Members were to sever all connections with churches, and the party was to remove those who did not from its rolls. In exceptional cases, believers who had rendered distinguished service to the party might be accommodated temporarily, especially if such service had involved personal risk, but they were to be reeducated in the "orderly, scientific Marxist worldview that alone can exterminate religiosity." Similarly, peasants who had married in the church because secular alternatives were not available in their area or who had attended the religious funerals of family members might be considered for candidacy and membership, but only with appropriate recommendations on their behalf. The resolution cited no other exceptions.[68]

But as the party admitted more workers and peasants during the early 1920s, the leadership harbored no illusions that this cadre had internalized party precepts on religion prior to joining. When Zinoviev addressed new candidate members in Volodarsk *raion* in February 1924, he made a point to clarify the religious issue: "You cannot be in the party if you are a religious person. The party does not persecute religion, and is patient toward it. The party understands why there are still so many religious people among us [in society] and does not forbid fraternization with any worker or peasant only on the grounds that he is religious. But we do not take such a person into the party." Zinoviev then directed a pointed—and if not apocryphal, certainly embellished—story about a woman whose attachment to religion nearly caused her to be rejected for party membership. Only her willingness to rethink her position during Antireligious Month salvaged her case. He concluded that "there are many [such] golden people from the working class" ready for such a step, "[b]ut in general all need to know that the party and religion are two different things—either religion, or the party."[69]

Party activists, who routinely encountered attempts by the new cadre to renegotiate the issue of religion at the grass roots, did not by any means consider Zinoviev's secular sermon gratuitous. Once again speaking for the antireligious movement, Iaroslavskii explained that the thousands who joined the party following Lenin's death were not reluctant to express their opposition to the party's stand. Virtually all workers' meetings, he reported, raised the religious question and asked whether Lenin had not erred on this issue. For many otherwise qualified male and female workers, the ban on religion remained their only stumbling block to party membership.[70] Iaroslavskii's assessment was in no way idiosyncratic. Reports from other activists confirmed that propaganda work among women in particular frequently foundered on the single issue of religious belief, and where females predominated, as in the textile mills of Tver', promising prospective members made no secret that the Bolshevik position on religion stopped them from joining.[71]

In 1925, the worker correspondent Glukhov gave the issue its greatest visibility. His essay in *Rabochaia gazeta,* "On Leninism, the Family and Religion," brought together the most frequently raised questions. Are there nonnegotiable requirements on religion to which every party member must conform, and to what degree is the member responsible for religiosity among family members? Must a spouse who does not belong to the party conform to Bolshevik directives, can one allow the baptism of children if the very fate of a marriage hangs in the balance, and is it permissible in the interest of harmony to tolerate a parent who keeps icons and religious relics in the apartment of the extended family? Glukhov took a hard line, writing that a Leninist who joins the party must take down icons, and neither wife nor other relatives can keep them. In his view, tolerance of icons in the dwellings of party members was to end, baptism of party members' children was to cease, and party chilren were not to be sent or taken to church.[72]

The wide discussion and numerous citations to which Glukhov's article gave rise did not come, as the stereotypes of party propaganda would have it, from protoproletarians clinging to superstitions from their past experience. Instead, a letter from M. Kostal'skii argued that for the party glibly to order inflexibility on icons and church attendance simply passed the weight of the issue to the shoulders of local loyalists like himself. The policy not only deeply alienated believers among the relatives of the party member, he asserted, but also begged the larger question of instruction within one's own family. The answer for Kostal'skii lay in making one's spouse understand that an icon offended a communist no less than a propaganda poster next to the icon would affront a believer. Moreover, he added, too many wives of party members worked exclusively in the home and needed to be drawn more definitively into party work. "One of Many" wrote that forcibly removing icons made no sense if the wife still silently lived in the fear of God, and where parents of the couple resided in the household, only negative results could obtain. On a level both more revealing and more practical, "Komsomolets" noted that those who followed Glukhov's draconian advice would remain bachelors. It would be better to follow the procedure outlined in his local wall newspaper: not to take down icons as an end in itself, but to show how they could be used, for example, to replace missing windows of the bath house.[73] As frank as they were, these responses only began to suggest the complexity of an issue whose realities frequently transcended the narrow categories used in propaganda tracts. Contrary to expectations among the leadership, there turned out to be no demonstrable and predictable relationship between personal atheism and the decision to join the party. In 1929, Bukharin estimated that, despite a 300 percent rise in the number of atheists in the country in recent years, only 55–60 percent were party or Komsomol members. Conversely, 40–44 percent of citizens outside the party were atheists.[74]

The young proved to be a particular disappointment in this regard. If party representatives took heart from unexpected reports that among the "old beards" blind faith and church attendance were decreasing, the youth failed to match expectations of them. Members of the Komsomol who found themselves at risk of attack in their communities for following even such innocuous party instructions as singing revolutionary songs on holidays kept a low profile rather than playing their assigned role.[75] Elsewhere Komsomols eschewed antireligious agitation altogether since even attempting it could offend the religious sensibilities of fellow members and lead to the disintegration of the cell.[76] Often, though, carrying out antireligious acts also served to discredit the party and its message. One Komsomol member hid in the altar in order to scare the priest, but he was discovered before the beginning of the services and an outraged crowd tore him to pieces.[77] In Lysye Gory, several youths disguised as devils seized Father Ignatii during the winter of 1925 and doused him with water from head to toe before running away. The clothes of the priest froze before he reached his home at the other end of the village, and his resultant illness kept him out of church for two weeks. The same lads liked to disrupt services by banging on the church doors, and on another occasion they stole the priest's ewe. By the time Ignatii located the animal, which the boys had locked in the church, it had defecated there. To the annoyance of the antireligious press, this harassment raised sympathy for Ignatii and church attendance increased.[78]

Additional shortfalls surfaced in unexpected ways. Questionnaires circulated in the elementary schools of Moscow and Perm in 1928 revealed that roughly half of the students identified themselves as believers and that Pioneers were at least as religious as other students. They expressed their belief openly in their questionnaires, only a fraction attributing the source of their faith to parental influence.[79] Ethnographers grew accustomed to encountering religious believers among Communist Youth League members, and belief in the supernatural among adolescents was not limited to organized religion. The same people who sang revolutionary songs and *chastushki* in the Komsomol clubs of Kostroma also observed popular superstitions, whereas in the many areas where sorcery and pre-Christian practices survived, Komsomol members participated alongside nonparty youth. Everyone especially looked forward to the all-night celebration of the day of Ivan Kupalo and the pagan reenactments associated with Shrovetide.[80] Moreover, during the hiatus in the celebration of Komsomol Christmas and Easter between 1924 and 1928, young communists reverted to participation in the *gulian'e* and drunkenness. In short, the slogan that every Komsomolets was a member of the League of Godless did not survive scrutiny.[81]

Reports within the party as well as for public consumption even accused some party organizations of reinforcing religion. This was the case in the Donbass during the Cultural Revolution, where professional organizations in the Slavianskii and Kramatorskii regions supported manifestations of belief. The wall newspaper of the Krasnyi Khimik factory, for example, regularly published religious stories and poems, and the Secretary of the *okrug* Union of Soviet Trade Employees [*Sovtorgsluzhashchikh*] delivered religious lectures to workers.[82] Also, in a case that attracted national attention, a trusted party member who was also a student at the party political school in his province carried out an assignment to deliver an antireligious report in the countryside by getting drunk, breaking windows in the village, and going to the home of the priest to sleep, "where the scandal continued."[83] In other instances, the party used an even broader interpretation in deciding what constituted an action that aided Orthodoxy—violations, for example, of its stand against anti-Semitism. From the outset, Soviet policies equated anti-Semitism with counterrevolution, but by the mid-1920s, the Information Department of the Central Committee acknowledged that the continued existence of anti-Semitism in the party and in the Komsomol undermined every campaign to eliminate it in society. Nevertheless, when in 1925 one Comrade Brikhnichev sent a letter directed to Stalin, which criticized Iaroslavskii's (born Minei Izrailovich Gubel'man) handling of atheistic agitation, officials of the party Control Commission and Agitprop deemed the tone anti-Semitic. But the incident cost the author no more than removal from further antireligious work.[84]

The intensity increased when decisions struck close to home. Even generally dependable cadres wavered in the face of traditional holiday celebrations. Soviet directives thus continually preached a dual message of sobriety and the need to create didactic activities, and the volume of such homilies increased as Easter or Christmas approached.[85] Particularly unfortunate rank-and-file members found themselves between party policy and family discord. Uncounted numbers married both in civil and in religious ceremonies but were undetected. Others, like the member of the *raion* soviet in Balakhnin who bowed to family pressure and allowed his infant to be baptized in April 1929, lost their party membership.[86] A communist couple in the village of Navolotsk declared their intention not to christen the infant the wife was carrying, but one mother-in-law prevented the removal of icons from the home they shared. And although this husband was intellectually committed to the nonexistence of God, on practical matters he often "became confused" and lapsed into traditional village ways.[87] When the peasant Kal'kin returned from Red Army service, the mother of his child born out of wedlock demanded a wedding and a christening. He forbade the baptism, the wife and her parents raised a protest, and a soviet court ultimately awarded her alimony when she divorced him. The spouse of a communist who named his son Kim (Communist International of Youth) and refused to have him baptized waited for her husband to leave town, whereupon a priest christened him Ivan. In yet another instance, the wife of a village teacher threatened to leave if he removed icons from their home. So frequently did this scenario arise that one worker from Briansk province complained that discussions of *byt* and of family arguments over religion were dominating conversation in the local club. This violated his understanding of conventional behavior in his locality: men had their club and the women the church. For its part, the party offered no assistance stronger than repeated calls for expanded religious instruction in the home.[88]

Yet for many people, discussions that focused so strongly on party policies failed to confront important issues, including one paramount, immediately personal consideration: how was a person—even one whose house was politically in order—to have any fun? Winning the public and the party alike to Soviet rituals and holidays involved issues of literal belief, piety, and even pragmatism, but no new rite could take hold if people did not enjoy it. The prominent literary critic V. V. Veresaev criticized the lack of sensitivity to this reality in a widely cited series of articles on ceremonies that he wrote for *Krasnaia nov'* in 1926. Commenting specifically on *Pravda*'s description of the Red Wedding in Kineshma described in the previous chapter, he wrote: "'Difficult to sort out' [the large number of congratulatory notices] (it would be better not to be so fastidious!),—and speeches, [and] 'additional speeches?' What boredom! What drab, sober [*trezvaia*] boredom!"[89] Judging from the volume of reports in the antireligious press that reprimanded Bolsheviks for their behavior during religious holidays, a sizable number of party and Komsomol members, officials of local soviets, and Pioneers frequently agreed.[90]

BUILDING SOCIALISM AND THE INDIVIDUAL

As the issues of gender, generation, culture in the factory, and religion in the party have shown, social behavior possessed an internal logic that derived far more from variations on received experience than from direct attitudes toward ideologies old or new. Public discussions by opponents and supporters of religion thus captured, albeit often imperfectly, one or another aspect of particular episodes and issues. But these proved ultimately less important than the fluid combinations of old and new influences that citizens independently produced in inventive and often unanticipated ways, just as Orthodoxy had synthesized pagan and Christian elements in prerevolutionary society.

Hence, the evidence ethnographers gathered frequently led to conclusions far different from those presented in antireligious propaganda, despite the partisan nature of Soviet social science that we have already noted. The more balanced reports communicated, for example, that in comparative terms the existence of an adolescent lack of religious enthusiasm was itself unremarkable. By extension, the rejection by some Soviet youth of priests and Orthodox belief did not signify their allegiance to a Marxist worldview, especially when many lacked even an elementary knowledge of geography, natural history, and the social sciences, and philosophical questions such as the origin of life did not interest them. Despite their turn away from formal religion, such young people continued to attribute causation they did not understand to supernatural forces through their belief in devils, the evil eye, and spirits that could promote or disrupt family happiness. Other youth laughed at such ideas, to be sure, yet they might themselves observe still other common prepossessions. And a third group, which appeared generally more worldly, in times of distress or danger immediately looked to a priest for deliverance. The young villager who went to church only to attend weddings once or twice a year more typically displayed mixed rather than unequivocally hostile attitudes toward the priest. Nor were differences between urban and rural youth as sharply drawn in life as in propaganda. The rhythm of their respective lifestyles differed—town dwellers lived a more structured existence, whereas village youth worked virtually without respite during the summer and spent much of the winter in search of amusement—but they resembled one another in important ways. Thus, though it might appear that the brand of rough behavior that occurred during Komsomol Christmas and Easter was grounded in Bolshevik tactical brashness and the reach of urban influences, in a more convincing interpretation it reflected the hold of the village over the city as much as the reverse, especially since the general appearance of modes of rural ruffianism in towns predated 1917.[91]

For the females of whom antireligious activists so frequently despaired, the most important influences were the conflicting pressures they felt in postrevolutionary society and their own evolving expectations of life. Young girls were certainly found at the extremes of support for and opposition to religion, but the vast majority were neither the unthinking followers of parents and clergy nor the rebellious iconoclasts presented in the most tendentious antireligious writings. Bearing out the prevailing stereotype, adolescent females did outnumber males at church. Piety and purely religious motivations seemed to attract far fewer of them, though, than the significance of the church as a female gathering place to exchange news and gossip, view the latest styles, and possibly socialize with the diminishing number of males who attended. In the

typical young woman's hierarchy of priorities, the *gulian'e,* with its opportunities to observe girls from other villages and meet new boys,
ranked higher. Moreover, it frequently happened that the same young
woman who appeared regularly at services and might later have a religious wedding would also take the serious step of ceasing to wear a
cross, would stop going to confession, and would show indifference to
God and priests. After the revolution she typically began to skip or
greatly condense her prayers before the icon upon entering a hut, yet she
would dutifully clean the icon lamp before holidays so as not to embar-
rass her family when company called. Moreover, parental and societal
pressure gravitated strongly against any clean break with the church. In
an era when adults not infrequently pelted Komsomol members and their
banners during processions, as on the International Day of Youth, female
and male adolescents alike might express religious belief within the family but among friends away from home reject the existence of God.[92]

To emphasize the obvious, such behavior reflected strict definitions
of religion and atheism only for those determined to impose these categories on the situation. Individual Russians gave specific elements of
social continuity and change their own emphasis, and they independently mixed the old with the new in ways that were compatible as frequently as they were antagonistic. In this manner, those who eschewed
the Slavic round dance and traditional games on holidays in order to
dance frenetically in the so-called city style "as if to make up for lost
time" found themselves literally next to those who continued to celebrate with familiar forms. But the same young men who performed the
tango and the foxtrot also perpetuated brutal and proprietary customs
grounded in long-standing constructions of male gender and honor. One
who had to leave the village for a time, for example, might declare a
particular young woman "forbidden" to other suitors, which meant
there would be a knife fight on his return if another danced with her or
walked with her on a *gulian'e.* As one female *chastushka* lamented:

> The cat sits on the windowsill
> Her little paw bandaged.
> I have no chance for conversation
> I sit here forbidden.

One could also easily find both pro- and anti-Soviet political songs and
chastuski, and, although youth generally exhibited more positive attitudes toward the new regime, even those dedicated to finding examples
of pro-Bolshevik behavior admitted that vigorously loyal young people
were only "oases amid general slackness."[93]

This cultural syncretism was not limited to youth. Members of the older generation included the devout as well as those who indulged in freethinking, nonbelief, and anticlericalism. Ethnographers encountered no small number of God-fearing older women who were religious pilgrims or repeated stories of miracles, but others of the same cohort employed what agitators called the Solomon response; that is, they held that no one could say with assurance whether or not God existed.[94] And though we cannot accept uncritically the facile assertion that older citizens continued to attend church chiefly out of "habit" [*privychka*], more astute observers noted that emotion rather than religious feeling did govern such loyalties in the 1920s more strongly than before, an observation consistent with the character of popular religion under duress. Priests in Kostroma province complained of falling numbers of old men at services, a decline in clerical income, and slow payment for services performed. Interviews in Kursk province turned up one *seredniak* who supported Orthodoxy but opposed new churches because they would involve new expenditures; his neighbor claimed to be for the church but against the priest. Elderly men in Voznesensk who resented the Solovsetskii Monastery for extended work they had to perform there without pay early in life did not hold the experience against the faith itself; yet their fellow villagers who continued to attend church made the priest and his family the target of their ribald anecdotes. Other factors such as distance from church negatively affected attendance, and the opinion of neighbors strongly influenced citizens to continue baptisms and church weddings. Above all, absolutely nothing diminished the universal enthusiasm for celebrating church holidays.[95]

The experience of an unnamed clerk at the Petrovka department store in Moscow captures the spirit of what many individuals faced. She was among the workers interviewed by the Moscow Institute of School Workers in 1929–1930 to determine their religious beliefs and attitudes toward general living conditions, and her responses indicate how she interpreted her circumstances in the new socialist society. Any single case, of course, offers scant basis for generalization, but by the same token the assumptions that informed the description of her life illustrate one mode of perceived values at the grass roots not available through any other type of source. The clerk, desiring both sympathy and belief from her interviewers, did present her case in terms of what she understood to be commonly held opinions and standards. Even though her message therefore included an attempt to manipulate her audience, in the sense of presenting the facts in a manner that would convince others of the correctness of her point of view, any such manipulation would inevitably have to be framed in her perceptions of society.[96]

The respondent's rationale for abandoning her belief in God was both highly personalized and dependent on social and legal circumstances that did not exist in the pre-Soviet period. Born in the town of Mtsensk (Orlov province) of religious, professionally unskilled parents, she lived in poverty until she married a coworker in 1921. Since their marriage did not take place in church, the sisters of the husband never recognized it as valid, and they continued their campaign to marry their brother to one of their own acquaintances who had a good dowry. When the clerk fell ill and was hospitalized for four months, the husband left her and their infant in October 1923 for the woman his sisters had selected. By the time she recovered and divorced him, the department store clerk was already pregnant by a second partner. She terminated this pregnancy with an abortion but later bore the man a child. He too deserted her for another woman. This second man refused to support his child—he now had an infant son in his new relationship and felt that this relieved him of any responsibility for prior deeds—and the clerk sued. Rather than pay alimony and child support, the defendant fled to Novorossiisk for more than two years. By the time their case reached court upon his return to Moscow in 1925, the clerk was involved with a third partner, whom the second argued should provide support for her and her family. The court nevertheless awarded her one-fourth of the earnings of the father of her second child, which caused him to retaliate with a series of suits to lessen his obligations. These lasted through 1928, when the courts reduced his payments from thirty-six to twenty rubles per month. What is noteworthy is that relating this story in full was the clerk's way of answering the question of whether she believed in God. She responded in the negative but—more to the point—treated the description of her troubles as a self-evident rationale for having broken her ties to religion.[97] In the end, whether she was the voice of the people or merely a self-pitying neurotic, this respondent demonstrated in her single case a logic that had much broader applications in Soviet society during 1917–1932: personal, nonspiritual circumstances often significantly and directly influenced what one professed to believe.

THE OLD IN THE NEW

Ultimately, Russians displayed the same propensity to interpret experience for themselves following the revolution as they had before, but after 1917 the range of choices changed dramatically. In early Soviet society, citizens not only synthesized competing interpretations of belief in the supernatural, but, what is more important, they blended traditional with revolutionary values. These strategies of coping with unforeseen circumstances and pressures accounted for the presence of religious believers in the party, faith healers in the factories, members of the former upper classes who consulted shamans, and peasants who contradicted cultural stereotypes. They explained in part the reasons why young girls attended church and the existence of elderly Russians who viewed religion critically. Ultimately, every citizen and group worked out a strategy within society, and preexisting assumptions about class, gender, generation, and even political affiliation proved not to be reliable predictors of private and public behavior. The component elements of these strategies could not be quantified—their fluid nature and situational bases defied any attempt—but social experience repeatedly demonstrated both their existence and their significance.

These social realities ran roughshod over the party's bifurcated presuppositions about human experience. The Bolsheviks exhibited a variety of levels of sophistication and understanding on social and cultural issues, but the simple categories in which the party framed its understandings in public ultimately undermined the very thing it wanted to achieve through them. In short, during 1917–1932 the revolutionaries failed to find viable ways to lessen or compensate for the absence of a unified viewpoint on religion in personal spheres; direct public confrontations between Bolshevism and its intended constituency would turn out to be no less diverse.

5 Resistance, Circumvention, Accomodation

"I recalled the peasant meetings in the village five years previous. Women were heartbroken at the collapse of religion, and bewailed the self-assertiveness of their children, especially their sons. Now, in 1929, women no longer seemed worried about the collapse of religion. Not one of them had mentioned it throughout the entire evening."
—Maurice Hindus, *Red Bread* [1]

The range of reactions to Bolshevik antireligious initiatives demonstrated the diversity of cultural aspirations in early Soviet society and the disparate relationships represented by the state. We have already seen the extent to which complexly motivated and often largely reflexive responses governed the rhythms of personal comportment. By their nature, though, revolutions also compel individuals to make definitive public choices on issues they identify as crucial, and atheism occupied just such a place in the Russian Revolution. However flawed their conception and execution, cultural-enlightenment and antireligious campaigns made clear even to the politically inattentive that no one could escape taking a public position on this central question. Every choice between belief and nonbelief now required justification. Those with intense convictions made their decision unhesitatingly and regularly backed their words with acts of resistance or circumvention. But for the majority during this revolutionary transition—this time when party members retained religious ties, yet clergy complained of a dramatic drop in the level of religious observance; when pockets of religiosity prospered in industrial enterprises, but the willingness to defend Orthodoxy varied even between neighboring villages—the answer was seldom clear-cut.

From the Bolshevik perspective, a major problem rested in the fact that the party and the state exercised extensive influence in defining the issues of contention, but they could not configure a desired outcome.

Soviet propaganda, through broad dissemination and repetition, therefore communicated the parameters of interaction and negotiation and in so doing framed public debate. It did not, however, fundamentally change what most people considered to be their most deeply held convictions in either secular or religious spheres. The critical mass between the extremes of activist commitment consequently maneuvered among multiple priorities, and the extent of their attachment to atheism or religious belief depended above all on how they chose to integrate spiritual with nonspiritual concerns. As this nonmilitant majority tried to fashion some palatable accommodation, issues of personal conscience, family harmony, community opinion, potential impact on their well-being, and the prospect of retribution all entered their thinking, but the decision involved more than degrees of fear. And for most Russians during the turbulent period 1917–1932, the position they took required ongoing reassessment.

CULTURAL REVOLUTIONS AND REPRESSION

From the outset, cultural revolution was integral to the attempt to build socialism, even though the concept of cultural revolution was itself undergoing constant permutations throughout the early Soviet period. We have established that the Bolsheviks began to create the "new Soviet man" from their first days in power, despite a lack of consensus on the specifics of the society of the future and an absence of agreement on the desired tactics and tempo of change. Militants and voices of moderation clashed over how best to build a proletarian culture even while the revolution fought for basic survival during the civil war. And when NEP replaced internecine warfare, every Soviet institution included officials who, practicing a kind of politics by analogy, sought to rectify problems in areas from state building to social welfare to aesthetics through forceful intervention. Nonetheless, equally in evidence was the variegated group who viewed social revolution as a process of raising public consciousness. These advocates of the new order championed experimental over invasive methods in fields as diverse as criminal and family law, education, electrification, agronomy, public health and sanitation, and the arts. But by the mid-1920s, a renewed radicalism everywhere began to challenge gradualism, and rigidity inexorably displaced the spirit of experimentation. Multilayered and disparate cultural revolutions thus became *the* Cultural Revolution of 1928–1931, when coercive campaigns attempted to integrate into social spheres the character of the forced collectivization of agriculture, rapid industrial-ization, and political victory of Stalin that were taking place virtually simultaneously. The Cultural Revolution thus brought the draconian di-mension of Bolshevism definitively to the forefront. It did not, however, eliminate or even completely silence the influences of moderation.

The conflict between religion and atheism, as we saw in chapter 2, followed the same pattern. During the civil war, the Red Army became both an actual and a metaphorical army in the battle against Russian Orthodoxy. Soldiers' responses on questionnaires, to cite one example, indicated that atheism among them reached 75 percent in 1919, with perhaps another 15 percent close to adopting it.[2] One need not accept such figures at face value, however, to recognize that military service provided a political education for inductees and inculcated new values.[3] The evidence for this resided not with statistics but in a perception found then and later everywhere along the political spectrum: that Red Army soldiers and veterans identified with Bolshevik ideas far more readily than did other citizens.[4] Yet the actions of the military during the civil war inhibited the spread of atheism as much as they promoted it. The Red Army increased acrimony against Soviet power through its participation in episodes of repression against religion, even though the Ministry of Justice justified these as legitimate actions against anti-Bol-shevik groups masquerading as religious organizations. To exacerbate matters, in mobilizing the most politically reliable elements for service against the Whites, the army stripped the local areas of the people most capable of carrying out antireligious measures systematically. This made force the tactic of choice more often than was good for the cause, when overworked and frequently untalented or unscrupulous officials strove to carry out the nationalizations of church property ordered by the separation of church and state.[5]

During NEP, antireligious work replicated the mixture of coercion and suasion being used in other spheres. At the beginning of the decade, the leadership continued to expect the Liquidation Commission to carry out the separation of church and state as a legal and administra-tive enterprise. At the same time, they entrusted the multiple state and party propaganda organs then being created with promoting secular civic values through cultural enlightenment. To these ends, the party concentrated its assault at the national level on the institutions and the economic base of the Russian Orthodox Church, while at the grass roots the focus fell on the class character of religion and on priests. Ag-itprop soon pointed out, though, that approaching religion in this way led to underestimating the difficulty of the antireligious task, and early in NEP atheistic leaders such as Iaroslavskii offered frank correctives. Churches needed to be closed, he held, but not mechanically and without regard for intangible factors. Certainly mistaken was the impulse to shut all places of worship, as was being done in some regions, and to disregard the symbolic and historical significance of specific churches. Greater sensitivity was also required, in Iaroslvaskii's view, when deciding whether to remove icons from families who were economically destitute and, by extension, psychologically desperate. Rather, antireligious activists needed to anticipate the impact of the ill will of an alienated minority, even where a majority might accept a church closing or had ceased practicing religion. In this connection Iaroslavskii singled out the bitter 1925 affair at the former Putilov factory that we examined in chapter 4 as a particularly negative example.[6]

One overarching problem was that responsible organs were not carrying out on a mass scale the cultural-enlightenment work intended to provide the accompanying explanation for antireligious actions. For example, a large number of the trade unions that were supposed to act as conduits of antireligious messages declared a position of neutrality on religion. Others took symbolic but unproductive steps such as excluding religious believers from membership, which party leaders felt injured the unions more than those not allowed to join. Experiences like these, in combination with a chronic lack of adequate funding, produced not the anticipated network of organs striving to promote atheism in a coordinated fashion, but national and local institutions who knew each other chiefly through written communications and published resolutions. Well before mid-decade, antireligious leaders ordered new campaigns more strongly grounded in materialist philosophy and better organized.[7]

This task of radical secularization also foundered when citizens expressed nonspiritual concerns through their reactions to cultural-enlightenment initiatives. When Iakov Iakovlev led his group of ethnographers into the village of Polevaia (Kursk province) in 1923, the size of the expedition caused peasants immediately to fear that it could only be tied to the imposition of a new tax.[8] Doctors and agronomists encountered the same suspicion in villages elsewhere;[9] women stayed away from an organizational meeting in Mamenko (Voronezh province) in 1923 when a local rumor held that the real purpose was to collect a tax on spinning wheels. A variation of the same story hampered the *Zhenotdel* in Novokurlai *volost'*, where a tax ranging from three to ten arshins of canvas was said to be levied on those who attended such gatherings. According to gossip in the village of Krasnyi, every newspaper subscriber would have to register with the *raion* militia and pay a fee. And a story that originated in Kazin and Borisov *volosty* of Voronezh province spoke of a tax to reimburse the dispossessed for their nationalized property.[10]

By 1923–1924, therefore, the leadership recognized the need to reorient cultural-enlightenment, antireligious work in ways great and small. In July 1923, the Commission on the Separation of Church and State admitted the problems of having failed to differentiate among religions in its previous efforts and promised specific new instructions for each denomination.[11] Two months later, Agitprop recognized diversity among the population in a different way when it created a special subcommission solely for antireligious propaganda in the village.[12] In addition, leading atheists denounced the pitfalls of proletarian prudishness under the guise of zeal—the expulsion of a member of the Society of the Friends of the Newspaper *Bezbozhnik* simply for being spotted in a beer hall[13]—and demanded greater support from agencies such as the State Film Company, Goskino, which went more than a year without producing a single work on an antireligious theme in its films for the village.[14] Reflecting this combination of determination and frustration, in November 1923 Mikhail Gorev strained to find merit as he reviewed the opening of the country's first atheistic theater. Noting the awkwardness and discomfiture of the workers and peasants who performed Polivanov's "Tarquin the Priest" in cramped surroundings in Moscow, Gorev nevertheless recommended that this nonprofessional troupe perform widely in factories and workers' clubs throughout the region.[15] In February 1925, leaders of the antireligious movement outlined a detailed eleven-week curriculum of twenty-two lectures for presentation by regional organizations, and at the end of the year the Central Council of the League of Godless explained in detail what the new orientation specifically required of local units in addition to these specialized campaigns: not less than one lecture per week; a monthly antireligious evening that would split its agenda equally between a report and various forms of entertainment; the organization of scientific and nature excursions; and, not least important, establishing the financial independence of cells through the regular collection of dues.[16]

The mid-1920s in this way witnessed a change in the predominant tenor of antireligious work, but not a significant improvement in its effectiveness. The criticisms raised during 1923–1924 found full expression in the pivotal party plenum declaration of April 1926, which called for more systematic and focused agitation among the population. Above all, propaganda now should look beyond the problems of the moment and stress natural science, but without lapsing into crude and simplistic formats.[17] But the prevailing strategy of charging virtually all state, party, and social organs with responsibility for antireligious work did not accomplish even these general goals. Within the city of Moscow itself, organs did not uniformly adopt a newly instituted Elementary Course in Godlessness [*Politgramota bezbozhiia*], for example, but either rejected its contents from the outset or abandoned it as unusable after a few lessons. As before, experiences such as these resulted in an absence of leadership, plan of work, or anything resembling a system.[18] As it turned out, so few qualified cadres existed as late as 1927 that the antireligious leadership debated whether to use only trained agitators or enlist virtually anyone available.[19] Maxim Gorky could tell the second national congress of the League of Godless not to tear down churches but to persuade the population to forget about them, but such exhortations failed to grasp the character of experiences in the field.[20]

The increasing mood of radicalism combined with revolutionary petulance that crystallized into the Cultural Revolution in 1928 therefore resulted in still another new approach to promoting atheism. The Fifteenth Party Congress, held in December 1927, had in fact outlined a cultural broadening of antireligious work,[21] but this ultimately ran its course in ways far different from the resolutions passed there. Even though antireligious propaganda soon linked the intentions of the congress to the Cultural Revolution,[22] the promulgation of the 8 April 1929 Sovnarkom directive on religious associations provided a different orientation to militancy. We have already seen that with this decree the Council of People's Commissars eliminated the right to conduct religious proselytizing and education, required the prior registration of religious groups with the government, and further limited rights of assembly and property for the church. Specifically, the "freedom of religious and antireligious propaganda" guaranteed by the Soviet Constitution became the "freedom of religious belief and of antireligious propaganda for all citizens."[23]

The letter of "On Religious Associations" thus effectively rescinded many of the protections afforded religious associations since 1918, yet in a larger sense it was the spirit of the document that even more foreshadowed the imminent deepening of the attack on religion. Before the end of 1929, the political police once again increased their role in repressing religious organizations and put pressure on other organs to do the same,[24] while the predominant tone of public materialist and antireligious messages became still more schematic and crude.[25] Above all, the beginning of the forced collectivization of agriculture included renewed assaults against the institutions and the people perceived as associated with the former order, and as the campaign proceeded churches in particular became a focus of attack. The number of closings rose dramatically, often without the requisite prior authorization from above.[26] And when those who carried out these acts did observe Soviet law, the sheer volume of new work sometimes reduced VTsIK and its subordinate soviets to approving long lists with only cursory discussion, as when a meeting on 19 February 1932 approved ninety-three church closings at a single sitting.[27]

Confrontations took on an intensely personal character. In late 1929, militants in Balashov *okrug* awakened the priest Nikolai Lavrov at two in the morning with an order to leave the parish immediately or face arrest, and soon after they gave the priest Evgenii Rudakovskii twenty-four hours to make the same choice. Local officials in Viazovsk *raion* (Saratov province) deprived clergy of housing and forbade believers to baptize infants and lay deceased relatives in state in their homes. Local officials routinely took from believers even what was necessary for family maintenance; they rounded up the religious without regard for age, gender, or health to clean pigsties and perform janitorial work. Some were banished to other parts of the country for a number of years, and in Murom, clergy as old as seventy were assigned to timber cutting. Multiple reports of this type reached VTsIK from virtually every place where collectivization occurred.[28]

Officials also used economic weapons. In April 1929, VTsIK took action against the abuse of tax laws against religious entities by ordering republic, *krai,* and *oblast'* soviets not to tax them above established norms or at a rate in excess of 30 percent of their general revenue. Regional soviets frequently disobeyed, employing various forms of financial leverage, especially in dealings with clergy. Officials in Moscow *oblast'* charged Metropolitan Sergei four hundred to five hundred rubles a month for his apartment; in Rybushka (Saratov *okrug*), tax collectors gave the priest Alexei Sheremet'ev only twenty-four hours to submit ten poods of beef. Similarly, in Bol'shaia Dmitrievka, the priest Anton Krutitskii and deacon Vasilii Iastrebov were ordered to pay their taxes in rye and wool, that is, a crop they had not sown and a commodity they did not possess. A court consequently sentenced them to two years in prison and five years of exile from the area. At noon on 31 October 1929, officials ordered the priest V. P. Pokrovskii of the parish of Il'itsk on the Moscow-Kazan railway to present 250 poods of potatoes, of which he paid 103. The fifty-seven-year-old cleric and three companions then worked all night by the light of a lantern so that he could deliver the remainder to the collection station nine versts away early the following morning. Officials nevertheless rejected the delivery on a contrived technicality, after which the local court sentenced Pokrovskii to eight months in prison and the loss of a thousand rubles in property. Beyond actions such as these against clerics, the People's Commissariat of Finance worked to provide local officials the means to abrogate arrangements between religious organizations and VTsIK, particularly those that under Soviet law allowed registered religious organizations the free use of buildings for worship. On 20 February 1931, the finance commissariat decreed that parishes must pay general as well as local taxes and, of greater significance, that they owed rent for the use of the land *beneath* the places of worship they used without charge. Should parishes not pay within two months, the local financial organ could petition to confiscate the prayer building.[29]

Nor did these economic assaults spare individual believers. The presidium of VTsIK was fully aware of the extensive degree to which local soviets ignored its directives and continued to tax religious followers according to their own predilections. In 1929–1930, it was by no means only the soviet of the Ivanovo Industrial Region, whose actions were particularly well documented, that brought those who could not pay exorbitant levies to court or confiscated their property. Attempting yet another corrective, VTsIK consequently decreed on 30 August 1930 that religious groups not pay at a level higher than 75 percent of their 1928–1929 tax if their income from agriculture had not risen, nor more than 100 percent if it had. Religious followers in Ivanovo-Voznesensk, Rostov-on-Don, and elsewhere, however, complained that in spite of this, local officials in 1930 assessed thirty to seventy times what believers had paid in 1928–1929, even though for many of them their income did not increase. Despite further orders to desist, reports that local officials continued to disregard central directives and taxed according to their own whims inundated the center in 1931 and thereafter.[30]

. . .

In these various ways, the overarching tactics of the Cultural Revolution grouped the announced enemies of the Soviet power together as the objects of a combined assault. Between 1928 and 1931, liquidating kulaks, implementing collectivization, and eliminating counterrevolutionary elements who ranged from clergy to Nepmen to recalcitrant factions within the party went forward together.[31] Consequently, in addition to their raison d'être, antireligious organizations were also expected to identify with the broader economic goals of industrialization and collectivization—"We are not simply a propaganda society," declared Iaroslavskii—while keeping a vigilant eye open for political deviations on both the right and the left. In cities and industrial enterprises, mass mobilization campaigns were to raise productivity when workers demanded, for example, the removal of religious holidays from the schedule of days of rest.[32] In the countryside, grain procurement and battling religion were inseparable, declared the Central Council of the League of Militant Godless. Kulaks, clergy, and sectarians had all exploited religious organizations in the past to protect their economic and class interests, the argument ran, and at present they worked together to impede grain collection. Antireligious work therefore now had to consist simultaneously of occupying the front rank in seizing grain; organizing *bezbozhnik* shock brigades, collective farms, factories, and shops; carrying out mass propaganda; eradicating illiteracy; and capturing the religiously oriented materials produced by the class enemy. By the time of the anti-Christmas campaign of 1930–1931, which mobilized 444 newspapers for publicity, antireligious goals were increasingly subsumed under broader party political objectives. Campaign slogans placed far more emphasis on eliminating rivalries within the party, liquidating bottlenecks in industry, and promoting shock work and collectivization than on atheism and criticisms of priests.[33]

Viewed from one perspective, this approach brought about the fusion of institutional energies against religion that the Bolsheviks had sought since 1917. Soviet, party, and Komsomol groups led the way in enrolling collective farms, factories, unions, and educational institutions into the League of Militant Godless en masse, which resulted in exponential growth for the league and caused members of the Central Council publicly to approve when atheistic brigades were mobilized for broader projects such as sowing campaigns. As the league was growing in this way and presenting itself as a mass organization more closely identified with the full range of contemporary political priorities, its publications prominently featured *bezbozhnik* work brigades and the sparkling dining facilities and happy children on godless collective farms.[34] Atheistic organs exulted in reports of believers exiting religious communes, a drop in the number taking holy orders, occasions of church closings, and the disappearance of religious holidays.[35] During the 1931 anti-Christmas campaign, the league reported that factory production continued unabated, only insignificant numbers attended church, and the lack of discipline usually associated with church holidays was no longer in evidence.[36] Even where previous propaganda had foundered, a small number of energetic activists could invigorate antireligious work.[37]

With an irony unpleasant for leading antireligious militants, however, the Cultural Revolution delivered a blow from which the League of Militant Godless would never fully recover. The league had previously occupied the most visible place in disseminating antireligious propaganda, but it proved too disorganized and underfunded to maintain its leading position once the Cultural Revolution increasingly turned to church closures, seizures of icons, expropriations of church bells, and the persecution of believers. Party and soviet organizations—in combination with Komsomols, the army, the political police, trade unions, various propaganda organs, and special brigades of workers mobilized for collectivization— now carried the greatest load; in terms of its own self-criticism, the League of Militant Godless accomplished the least.[38] Even as it publicly celebrated its successes, small but significant signs—photos in *Bezbozhnik* of state cooperatives selling Christmas ornaments and other holiday items[39]—testified to a different state of affairs. According to the Central Council's own internal assessments, the rapid enrollment of five million members amounted not to a mass organization in any operative sense but a cadre that existed largely on paper. As the league took stock of itself in 1932, it found few functioning godless cells in the collectives, its "plan" amounted to no more than a constant barrage of directives, members failed to pay dues, professional agitators had not received their salary in three months, and tying antireligious work to collectivization had not improved the quality of propaganda. The Central Council most commonly defended itself only by arguing that the league now worked better than in the past and that it was receiving inadequate support from the party, especially at the local levels.[40]

Though the League of Militant Godless thus lost its prime authority over antireligious activism, it nevertheless continued to absorb much of the blame for failures. In March 1930, Stalin's article "Dizziness with Success" took to task the excesses of early collectivization. Soon a variety of sources, not least the league itself, were raising parallel criticisms of antireligious work, which mitigated attacks on churches and enabled some to reopen.[41] If some villages even in close proximity to industrial towns had not seen a single antireligious agitator by 1928,[42] the new militance was not the solution. Combining the liquidation of kulaks, the general class struggle, and the building of collective farms with the undisciplined closing of places of worship, violence against clergy, and seizure of church bells over the next four years only made matters worse, critics charged. Outrages against the symbols of religion had galvanized resistance from Orthodox supporters and sectarian "fanatics" alike, with the ostensible natural allies of Bolshevism, the most impoverished stratum of the peasantry, often setting a religious mood that caused whole collective farms to disintegrate.[43] In this analysis, the fault lay not with the party line but, in the language of the era, with deviationists who sabotaged it. In an expedient tautology, every failure fit one category of deviation or another. The so-called left misunderstood the social dimension of religion and committed excesses; the deviation on the right underestimated the political aspect of the class struggle against religion and did too little.[44]

RESISTANCE AND RETRIBUTION

Throughout 1917–1932, Orthodox believers did not tolerate repression passively but regularly countered it with insubordination and force. They used violence for self-defense and resistance, but also for retaliation and intimidation. During the civil war, this predominantly took the form of armed support for the opponents of the revolution and against local acts of the separation of church and state. With the Bolshevik victory, it became of necessity ad hoc. After 1928, the use of brutality on all sides increased.

Active resistance occurred from the very beginning of Bolshevik rule. So frequently did the revolutionary state encounter opposition couched in religious issues—and so deeply was the link of religion to anti-Soviet behavior ingrained in Bolshevik thinking—that in March 1919 Narkomiust included a query on the number of appearances of Black Hundreds under the influence of clergy in a routine questionnaire to local organs.[45] Less stilted reports did not use such simplistic categories to make their point, but they nevertheless found significant sabotage against Bolsheviks when the closing of religious buildings and related acts took place.[46] The journal *Nauka i religiia* might therefore celebrate the arrest of Bishop Viktor of Tomsk and a group of priests in late 1922 for leading resistance to the Soviet state through their churches, but *Bezbozhnik* by no means considered the problem of religiously rooted, underground resistance to the Soviet state resolved. Throughout the mid-1920s the paper consistently maintained that clergy coordinated local actions in a united front against the revolution, cited monasteries as particular breeding grounds of opposition, and seized every opportunity to report proreligious demonstrations.[47] Internal party documents, which were classified at the time, reinforced this assessment. During the second half of the 1920s, party organs in Nizhnii Novgorod continued to encounter a significant number of religious groups that effectively circulated anti-Soviet political materials,[48] and similar communications that legal religious organizations served as fronts for oppositional activity reached party leaders from a variety of other locales as well.[49] In addition, reports of threats and acts of violence against antireligious agitators were by no means uncommon throughout the decade, increasing at its end, even before the onset of forced collectivization. Thus, in early 1929, unknown assailants killed a Komsomol member conducting antireligious work in the workers' settlement of Barvenko in the Donbas, and on the eve of Easter the Komsomol musical group there received an ominous threat not to play on the holiday. In Sredensk *okrug,* clergy played an instrumental role in organizing a Union of Michael the Archangel for violence against atheists, and in another locality a group of workers unmercifully beat a schoolteacher for entering into an antireligious disputation.[50]

When collectivization began in earnest, violence increased on both sides, and not only in the countryside. At the time when the use of force against the population was increasing, new reports of murdered antireligious agitators reached the center from points as diverse as the highly industrialized Ivanovo *oblast',* the largely agricultural Middle-Volga *krai,* and Chita *oblast'.*[51] Peasants in Vladivostok *okrug* circulated a "letter from heaven," which absolved from sin all those who killed atheists: "Whoever will believe will be delivered from their sins, even when the sins are stained with blood. Whoever adheres to the commandments will have all his sins melt away like snow."[52] It should therefore not be surprising that virtually no antireligious circles existed in either town or village schools in Syzran' *okrug* because agitators feared the consequences of attempting to organize them.[53] In Stavropol, the priest Pomrianskii led a group that killed Nikanorov, a member of the rural soviet. And during the night of 31 July 1930, when the local League of Militant Godless was preparing an antireligious day, "hooligans" broke into the local club. They rifled the document files and bookcases, scattering and defiling the contents. They also broke the movie projector, tore off half the screen, and in general vandalized the premises. In Orenburg *okrug,* churchmen participated in a night raid of the Griazno-Irtek *kolkhoz* in 1930. Surrounding the collective on three sides, they intimidated a significant number of families into fleeing.[54] And when local officials in the village of Karel' rapidly carried out full collectivization in 1930, closed all churches, and arrested clergy, the local old women [*baby*] reacted with a traditional stratagem: they staged a demonstration from which males abstained and won the release of the local priest.[55] One atheistic publication counted no fewer than twenty such reported "excesses" by female "fanatics" in a single year.[56]

Clergy also led civil disobedience. Where support for Soviet power wavered, priests easily blamed the state for problems of food procurement, rationing, goods shortages, and the international situation, but they also attributed local calamities to the regime. Thus, the fact that a fire broke out in Igelkino in 1929 during the showing of a film gave the priest all the opening he needed to condemn film in general and its party and Communist Youth League sponsors.[57] The deacon Ivan Kiselev in the village of Pustosh (Moscow province) headed a group that encouraged peasants not to pay their taxes or turn over required grain requisitions.[58] In Khyr-Kasinsk, churchmen and believers publicized the end of the world and the inevitability of war in order to encourage an exodus from the *kolkhoz*.[59] And throughout 1929–1930, security organs failed in their attempt to prevent the believer K. A. Odintsev—who predicted the end of Soviet power and gathered collective farmers to criticize the taking of land and levying of taxes—from publicly encouraging peasants to rise and overthrow the state. "This is not a government, but bandits," declared Odintsev publicly.[60] In Orekhovo-Zuevo *okrug,* the priest in Selivanikho labeled the collective farm "the road straight to Hell," and in nearby Petrushkino the priest Tretilov and a lay sympathizer declared that "the *kolkhoz* comes from the Devil and the tractor from the Antichrist."[61]

The strategic use of rumor often drove such direct resistance and civil disobedience. Given the capacity of this device to influence a large audience virtually without fear of accountability, rumormongers found their voice from the very beginning of the Soviet period.[62] Not all such rumors involved forces of religion working against the Soviet state, but a kind of story oriented generally toward behavior harmful to the announced objectives of the revolution—and favorable to positions commonly supported by religious believers—appeared in significant numbers in both town and village. Broad predictions of the coming of the Antichrist and the end of the world understandably caused anxiety, but less ominous stories were often equally disruptive. As Lenin lay critically ill in 1922–1923, rumors related to his death abounded. One held that as a result of his death, Soviet power would end by 15 April 1923; in a different version, all churches would be converted into movie theaters when he died. Another canard spoke of the French army's having already conquered Berlin and being on the march toward Moscow.[63] Still more localized was a tale that the Antichrist would arrive at noon and put his mark on school children, which caused mothers and sisters to gather outside the Fedoseevo-Pustinskaia school and demand that students be dismissed immediately. Although the children remained through the end of the lesson, relatives took them home during recess. The Soviet government interpreted this 1918 incident as an attempt to combat the recent separation of church and school.[64]

Yet, even when circumstances did not suggest a direct causal connection, many rumors expressed a kind of anti-Soviet attitude by implication. In one anti-Bolshevik, anti-Semitic story during the civil war, a Jewish commissar shot an icon but died himself when the holy image deflected the bullet back toward him.[65] The year 1924 witnessed what one newspaper called "an epidemic of miracles," as reports of icons being spontaneously restored, lamps without oil that lit themselves and burned for a long time, and similar tales made their way into towns and especially through the countryside.[66] In Saratov in 1926, the priest Vorob'ev confounded antireligious work simply by telling villagers that Marx was a religious believer,[67] and monks selling crosses in Staryi Dondukovskii (Maikopskii *okrug*) shouted threats to passersby that approaching bandits would chop up anyone who did not have one.[68] God would punish Voskresensk *volost'* (Iaroslavl' province) for atheism with uninterrupted rain, ran one story of the second half of the 1920s; another predicted that an old man would be found in a coffin, beneath which was to be an inscription predicting famine and war.[69]

Those who opposed collectivization often used religious categories to express their position,[70] and rumors of divine intervention against those who cooperated with the Soviet state proliferated. The village priest in Sendavko (Orenburg *okrug*) at night heard "the voice of the Lord" tell him that "whoever enters the *kolkhoz* passes into the hands of the Antichrist." In the village of Rybkin, a sectarian wrote letters to *kolkhoz* members, signed by Michael the Archangel, that influenced families to flee and thus seriously disrupted sowing. And in Samara *okrug* the churchman Nikishin brought about a similar exodus when he warned that all would perish in the collective.[71] God allegedly authored a letter warning that the *kolkhoz* was the sphere of the devil: "Whoever is not tempted into the *kolkhoz* is saved; all *kolkhoz* members will be annihilated in the next few days." A variation of this document advised peasants "to exit the collective and take up shock work [*udarnichestvo*] to bring about the collapse of the collective farms." And a letter attributed to the Mother of God in Berezovsk warned of the nearness of the final judgment and the need to battle collectivization and atheism.[72]

Typically, rumors addressed multiple targets. Clergy claimed a miracle just before Easter in 1930 in Lukino *raion* (Mordovsk *oblast'*). The report brought forth a larger crowd than usual on Easter not only from

Mordovsk, but also nearby areas. Clergy, invoking what were by then stock phrases, told the throng of the arrival of the Antichrist, the end of the world, and "the nationalization of women under collectivization."[73] One of the more direct rejections of Bolshevik materialism and faith in technology came from the village of Stolpino (Ivanovo *oblast'*) in 1931. Rumors spread there by parishioners convinced other peasants that the tractor was a "Satanic force" that "will plow up the bones in your parents' graves." Many consequently refused to use tractors in the fields.[74] In this environment, as the *bezbozhnik* Shokhol' reported to the Central Council in January 1930, it was fanciful to close a church one day and stage an antireligious meeting there the next night. All that accomplished was to place antireligious forces "in a stupid position."[75]

REVOLUTIONARY LEGALITY AND CIRCUMVENTION

The lower classes more frequently preferred tactics of circumvention to fomenting confrontation. Since open resistance to tsarist officials and nobility had ultimately proved futile in the past, disfranchised elements—including but not limited to the peasantry—long ago had devised ways to derail unwanted initiatives from above or set their own initiatives into motion. Emerging Soviet law and the Bolshevik concept of revolutionary legality unintentionally provided them with new opportunities.

After 1917, religious believers drew heavily on past experience and guile. Supporters of Orthodoxy used their numerical superiority, for example, to infiltrate antireligious education groups in Nizhnii Novgorod province and substitute a close reading of religious texts for the intended Bolshevik activity. In Revdinsk (Urals), the church elder and lay supporters took over the leadership of the local antireligious circle, and a deacon headed one in the village of Novyi Tan'in (Middle Volga). In a number of areas, cells of the Friends of the Newspaper *Bezbozhnik* regularly enrolled not only believers, but wives and daughters of priests as well.[76] And during collectivization, in some cases a priest or other religious figure even managed to become head of a *kolkhoz*.[77]

But this infiltration of institutions paled beside the success of clergy and activist laity in subverting the Bolshevik concept of revolutionary legality. Ideally, the observance of Soviet law in actions against religious organizations would help establish regularized state procedures and at the same time inculcate a new legal consciousness in society.[78] In pursuit of both of these aims, a joint NKVD-Narkomiust instruction of

19 June 1923 declared that only the executive committees of provincial and *oblast'* soviets would decide the fate of places of worship. In view of the poor judgment already used in the closing of churches, the two organs felt that care had to be used in deciding even which soviet committees should be so empowered.[79] In this spirit of revolutionary legality, the VTsIK Commission on Religious Issues also persistently called for actions to be taken against parishes only with the prior approval of higher organs, in keeping with the resolutions on antireligious work adopted at party congresses, and especially without any violations of Soviet law. At a meeting of the presidium of VTsIK, N. V. Krylenko of Narkomiust took a strong stand against a tactical reliance on repression over law: "It is not in the spirit of the general policy of the Soviet state to stand exclusively on repression with regard to the church. Repression is not the path which will produce the immediately desired results."[80]

This Bolshevik revolutionary legality was, to be sure, a legality of pragmatism rather than of principle or compassion. It strove for the maximum number of church closures with the minimum disruption of the local community, as when the Moscow Committee of the League of Militant Atheists in 1929 carefully distinguished between the ongoing goal of closing churches and the need to replace counterproductive tactics in doing so.[81] VTsIK and the Commissariat of Finance also exhibited far greater concern for legality when a church seizure involved objects of gold, precious icons, or historically significant buildings.[82] And Soviet law, of course, worked in both directions. If a church were not functioning, had no historical significance, and the local soviet could demonstrate some alternate use for the building, petitioning to reverse a nationalization already implemented was difficult.[83] Finally, various local authorities disregarded law altogether. Some 230 workers in the railroad settlement of Babaevo learned this lesson when, at the beginning of 1919, the construction committee of a proposed church was arrested and the money they had raised confiscated.[84]

Nonetheless, even a politically pragmatic commitment to legality placed an efficacious weapon in the hands of Russian Orthodoxy. Clergy and activist laity did not, of course, give credence to the Bolshevik distinction between sanctioned and unsanctioned acts against the church, but they did fully recognize that concern among the Soviet leadership for observing the letter of the law was an opportunity to subvert its intent to their own purposes. Partisans of Orthodoxy therefore cited law whenever possible in direct confrontations, and if unsuccessful at the local level they appealed to central authorities in the hope of having lower decisions overturned. Believers succeeded often enough that this practice continued well into the 1930s. As a result, Mikhail Kalinin, chairman of VTsIK, gained a reputation as a sympathetic figure to whom the wronged could turn, and scores of entreaties to "Little Father" Kalinin reached central authorities through the VTsIK Commission on Religious Issues. Voicing a common objection, antireligious agitators in Nizhnii Novgorod province complained that "believers know the path to VTsIK and Mikhail Ivanovich [Kalinin] very well."[85]

Workers and peasants certainly required no instruction in composing petitions. Even at the height of the civil war, workers in Vitebsk did not hesitate to produce scores of signatures demanding the release of the priest of the Pokrov church.[86] When the 1918 law on the separation of church and state made possible the transfer of nationalized places of worship to registered communes of believers, congregations quickly recognized the potential thereby to gain control of their parishes. The application of the Moscow Nikolaev Church on 23 October 1918 provided a textbook example of a correct registration. The requisite inventory listed all church property ranging from icons to the clock, tables, and carpeting, complete with measurements.[87] A parish of the Old Believer sect carefully quoted the 1918 decree on the separation of church and state and the Narkomiust instruction on its implementation in their 1921 petition to the Administrative Department of the Moscow City Soviet for their return of a church on Malaia Anron'evskaia Street.[88] These cases were far from unique: city and regional archives contain hundreds of the similarly thorough documents that poured into local soviets, which frequently gave church buildings back to the petitioners.[89] Believers employed state procedures so consciously and adeptly that by 1926–1928 the language of state decrees and that of many petitions was virtually identical.[90] And where haste had been used in ordering churches closed, the Commission on Religious Issues canceled such authorizations, sometimes in large numbers.[91]

The expansion of sectarianism during the 1920s created additional opportunities to bend the law. During the first decade of Soviet power, the Bolshevik approach to the state-church conflict changed from an initial focus overwhelmingly on Orthodoxy to serious concern about the growing number of indigenous sects and foreign denominations.[92] Orthodoxy itself became a moving target as it fragmented even further internally, and non-Orthodox religious groups that had operated underground during the tsarist period now did so openly. At the same time, foreign proselytizers entered the country with resources that exceeded anything Bolshevism or Orthodoxy could marshal and gained significant numbers of converts by the second half of the decade. Those who

abandoned Orthodoxy, therefore, often did so by joining another denomination or minority sect, to the consternation of the Soviet state and
the Orthodox Church. This was a concern in the countryside, but it also
occurred conspicuously among the peasants who were moving into industrial centers, where the ability to build churches and schools en-
hanced the attractiveness of the foreign denominations in particular.[93]
This phenomenon spawned additional circumventions of Soviet law.
Religious organizations capitalized on the opportunity to form economic communes voluntarily; by 1926 some thirty-five religious communes operated legally, and an undetermined additional number ille-
gally, in Votskaia *oblast'* alone.[94] When a number of denominations
intermittently received exemptions from the military in favor of alternative service, accusations arose saying that religious groups used avoid-
ance of service as a recruiting tool and that some groups became non-
combatant only after exemptions were granted on religious grounds.[95]
Finally, Soviet law allowed for acts of sectarian partisanship, as when
non-Orthodox denominations reportedly closed ranks with nonbelievers
to vote for the closing of Orthodox churches.[96]

Acts of physical intimidation did not necessarily diminish the
propensity of religious believers to appeal to law. When party and
Komsomol activists, backed by armed militia, attacked the church of
the Diat'kov commune (Briansk province) on 4 March 1929, a sophisticated complaint from local leaders made its way through the bureaucracy to the republic procurator at Narkomiust within nineteen days.
The document included both a bid for sympathy in the form of a detailed description of the event as well as strong and precise legal substantiation for the position of the commune. The representatives of Diat'kov related how the attackers had destroyed the living quarters of the
caretaker of the church and thrown his family with their belongings into
the street in only twenty-four minutes. They described the seizure of sacred vessels; the smashing of doors, windows, icons, and the iconostasis; and the chopping up of the altar. Of greater significance for the legal aspect of their appeal, they also furnished exact references to
numbered documents from 1919, 1924, and 1927 in which VTsIK had
granted the church to the commune. This was sufficient for VTsIK to
order an investigation, which broadened to include other issues as each
side accused the other of misrepresenting what took place.[97]

Believers also did not let the abuse of tax laws go unanswered. Des-
peration undoubtedly motivated specific petitions as much as guile, to
be sure, but VTsIK officials did not simply dismiss breaches of law
against the religious. Even during the tumultuous year 1930, Kalinin's

secretary candidly criticized illegal actions against believers: "There exists no sign of elementary revolutionary legality toward them as *lishensty*. There reigns in the local areas complete arbitrary rule and a lack of understanding of the policy of the party in this politically important process."[98] And although one might be tempted to disparage such pronouncements as disingenuousness masked as self-criticism or as the creation of scapegoats, the actions of VTsIK officials frequently proved consistent with these words. In a representative case, an appeal by V. F. Trusov resulted in the lowering of his agricultural tax from 521.50 rubles to 231.[99] Others who did not appeal tax abuses on their own contacted the Holy Synod, which represented collective grievances.[100] Finally, in an ironic twist of intent and implementation, a 1929 VTsIK decree that placed an upper limit on the level of taxes for religious believers had the result that followers of Orthodoxy paid significantly less than other households on collective farms in subsequent years.[101]

Capturing the essence of revolutionary legality, an incident in the village of Verovka (Rykov *raion*) demonstrates how both sides in local disputes tried to influence central authorities. In their petition to the Presidium of VTsIK, religious citizens there described a church closing in January 1929 that ran the gamut of legal and illegal tactics. According to the document parish representatives filed in protest, local antireligious activists first took steps toward the closure of the Nikolaev Church, and parishioners countered with a registration of believers in order to regain it. When only 709 of a potentially much larger number had signed, however, the head of the local party organization intervened and confiscated the registration book. Angry church supporters sent representatives to the *Raion* and *Okrug* Administrative Departments, but officials turned them away. A rumor then began to circulate that the church would close by 1 May. This became a reality on 25 April when the chairman of the Rykov regional soviet executive committee, Ivanenko, officially notified the clergyman and church elder. At five o'-clock the following morning, a group of church members arrived at the Artemov *Okrug* Administrative Department to protest what they contended was an illegal closing of their church. But at the same hour, the Rykov militia, local Komsomol members, and the secretary of the local party cell were bursting into the church, smashing the iconostasis, defiling the icons, and carrying off all church goods on two trucks.[102]

The Administrative Department then pressed the offensive. Far from acceding to protests on 26 and 28 April, they declared the seizure to be legal and announced that the clergyman and church council would be held responsible for any disorders. "We [parish members] were especially exasperated when we saw that a room for a movie house was being added to the church. On 30 April this agitation became a riot [*bunt*]. A crowd of thousands from Verovka and [other] parish villages appeared at the church, drove out the invaders from the place of worship, and sounded the alarm. Parents and children exchanged shouts and fisticuffs." When the regional militia arrived and firefighters doused the demonstrators with cold water, a generational dimension of the affair came into play. Komsomol members beat mothers, and mothers trampled Komsomol and militia members. The believers retained control of the church for five hours, and in the aftermath soviet forces banned believers from the building altogether and posted a guard night and day. According to the religious petitioners, brother fought brother and fathers opposed sons, but the believers desisted rather than cause further violence within families.[103]

But local officials reported a decidedly different story to VTsIK. They had collected more than fifteen thousand workers' signatures in favor of closing two churches in the area, they said, and on 24 April the central executive committee of the district soviet gave its approval by telegram. Not a "crowd" of believers, but "twenty to thirty women" protested at the church on 26 April. The rapporteurs also appealed to official disapproval of anti-Semitism by including that the Orthodox mainly questioned why their church and not the nearby synagogue was being seized. The "thousands" that the parishioners said had protested on 30 April appear as 150 in the report by local officials, and the extensive fighting was reduced to one Komsomol member being briefly hospitalized after being hit with a rock. Central officials did not attempt to reconcile such disparate accounts from a distance and after the fact, and neither side achieved full satisfaction. The church remained closed, but the political police, based on the fact that any incident at all occurred, launched an investigation of the local officials' handling of the affair and of their fitness for office.[104]

In addition to expressions of legitimate grievance, believers filed disingenuous petitions. The central executive committee of the Middle Volga *Krai* Soviet complained that Kalinin's frequent intervention on behalf of church members and his support of false petitions undermined local authority. Middle Volga officials, for instance, had closed a nonfunctioning church in the village of Bogdanovka in 1929 in accordance with the precepts of Soviet law, that is, with a prior petition by the local population and the transformation of the building into a house of culture, elementary school, and machine tractor shop. Local supporters of Orthodoxy reacted by sending a single representative, one Kriventsov, directly to the VTsIK Commission on Religious Issues. On the basis of his appeal, which included the presentation of signatures of those who in some cases later turned out to be children less than ten years old, the commission overturned the closing. The Middle Volga *Krai* Soviet furnished additional examples of how a small number of believers could manipulate the process if they were willing to address central officials directly, as when fabricated versions of events had brought about reversals of closures in Khvorostianko (Privolzhsk *raion*) and elsewhere in the region. The Middle Volga central executive committee demanded that Kalinin desist.[105] Far from being intimidated, though, the Orthodox often pressed their advantages. VTsIK chastised the leadership of the regional soviet in the town of Azarmass, which in 1921 had thirty-six churches, not only for closing the final two in the early 1930s, but also for employing administrative methods in doing so. Believers seized the opportunity to demand the reopening of all thirty-six.[106]

ACCOMMODATION AND INDIFFERENCE

In the larger context, far more citizens everywhere practice accommodation than ever take up activism. The largest number conform generally to the broad dictates of their respective societies, but not primarily in order to launch acts of conscious circumvention of the kind we have just examined. Rather, they work within the prevailing framework above all to reconcile their personal agendas with the constraints imposed by the social, political, economic, legal, and moral environment. As they thus negotiate between conformity and will, individuals create modes of survival and fashion the means for personal empowerment, redress, and self-aggrandizement. In short, strategies of accommodation do not preclude active participation in society but facilitate it to the potential benefit of the practitioners. This was particularly important during the early years of Soviet power, when both state and church subjected citizens to opposing pressures on the religious question and, by extension, on the future of society itself. The majority responded with infinitely varied combinations of spiritual and nonspiritual priorities.[107]

Accommodation consequently had an undeniable impact on the social history of atheism and religion in revolutionary Russia. Despite their high visibility in the battles between state and church and in subsequent historiography, only a small proportion of even the most dedicated either died for or committed violence in the name of Russian Orthodoxy. And for the much larger group who participated in resistance or circumvention—joining a crowd to battle the closing of a church or signing a petition—the experience demanded only episodic and for that reason flexible activism, not complete and irrevocable commitment. And in the opposite camp, acts of militant atheism involved but a small fraction of those who identified with Bolshevism. Even if one includes the hooligans who attacked churches and clergy for reasons that only weakly intersected with the goals of the Bolshevik leadership, the activist core against religion was minuscule. It was also a group insignificant by other measures, since revolutionary institutions never gave their most valued cadres, adequate funds, or systematic effort to antireligious work. In the end, although the elimination of religion was an early Soviet desideratum, it was also demonstrably less than a de facto high short-term priority. Making these statements does not trivialize the sacrifices by clergy and others who did pay the ultimate price for their beliefs. Neither does it denigrate the sincerity and depth of outrage felt by those believers who were nevertheless capable of only situational resolve in defense of Orthodoxy. Expressing such sentiments also does not question the earnestness of the Bolshevik determination ultimately to create a society free of religious influences, nor does it dismiss the reasons that the leadership considered such a step necessary. But it does emphasize the importance of accommodation as the most common personal strategy of choice during the Russian experiment in communism.

Noting the widespread existence of strategies of accommodation, however, is easier than measuring them. Neither state nor church formally recognized the legitimacy of individual adaptations to revolutionary conditions in Russia. Both characterized behavior that fell short of their respective ideals as personal failings and problems to be rectified, not as rational responses by individuals to multiple pressures in an unstable environment. Given Tikhon's anathema against the Bolsheviks and the corresponding secular excommunication the party practiced against believers in the ranks, citizens in particularly difficult situations were vulnerable to sanctions and retribution from more than one source. As a result, strategies of accommodation did not enter the historical record as discrete analytical categories employed by any major actor. Instead, they appeared within the context of the voluminous reactions by state and church to perceived negative behavior, which both elected to publicize as aberrations. On the personal level, individuals also did not make their feelings known in ways that could be quantified or readily categorized but rather through their daily actions and other indirect methods—general conversations in workers' clubs, for example, or even pointed questions in public meetings—for which they typically would not be held seriously accountable. Thus, strategies of accommodation revealed themselves through evidence that was oblique, frequently anecdotal, and at times impressionistic, *but such revelations were above all ubiquitous.* Even though state and church habitually paid more attention to the manifestations of accommodation than to its true roots and described it in the terms they used to measure their own priorities—a perceived fall or rise in church attendance, for example—the constancy of their preoccupation kept the issue of how individuals carved out their existence never far from the center of attention.

One additional point deserves explication. Accommodation should in no way be confused with the expressions of religious doubt that Western students of theology, psychology, and philosophy have variously called "indifference," "indifferentism," "ambivalence," "antitheism," and the like. In *Essai sur l'indifférence en matière de religion,* the seminal treatise on the subject, Félicité de Lamennais in 1817 defined indifference narrowly as an intellectually bankrupt negation of faith that "does not give rise to any doctrine, since those who are indifferent in reality neither deny nor affirm anything." Lamennais characterized it as "a systematic error, a voluntary slumber of the soul . . . a pervasive numbness of the moral faculties."[108] Subsequent magisterial works— the writings of Emile Durkheim, Sigmund Freud, Roman Malinowski, and Max Weber stand out—refined and extended this focus as they linked the intellectual dimension of religious zeal and doubt more definitively to the social realm. In a large sense, though, this literature and especially the more recent works that derive from it share one crucial assumption: they move generally outward from the inner life to the social manifestations of belief.[109] Such an approach does not explain Soviet society in 1917–1932 well. In early Soviet Russia it was not a personal act of intellectual negation or affirmation that in the first instance set in motion changes in social norms, but the interactions between forms of belief and pressing but fluid social circumstances—a process already under way before 1917. Will and spirituality therefore undoubtedly informed personal behavior in revolutionary Russia in crucial ways, to be sure, but for the majority of the people the intense external pressures generated by transition to socialism played at least as large a role. Thus, the Russian case makes greater sense when inner and social factors occupy a more equal plane. Clifford Geertz describes this interaction: "In religious belief and practice a group's ethos is rendered intellectually reasonable by being shown to represent a way of life ideally adapted to the actual state of affairs the world-view describes, while the world-view is rendered emotionally convincing by being presented as an image of the actual state of affairs."[110] And what was intellectually reasonable and emotionally convincing for the majority in early Soviet Russia stopped short of overt risk and might change in response to shifting circumstances.

Thus, in the course of pursuing their general concerns, the Bolsheviks could not help but confront diverse symptoms of accommodation. Even the use of force yielded results that were far from uniform. On the one hand, compulsion worked more or less effectively within a restricted range of objectives. Not surprisingly, the number of churches closed in areas that experienced collectivization ran well ahead of the ostensibly more politically conscious, less religious urban centers. Similarly, the size of the antireligious demonstrations that occurred during the Cultural Revolution would defy explanation in the absence of intimidation. Certainly the rise of anticlericalism and the evidence of opposition to religion of the late tsarist period, even if combined with the acts of postrevolutionary hooliganism against religious symbols, would prove woefully inadequate to explain the scale of public participation. The three thousand, for example, who turned out for a jointly sponsored party, Komsomol, and union demonstration in March 1929 to demand the liberation of the masses from religion and the transformation of churches into schools sharply exceeded the common level of activism either before or after the Cultural Revolution.[111] The same must also be said of the petition from 50,000 workers and employees in Novosibirsk to the local soviet that all churches be closed, a similar demand from the 1,556 workers of the Lantsuskii factory in Gomelo and the 1,440 residents of Starovo (Vladimir province), the unanimous call by the peasants of Sel'tso (Viaznikov *raion*) during the collectivization of their village for the conversion of their two churches into a People's House and a school, and the rapid closure of the thirty churches of the Babinsk region (Kaluga *raion*). Nor can one accept as spontaneous the resolution of 8 February 1930 at the writing paper factory in Okulov that "from this day forward there will not be a single icon in our apartments," the more so since its passage was followed by the forcible seizure of icons from workers' apartments and their mass public burning.[112]

On the other hand, responses to force even within the same area varied; the aspects of building socialism that did not lend themselves to its applications gave rise to further evidence that the rank and file were to a significant degree acting according to their own priorities. In Moscow *oblast'*, for example, by January 1930, 17 of 22 churches had closed in Malokhovsk *raion*, as had 22 of 36 in a neighboring region. Yet in nearby Bezhetsk *okrug*, closings had occurred at only 12 of 320 churches.[113] Central leaders interpreted such variations in terms of what they vaguely labeled the local "mood," which they instructed factory committees to assess before and after the closing of a church.[114] In so doing, officials were tacitly recognizing the existence of behaviors and attitudes that lay beyond the sway of compulsion, even as they strove to alter them. And in spheres where the potential of suasion to accomplish social transformation was greater, the primacy of personal concerns was even more pronounced. To cite one quintessential example, a discussion of the economics of social welfare in *Antireligioznik* in early 1928 inexorably led to observations on the true priorities of the rank and file. While lamenting the difficulty of convincing citizens to accept a nonreligious understanding of the family as a prerequisite to building socialism, this article frankly expressed that those expected to do the actual building were most intensely preoccupied at present not with abstractions but with the care of children, general household maintenance, and the manifestations of the inherited hierarchy of gender within the family.[115] In sum, if compulsion and intimidation could generate acquiescence in public affairs—a visible and uncomplicated form of accommodation—their efficacy diminished the more deeply the revolutionary process probed the personal sphere. In the absence of widespread enthusiasm for Bolshevik goals, therefore, the success of the social revolution hinged on the degree to which individuals and groups were willing to practice accommodation in its more nuanced form: preemptive obedience without direct coercion.

The revolution thus experienced its most significant encounters with accommodation in areas where citizens found the most latitude to exert their own priorities. The party members who retained religious ties had obviously constructed a strategy of accommodation that, to invert the proposition, meant that some Orthodox families had done the same vis-à-vis the party. Accommodation also manifested itself in the range of religious and secular rituals found in the celebration of holidays as well as in the variety of community attitudes toward Soviet schools. It underlay the propensity of citizens to couch personal concerns in religious language and, conversely, to work through state political institutions to protect religion.[116] Those who could not commit without reservation to either Bolshevism or Orthodoxy employed accomodation as they clung to the occult or opted for sectarian alternatives, and it dominated life in the workplace. In these circumstances, a rejection of religion in no way equaled an allegiance to Bolshevism; rather, it produced a field of hybrids. Antireligious publications that approvingly noted how religious observance had all but ceased in the many industrial areas before the beginning of the Cultural Revolution also observed only weak pressure to close even nonfunctioning churches there.[117]

This synthesis of acceptance and passivity—acquiescing to the elimination of much of the old without enthusiastically embracing the new—became an important mode of behavior in Soviet society. When expatriate journalist Maurice Hindus returned to his native village after collectivization, he found neither widespread smoldering anger at the demise of religion nor a community in fearful subjugation. Himself a religious sympathizer eager to find signs of sustaining spirituality, Hindus instead encountered reactions that ranged from resignation to indifference even from former guardians of community morals. Moreover, despite the presence of party militants and youth generally hostile to religion, most residents readily and openly expressed their ideas and exchanged views.[118] Since behavior such as that observed by Hindus was primarily a reaction to the immediate environment, it largely eluded the scope of Soviet social engineering. As a politics of attitude and not of policy or ideology, it lay beyond the reach of what the party did well and could best be addressed by the methods it used least well. And in placing the personal above the collective, it stood at odds with the fundamental tenets of Bolshevism.

Finally, the diversity of personal accommodations undercut supporters of the party as they attempted correctives. There was no hesitancy to seek information, as when the Russian Geographic Society surveyed the residents of Viatka on the size, configuration, and even window and door placement of peasant huts; the prevailing usage of land, firewood, and nearby terrain for hunting; the diet, including the predominant grain for bread, beverages other than water, and the most popular vegetables; and attire, including the length of males' hair.[119] Beyond such inquiries relating to *byt,* however, institutions also probed attitudes, where replies were nearly as diverse as the respondents themselves. In reaction to the mixed signals the regime sent, citizens like the Moscow and Leningrad workers who answered questions on life and religious belief from the Moscow Institute of School Workers in 1929–1930 recognized that there were issues on which one could be truthful, others that required dissembling or shifting blame on others, and still other topics for which repeating a platitude was the only safe answer. They were not unanimous, however, on where to draw such lines.

Through their replies in interviews and questionnaires, respondents revealed their perceptions of what was expected and how far they were willing to comply; some gave only safe, formulaic answers. The army veteran Roshin of the Burevestnik factory elected only to praise Soviet power in phrases common to propaganda. Condemning religion, Roshin claimed to have burned the family icons and, speaking also for his wife, expressed hatred for the priest. Although none of their four children had been Octobered, they neither prayed nor received any religious education.[120] An unnamed female worker from the Babaeva factory exploited the association of religion and vodka common to party discourse as she blamed her alcoholic husband for the icon in their former apartment. In a stilted revelation, she also stated that her six-year-old daughter had volunteered, "Mama, we have no god" (l. 3). A male worker at the 1905 factory in Leningrad had as a child attended a parish school, believed in God, and practiced Orthodoxy actively with his family until he left for the city, but he joined the party following Lenin's death and, he said, began rearing his two children as atheists (l. 5). Anna Iazeva of the Bukharin trolley park gave up her belief in God when she married a party member and mothered two Komsomol members (l. 10). The party also received credit for a Moscow textile worker's achievement of literacy at the age of twenty-seven, the same year she became a candidate member of the party. Boasting of having abandoned her religious spirit and that her children were in the Komsomol and Pioneers, she answered queries about her personal circumstances predominantly by railing against the bourgeoisie and praising the uninterrupted work week (l. 11). S. M. Zil'derbrand offered that "my character was not to be religious, because I never believed in God" (l. 15), whereas F. G. Goriachev declared himself an ardent *bezbozhnik* in the process of recruiting his wife (l. 36). And an unnamed female worker from the 1905 factory couched one important truth in generally pro-Soviet terms. Although she said she had attended church as a child only because those who did not were not fed, she presently would not remove her icons "because it would be a pity to throw them away" (l. 4).

Others treated the interview chiefly as an opportunity to articulate economic grievances. Another unnamed clerk from the Petrovka department store dismissed any question about religion by turning the discussion to economic hardship, exhaustion from her labor, and duties at home, which she enumerated in detail. Perhaps sensitive to party litany, the woman attributed the ownership of an icon in her apartment to her mother but stressed that her twelve-year-old son was a Pioneer. These, however, were asides in her overarching expressions of dissatisfaction about work and housing (l. 9). Similarly, textile worker Kudinova spoke far more extensively about her personal life than her decision to join a godless cell in 1929, and neither religion nor atheism figured centrally in her questionnaire. The same could be said of her coworker R. K.

Zenina (ll. 13–14). This group, in short, treated the experience as a catharsis. The weight they gave to material circumstances, in marked contrast to their slim replies on religion, suggests an important difference between their agendas and those of the interviewers.

Additional respondents tacitly redefined the categories of church-state conflict by trivializing religion and atheism simply as products of different periods. A third unnamed clerk at the Moscow Petrovka department store had received a religious upbringing in the village "in the old tradition," and even the two-and-one-half-year sentence an older brother had served in a tsarist prison for revolutionary activities as a seminary student did not directly shape her present attitude toward religion. Rather, the demands that work at home made on her free time explained why she was "passive" toward it, kept no icons, and furnished it no monetary support. She brought up her four children "in the contemporary spirit," though, and all entered the Komsomol, the Red Army, or the factory school (l. 6). Similarly, the formerly devout Vasilii Arkhipov volunteered, "I am bringing up the baby according to the new *byt*." His explanation for breaking ties to his religious upbringing rested on allusions to the long hours of an apprenticeship he undertook at the age of twelve and the demands of life thereafter (l. 7). Another Moscow textile worker claimed to have had a detached attitude toward religion at all stages of her life. She was never religious in childhood, yet her family walked four versts to church because "at that time religion existed for everyone." Neither of her two marriages took place in church, however, and her words suggested that her break with religion did not involve inner turmoil: "If you're alive, then you can live without a priest. And if you're not alive, the priest and the church can't help" (ll. 19–21). Chief electrical mechanic I. A. Poliakov attributed his former religious belief to a "time [when] the Law of God was widely taught in school," even though his own God-fearing parents did not attend church for want of proper clothing and prayed at home instead. The two icons in his present home were, he said, a concession to his wife (l. 33). Finally, a construction worker whose parents believed in God explained that he kept no icon in Moscow only "because I live in a dormitory" (l. 26). Such matter-of-fact answers did not fit the causal relationships and introspection on decisions regarding religion that the questions presumed.[121]

Others fashioned their own approaches, including telling the apparent unvarnished truth. Said one worker: "I believe in religion for the present, go to church rarely, but I do go. There are no icons in my husband's room, but in mine there is" (l. 27). A fellow textile factory worker neither kept icons nor attended church yet did not feel inhibited to express her belief in God (l. 32). In a unique twist, an unnamed non-party worker confessed to devout religious belief before the revolution and having come under the influence of Tolstoy at the age of twenty; he explained his present atheism in tones of religious fervor (l. 64). The worker Praskov'ia Plekhanova expressed a belief in God despite not praying or attending church for lack of time, and she closed with comradely greetings (l. 76). In the end, such a sample does not enable us to draw precise conclusions about what Russians of this period considered, to use Geertz's terms, intellectually reasonable and emotionally convincing. But although we cannot say with certainty what respondents *thought,* their answers do indicate what they *thought about.* And the evidence strongly suggests that their priorities transcended the chief preoccupations of both state and church as the majority attempted to fashion a personal accommodation with pressing realities.

THE BEGINNING OF HISTORY

Citizens used combinations of resistance, circumvention, and accommodation throughout early Soviet society. As economic hardship and social transformation converged, individuals and groups practiced at least one such strategy, and any current position could subsequently be renegotiated. Such experiences during the formative years of the revolution left an indelible imprint. They placed a premium on consensus above competence; rewarded acquiescence more than initiative; and fostered rationalization in place of responsibility. The choice between religion and atheism therefore did not result in a clear victory for either side in the conflict. Rather, this conflict stood at the center of—and served a didactic function in—inculcating the behavior of the "new Soviet man." In the end, the relationship between ideals and observed experience gave rise not to a population intensely religious or materialist, but to a predominant ethos of misdirection and dogged self-preservation.

Epilogue

"Not one of those boys is alive today. Some were killed in the war, some died from sickness, some disappeared without a trace, while others, though still alive, have turned into different people; and if by magic those different people were to meet their past selves they would no longer know what to say to them. I fear, in fact, they would not even guess they were meeting themselves."
—Iurii Trifonov, *The House on the Embankment*[1]

When the Bolsheviks attempted to create the world's first assertively atheistic society, neither state nor church achieved its full objectives. The acrimonious conflict between competing versions of singular truth produced no definitive victor; all combatants compromised themselves in the process. The highest impulses of revolutionary Bolshevism aspired to a prosperous society firmly grounded in egalitarian values and a materialist worldview, but the nature of the tactics employed at the lowest reaches of the movement motivated citizens to create avenues through and around Soviet policy. The reliance of the party on bifurcated social categories rooted in crude caricatures of Marxist ideology directly undermined its ability to gauge the full dimensions of the task ahead and to communicate its message broadly. Russian Orthodoxy similarly violated its basic precepts. It vacated the moral high ground when its advocates resorted to violence, and the laity exploited the faith when they broadened religious understandings to encompass the defense of what was familiar, convenient, and rooted in self-interest. Soviet society would long feel the ramifications of these early battles.

The competition between religious and antireligious views entered a new phase in 1932. Rather than resolving the religious issue and other contentious points definitively, the Cultural Revolution ended with a sharp turn away from bombast and toward pragmatism. This affected spheres such as economic planning, social welfare, aesthetics, and education, and it eliminated campaigns that could be destabilizing in favor of a return to traditional standards and mores. The antireligious movement accordingly suffered. Cells of the League of Militant Godless disappeared as rapidly as they had materialized, and the five million members at the height of the Cultural Revolution soon contracted to a few hundred thousand. In spite of the passage of an ambitious so-called godless second five-year plan by the league, rural representatives continued to give negative assessments of effectiveness. The antireligious movement also found it difficult to reinvigorate urban activism, which it had neglected during collectivization, and even Moscow and Leningrad lagged. The pivotal newspaper *Bezbozhnik* suffered a decline in circulation beginning in 1932 and closed permanently in 1935; many other antireligious publications experienced the same fate. Criticisms of lack of organization, faulty agitation among women, institutional conflict, and general impotence similar to those voiced during the 1920s continued to be heard. The anticipated third national congress of the league never met. Outside the league, the party leadership continued to fail to project a unified antireligious policy at any given moment, and even its general orientations repeatedly shifted. Following the lull after the Cultural Revolution, activists changed course again and stepped up antireligious repression in 1937 as Stalinism became more repressive, but even this proved ephemeral. With the German invasion in June 1941, state and church began to cooperate; the public activities of the League of Militant Godless ended.[2]

After the Cultural Revolution, however, Russian Orthodoxy could not simply return to the pre-1928 status quo.[3] No fewer than half the churches still in operation at the beginning of collectivization had been closed, including as many as 80 percent of the village churches. Whereas the census of 1926 had counted seventy-nine thousand clergy in the country, the 1937 census recorded thirty-one thousand. Orthodox believers had difficulty finding priests to perform weddings, baptisms, funerals, and ordinary observances, and they often lacked places to hold them. Sectarian groups continued to gain ground, sometimes with the participation of former Orthodox priests who had lost their churches. The total number of members of Christian denominations fell only slightly between the late 1920s and 1937, which meant Orthodoxy had absorbed a disproportionate part of the blow against religion. In response, the laity practiced self-ordination and conducted services, often from a private home; but without proper clergy, reports of a further drop in observances were common in the 1930s. The young in particular were not initiated into the patterns of regular worship. Moreover, with the reinstitution of repression in the late 1930s came renewed harassment of believers. The 1939 census dropped its question on religious belief.[4] In the long term, vicissitudes of church-state relations continued throughout the Khrushchev and Brezhnev periods.[5] And in post-Soviet Russia, the Orthodox Church came to be the only national institution to enjoy wide public trust, yet it also endured embarrassing revelations regarding its cooperation with the state during the late Soviet period.

In the end, the formative revolutionary experience of 1917–1932 involved above all a fundamental clash of cultures. The party leadership, who understood culture as an attained level of consciousness, approached social change as an exercise in mass enlightenment. Philosophical materialism was to replace the prevailing, misguided worldview through instruction. Equally important, the regime would create symbols, customs, and traditions that would inspire loyalty because of their demonstrated utility. These party creations therefore did not reflect long-standing custom or prevailing shared values but rather embodied the ideals Bolshevism wished to inculcate and promoted new behavioral models. As the party thus fought to establish the legitimacy of its revolutionary endeavors, its propaganda identified those who agreed as conscious, a level those who disagreed had not reached.

But the party misunderstood and underestimated the strength of the beliefs that explained personal and collective experience for the masses. Bolshevism had not devoted significant attention to the techniques of promoting atheism prior to 1917; and when it acted on its largely untested presuppositions thereafter, it failed to take into account the sensibilities of its intended audience. What the party dismissed as superstition was actually deeply embedded in mass consciousness: aggregations of divine, magical, and pagan precepts that many in society employed to fathom and control the present and future. Regardless of the dismissive attitudes found in Bolshevik pronouncements, therefore, these variegated belief systems demystified nature and the human environment, provided plausible explanations of observed reality and the unknown, and lay at the foundation of social and family structures. Recourse to religion made possible salvation after death, and it provided access to benign supernatural intervention in earthly events.

In sum, what took place between October 1917 and the end of the Cultural Revolution did not convince the majority of Russians completely to change their basic convictions, but it did foster important changes. Russian Orthodoxy survived even though, as prior to the revolution, its resilience did not derive from any unfailing ability to govern personal, collective, or institutional behavior. Rather, as the predominant means for the expression of spirituality in society, it exercised influence because it still extensively shaped the environment in which such behaviors took place. And though Orthodoxy could not impose universal submission to a specific code of morals or even adherence to a unified doctrine, it nevertheless informed the collective values and rituals from which none in society were free. Indeed, the fact that many Russians across the social spectrum had based their spiritual allegiances before the revolution on symbols rather than texts and had even equated religious symbols with the faith itself only exacerbated every attempt to remove the traditional in favor of the new. And while members of society contended the specifics of the antireligious effort, their proclivity also to express social and political objectives inimical to the regime through conflicts over faith complicated efforts on all fronts. The chief antireligious issue therefore transcended the replacement of the church as an institution, even though that was no small undertaking. Soviet power faced a task more daunting than the replacement of one set of regularized observances by another. Success depended on the public acceptance of Soviet values as a belief system capable of providing the same range of functions and benefits as those grounded in the supernatural.

Yet, although the early years of Soviet power did not witness the widespread and unalloyed acceptance of party ideals, they significantly altered the way society approached belief itself. The failure to achieve maximum programs notwithstanding, the general tenets and policies of Bolshevism undeniably gained significant support in Soviet Russia after 1917, and the Bolsheviks enjoyed the manifold advantages that accrue to any party in power. This enabled the basic message of the party at least to reach the majority in society by 1932, despite the internal and external criticisms of the character of antireligious work. Continuous communication of the message alone, of course, did not transform the rhythms of daily life for those not receptive, but it did effectively create a new, competing ideal of behavior that all now had to take into account. Even though this alternative model predominantly rested on bifurcated understandings of social reality that were at odds with observed experience, it enabled Soviet power repeatedly to counterpose its vision of socialist egalitarianism to the complementarity of social roles on which the old order had relied. Encouraging individuals to throw off religion in this way—and observance did in fact decline after 1917—did not lead reflexively to the enthusiastic adoption of Soviet values. It did, however, create circumstances in which individuals and groups not only had the opportunity to reevaluate their relationship to the sacred, but indeed could not escape doing so. In this environment, Soviet power and Russian Orthodoxy both claimed possession of the ethical and philosophical truth that would underlie the better future for Russia. After 1917, Russians thus faced no fewer alternative belief systems than before. The range of possibilities changed, though, and the influence of the nonspiritual increased.

Glossary

Agitprop: Agitation and Propaganda Department of the Communist Party formed in 1920.

Antireligious Commission: See *Commission on Antireligious Propaganda.*

arshin: A unit of linear measure equal to approximately twenty-eight inches.

artel': A collective of laborers, initially of peasants performing seasonal labor away from the village, who contracted for wages collectively, divided assignments, and frequently lived together for the duration of their work. The Soviet government co-opted the form in various industrial campaigns.

bedniak: The lowest economic stratum of the peasantry—in Bolshevik thinking, the stratum with the most to gain from revolutionary upheaval and, by extension, from supporting the party, although experience frequently did not bear out this assumption.

bezbozhnik (pl. *bezbozhniki*): Literally "one without God" or, more idiomatically, "godless." This is the most common term used in Russian to refer to atheists; it is employed far more frequently than *ateist* [atheist].

Black Hundreds: Bands of ruffians who during the tsarist period were best known for their participation in anti-Semitic pogroms and the repression of labor disturbances. After 1917, the term became a shorthand to identify any group willing to use force against Soviet power.

bourgeois specialists: Managers, engineers, and others with technical expertise who had held positions of responsibility under tsarism and were necessary to the functioning of the economy after the revolution. The preference in rations, wages, and housing that the Soviet state showed them caused deep resentment in society.

Central Committee: The governing organ of the Soviet Communist Party that, in theory, was elected by lower party organs and in turn elected the members of the ruling Politburo.

chastushka: A topical, single- or multiple-verse song consisting of series of couplets. Peasants originated these popular rhymes, which later entered urban mass culture, to express love, humor, and social criticism.

Cheka: Acronym for the Chrezvychainaia Kommissiia [Extraordinary Commission], the Soviet political security police established on 7 December 1917 and later superseded by the GPU (State Political Administration) [Gosudarstvennoe Politicheskoe Upravlenie] on 8 February 1922, the OGPU (Unified State Political Administration) [Obedinennoe Gosudarstvennoe Politicheskoe Upravlenie] on 15 November 1923, and the NKVD (People's Commissariat of Internal Affairs) [Narodnyi Komissariat Vnytrennykh Del] in 1934.

Commission on Antireligious Propaganda: Created by the Politburo in October 1922 under Agitprop to establish links with other institutions involved in antireligious work, it was also known as the Commission for the Implementation of the Separation of Church and State under the Central Committee of the Russian Communist Party (Bolsheviks) or simply as the Antireligious Commission. It was dissolved in 1928.

Denikin, Anton: White general during the Russian civil war.

desiatina: A measure of land equal to approximately two and one-half acres.

feldsher: A category of paramedical professionals dating from the prerevolutionary period who worked either in conjunction with or, frequently, in place of doctors.

Glavpolitprosvet: The Narkompros Central Administration of Political Education, created in 1920 to oversee the conduct of all national propaganda.

GPU: See *Cheka.*

guberniia: Main administrative units of early Soviet Russia were the *krai* (at this time, more than one province), the *guberniia* [province], and the *oblast'* (a large subdivision of a province or an administrative unit consisting of parts of more than one province). Provinces were further subdivided, in descending order, into units named *okrug, raion* (which could also be a region within a city), *uezd'* [district], and *volost'* (which could be either a village or a section of an urban settlement).

gul'iane: A traditional courtship promenade.

intelligent (pl., *intelligenty*): A member of the intelligentsia, that is, in prerevolutionary Russia a self-defined group of critically thinking people who addressed questions of general social existence and change. The term was first used in the first quarter of the nineteenth century.

Kolchak, Alexander: A former tsarist admiral who headed anti-Bolshevik forces in Siberia during the Russian civil war.

kolkhoz (pl., *kolkhozy*): A collective farm.

Komsomol: Communist Youth League.

Kronstadt: A northern naval base and the site of a symbolically important anti-Bolshevik uprising in March 1921.

krai: See *guberniia.*

kulak: The most prosperous peasants, who were reviled as bourgeois by the Bolsheviks and persecuted during the collectivization of agriculture.

lishentsy: Literally "deprived ones," that is, those without rights of citizenship in the 1920s because of their class, economic, professional, legal, or prerevolutionary status or because of acts of opposition to the Soviet state.

Metropolitan: Clerical rank below Patriarch but above archbishop and bishop in the Russian Orthodox Church.

Narkompros: People's Commissariat of Enlightenment.

Narkomiust: People's Commissariat of Justice.

nekul'turnost': The lack of "culture," that is, a pejorative to characterize those who lacked the consciousness and cultivated behavior that derive from education and enlightenment.

NEP: The New Economic Policy adopted at the Tenth Party Congress in March 1921.

NKVD: See *Cheka.*

oblast': See *guberniia.*

OGPU: See *Cheka.*

okrug: See *guberniia.*

Patriarch: Head of the Russian Orthodox Church.

Politburo: Political Bureau of the Central Committee of the Communist Party, created in 1919; the de facto ruling body.

pood (or *pud*): A unit of weight equal to slightly more than thirty-six pounds.

Populism: A revolutionary movement based on peasant socialism that took root in Russia during the second half of the nineteenth century.

prestol'nyi holiday: A patron's or church's name day; the day of the saint or event for which the church was consecrated.

Primary Chronicle: Annual record of important events kept during the Kievan period.

raion: See *guberniia.*

Reds: Bolsheviks and pro-Bolshevik elements during the Russian civil war of 1918–1921.

Rus':   Slavic tribes residing in the basin of the Dnieper River prior to the arrival of the Varangians; also the collective term to describe Russia in the Kievan, Appanage, and Muscovite periods.

Russkaia Pravda: Compiled in the eleventh century, this was Russia's first written law code.

seredniak: The middle, and consequently the largest, economic stratum of the peasantry. In Bolshevik thinking, the stratum the party had to win over from the influence of the kulaks if the revolution were to succeed.

Slavophile: Group within the intelligentsia that believed that Russia's successful future development depended on recapturing the collectivist spirit of its peasant past.

Socialist-Revolutionary Party: A party that advocated peasant socialism. The party's left wing (the so-called Left SRs) shared power in a ruling coalition with the Bolsheviks until March 1918.

soviet: The Russian word for "council," these grassroots institutions came into existence during the revolution of 1905 and played a major role in the events of 1917.

Sovnarkom: The Council of People's Commissars, which was formally the ruling political body of the early Soviet state.

uezd: See *guberniia.*

verst: A unit of measure equivalent to approximately two-thirds of a mile.

volost' (pl. *volosti*): See *guberniia.*

VTsIK (Central Executive Committee of the All-Russian Congress of Soviets): The operative center representing the hierarchy of soviets that oversaw day-to-day governance and administration.

Westernizer: A group within the intelligentsia who felt that Russia should reform itself along Western lines.

Whites: A generic term for the array of anti-Bolshevik forces during the Russian civil war.

Zhenotdel: The Women's Section of the Communist Party, disbanded in 1929.

Notes

INTRODUCTION

1. An overview of this literature can be found in Lewis H. Siegelbaum, *Soviet State and Society between Revolutions, 1918–1929* (Cambridge: Cambridge University Press, 1992).

2. Informed largely by the concerns of the Cold War and religious partisanship, existing historiography utilizes above all a state-versus-church framework of analysis and victimization as the principal basis of interpretation. Many of these studies have been carefully and even impressively researched, but they overwhelmingly present the promotion of atheism only as an ideological mandate or a prerequisite to establishing totalitarianism, or both, and thus they significantly underestimate its social dynamics. See John Curtiss, *The Russian Church and the Soviet State, 1917–1950* (Boston: Little, Brown, 1953); George Kline, *Religious and Anti-Religious Thought in Russia* (Chicago: University of Chicago Press, 1968); David E. Powell, *Antireligious Propaganda in the Soviet Union: A Study of Mass Persuasion* (Cambridge, Mass.: MIT Press, 1975); Matthew Spinka, *The Church in Soviet Russia* (New York: Oxford University Press, 1956); James Thrower, *Marxist-Leninist "Scientific Atheism" and the Study of Religion and Atheism in the USSR* (Berlin: Mouton, 1983); Dmitry V. Pospielovsky, *A History of Marxist-Leninist Atheism and Soviet Anti-Religious Policies,* 3 vols. (New York: St. Martin's Press, 1987–1988); Pedro Ramet, *Cross and Commissar: The Politics of Religion in Eastern Europe and the USSR* (Bloomington: Indiana University Press, 1987); John Anderson, *Religion, State and Politics in the Soviet Union and Successor States* (Cambridge: Cambridge University Press, 1994); Nathaniel Davis, *A Long Walk to Church: A Contemporary History of Russian Orthodoxy* (Boulder: Westview Press, 1995); Michael Bourdeaux, ed., *The Politics of Religion in Russia and the New States of Eurasia* (New York: M. E. Sharpe, 1995). Two important recent studies begin to transcend the view of church-state relations chiefly as a study of victimization: Glennys Young, *Power and the Sacred in Revolutionary Russia: Religious Activists in the Village* (University Park: Pennsylvania State University Press, 1997); and Daniel Peris, *Storming the Heavens: The Soviet League of the Militant Godless* (Ithaca, N.Y.: Cornell University Press, 1998). In contrast to the present work, Young concentrates above all on village semiotics as manifested in the use of village politics for the protection of religion. Peris casts his study more widely but filters his findings through the actions of the League of Militant Godless. I thank Daniel Peris for

making his manuscript available to me while it was in press.

3. This work employs the term *propaganda* in its British usage, that is, as the systematic propagation of a particular doctrine or practice. This reflects the Russian sense of the term, and it frees the word from a common American colloquial association of propaganda with falsehood.

4. On this point see R. E. F. Smith and David Christian, *Bread and Salt: A Social and Economic History of Food and Drink in Russia* (Cambridge: Cambridge University Press, 1984), passim.

5. See William B. Husband, "Soviet Atheism and Russian Orthodox Strategies of Resistance, 1917–1932," *Journal of Modern History* 70 (March 1998): 74–107, and the works cited therein.

6. This work will not distinguish between the Russian words *ateist* [atheist] and *bezbozhnik* [godless one]. This follows common practice in public communications in Russia during 1917–1932, even though *bezbozhnik* was far more commonly used. It also conforms to the definitions offered by S. I. Ozhegov, who uses the same expression "the denial of the existence of God" [*otritsanie sushchestvovaliia boga*] for both terms in his authoritative dictionary. S. I. Ozhegov, *Slovar' russkogo iazyka, izdanie sedmoe* (Moscow: Sovetskaia entsiklopediia, 1968), 29, 37.

7. Abbreviations herein follow standard Russian archival notations: opis' [inventory number of archive file] (op.), fond [archival collection] (f.), delo [archival file] (d.), dela (dd.), list [document page] (l.), listy (ll.), oborot [reverse side of page] (ob.).

1: BELIEF AND NONBELIEF IN PREREVOLUTIONARY RUSSIA

1. The quotation from Tolstoy is condensed without ellipses. The Hearne quotation is taken from Graham Midgley, *University Life in Eighteenth-Century Oxford* (New Haven, Conn.: Yale University Press, 1996), 2.

2. For commentary on the problems inherent in defining atheism in Europe precisely, see Michael Hunter and David Wootten, eds., *Atheism from the Reformation to the Enlightenment* (Oxford: Clarendon Press, 1992), 2–5, 17, 24, 25, 58, 70, 73, 131, 134, 222, 250, 287; David Wootten, "Lucien Febvre and the Problem of Unbelief in the Early Modern Period," *Journal of Modern History* 60 (1988): 703–7.

3. Lucien Febvre, *The Problem of Unbelief in the Sixteenth Century: The Religion of Rabelais* (1942; trans. Beatrice Gottlieb, Cambridge, Mass.: Harvard University Press, 1982), 131–32, 135–40. See also Paul Oskar Kristeller, "The Myth of Renaissance Atheism and the French Tradition of Free Thought," *Journal of the History of Philosophy* 6 (1968): 233–43.

4. A review article appears in Wootten, "Lucien Febvre," 695–730; David Wootten, "New Histories of Atheism," in Hunter and Wootten, *Atheism,* 13–53.

5. James Turner, *Without God, without Creed: The Origins of Unbelief in America* (Baltimore: Johns Hopkins University Press, 1985), 2–3.

6. Ibid., 9.

7. Emmanuel Le Roy Ladurie, *Montaillou: The Promised Land of Error* (1975; trans. Barbara Bray, New York: George Braziller, 1978), 33, 153–59, 169–71, 305, 308, 314, 342. On the discrepancy between church strictures against sexual permissiveness and public mores, see Jeffrey Richards, *Sex, Dissidence and Damnation: Minority Groups in the Middle Ages* (London: Routledge, 1991), 22–41; Gillian Clark, *Women in Late Antiquity: Pagan and Christian Lifestyles* (Oxford: Clarendon Press, 1993), 38–41.

8. Natalie Zemon Davis, "Some Tasks and Themes in the Study of Popular Religion," in Charles Trinkaus and Heiko A. Oberman, eds. *The Pursuit of Holiness in Late Medieval and Renaissance Religion* (Leiden: E. J. Brill, 1974), 308, and the works cited in 308 nn. 1, 2.

9. Turner, *Without God, without Creed,* 2.

10. On a different but related syncretism in the Scientific Revolution, see Keith Hutchison, "What Happened to Occult Qualities in the Scientific Revolution?" *Isis* 73 (1982): 233–53; Ron Millen, "The Manifestation of Occult Qualities in the Scientific Revolution," in Margaret J. Osler and Paul Lawrence Farber, eds., *Religion, Science, and Worldview: Essays in Honor of Richard S. Westfall* (Cambridge: Cambridge University Press, 1985), 185–216.

11. On reactions to plague, for example, see William H. McNeill, *Plagues and Peoples* (New York: Doubleday, 1977), 163–64.

12. Keith Thomas, *Religion and the Decline of Magic* (New York: Scribner's, 1971), 3–21, 25–27, 48–49, 210, 243, and passim.

13. Davis, "Study of Popular Religion," 308–12.

14. This definition of culture follows Clifford Geertz, *The Interpretation of Cultures* (New York: Basic Books, 1973); William J. Bouwsma, *A Usable Past: Essays in European Cultural History* (Berkeley: University of California Press, 1990); E. P. Thompson, *Customs in Common* (New York: New Press, 1993); Robert Darnton, *The Great Cat Massacre and Other Episodes of French Cultural History* (New York: Basic Books, 1984); Robert Darnton, *The Kiss of Lamourette: Reflections in Cultural History* (New York: W. W. Norton, 1990); Peter Burke, *Popular Culture in Early Modern Europe* (1978; rev. ed., Brookfield, Vt.: Scolar, 1994), xiv–xxvii. In Geertz's own words: "The culture concept to which I adhere has neither multiple referents nor, as far as I can see, any unusual ambiguity: it denotes an historically transmitted pattern of meanings embodied in symbols, a system of inherited conceptions expressed in symbolic forms by means of which men communicate, perpetuate, and develop their knowledge about and attitudes toward life." Clifford Geertz, "Religion as a Cultural System," in Michael Banton, ed., *Anthropological Approaches to the Study of Religion* (London: Tavistock Publications, 1965), 3.

15. On Anasazi beliefs, see Paul Horgan, *Great River: The Rio Grande in North American History* (Hanover, N.H.: Wesleyan University Press, 1984), 23–33.

16. Thompson, *Customs in Common,* 1; Eric Hobsbawm, "Inventing Traditions" and "Mass-Producing Traditions: Europe, 1870–1914," in Eric

Hobsbawm and Terence Ranger, eds., *The Invention of Tradition* (Cambridge: Cambridge University Press, 1983), 1–13, 263–67, 303–7; Thomas, *The Decline of Magic*, 422–29. The possibility of firsthand corroboration is by no means a universal condition of belief, and followers have been known to cling to what they accept on faith no less intensely than to that which they can confirm. Furthermore, satisfying the criteria for verification in the present is not a reliable predictor of what humans will regard as accurate in the future. The essays of Stephen Jay Gould offer multiple demonstrations of this, including "On Heroes and Fools in Science," in Stephen Jay Gould, *Ever since Darwin: Reflections in Natural History* (New York: W. W. Norton, 1977), 201–6. A broader treatment is Thomas S. Kuhn, *The Structure of Scientific Revolutions,* 2d ed. (Chicago: University of Chicago Press, 1970).

17. Thomas, *The Decline of Magic*, 25–34, 61–68.

18. Judith C. Brown, *Immodest Acts: The Life of a Lesbian Nun in Renaissance Italy* (New York: Oxford University Press, 1986), passim, but see esp. 105 for an account of the motivations of the representatives of the papal nuncio.

19. The relationship between the introduction of new collective social rituals and the ascent of Protestant piety is discussed in François Lebrun, "The Two Reformations: Communal Devotion and Personal Piety," in Roger Chartier, ed., *A History of Private Life: Passions of the Renaissance,* trans. Arthur Goldhammer (Cambridge, Mass.: Belknap Press, 1989), 101–9. For an example from a traditionally Catholic area, see Leroy Ladurie, *Montaillou,* 169.

20. As anyone who has celebrated Mardi Gras, dressed for Halloween, decorated a Christmas tree, or witnessed the fashionable resurgence of celebrations of the Day of the Dead in Latino communities can attest, these phenomena continue, even if in secularized, recreational, and commercialized forms.

21. Max Weber, *The Protestant Ethic and the Spirit of Capitalism* (1930; trans. Talcott Parsons, London: Routledge, 1995), 27, 40, 51, 55, 75, 89–90. There are many who disagree with this interpretation of Weber versus Marx. Talcott Parsons, in his introduction to a translation of Weber's *Sociology of Religion,* takes issue with the idea of *The Protestant Ethic* "as a counterattack against the Marxist assertion of the predominance of 'material' interests." In Parsons's view, "Only gradually has it become more generally understood that in Weber's broad plan of work [*The Protestant Ethic*] was intended as no more than an *essay* in historical-sociological interpretation." Max Weber, *The Sociology of Religion* (1922; trans. Ephraim Fischoff, Boston: Beacon Press, 1963), xx, italics in the original. A more recent argument that echoes neither Parsons's argument nor the one offered by this study, and is less sympathetic to Weber than Parsons, can be found in Jane Schneider, "Spirits and the Spirit of Capitalism," in Ellen Badone, ed., *Religious Orthodoxy and Popular Faith in European Society* (Princeton, N.J.: Princeton University Press, 1990), 25–27, 52–53. Such debates lie outside the scope of the present work, for which the short-term public perceptions of Weber's ideas, rather than long-term understandings, are most critical.

22. Marx and Engels articulated their position on religion in a manner more declarative than systematic. Characteristically, they stated in *The Commu-*

nist Manifesto that the bourgeoisie "drowned the most heavenly ecstacies of religious fervor" and incorporated religious institutions into a centralized power structure to manage "the common affairs of the whole bourgeoisie." Karl Marx and Friedrich Engels, *The Communist Manifesto* (New York: Penguin Books, 1967), 82. Their failure to elaborate fully on this issue left them vulnerable to the kind of crude popularization represented by the positions Weber attacked. Ultimately, the simplified interpretation that religion was nothing more than an instrument of oppression in the service of the bourgeoisie became the public face of the Bolshevik atheism. Philosophical discussions of materialism and related issues made their way into early Soviet scholarly discourse, but not into propaganda or public forums. By the 1970s, assorted snippets from *Capital, The Critique of the Gotha Program,* "The Communism of *Rheinischer Beobachter,*" and a handful of other works of Marx and Engels were considered sufficiently "classic," in the words of the editors, to introduce a Soviet collection of documents on religion and the church. *O religii i tserkvi: Sbornik vyskazyvanii klassikov Marksizma-Leninizma, dokumentov KPSS i Sovetskogo gosudarstva* (Moscow: Politizdat, 1981), 7–20.

23. In this regard, the Reformation worked in combination with other elements, especially the rise of the state and the spread of literacy. See Roger Chartier, "Figures of Modernity: Introduction," in Chartier, *History of Private Life,* 15–19 and passim.

24. Fernand Braudel, *A History of Civilizations,* trans. Richard Mayne (New York: Penguin, 1987), 351–56. The quotation is on 354.

25. Carlo Ginzburg, *The Cheese and the Worms: The Cosmos of a Sixteenth-Century Miller,* trans. John and Anne Tedeschi (Baltimore: Johns Hopkins University Press, 1980).

26. Ibid., xxiv; Wootten, "New Histories of Atheism," in Hunter and Wootten, *Atheism,* 13–14; Michael Hunter, "'Aikenhead the Atheist': The Context and Consequences of Articulate Irreligion in the Late Seventeenth Century," in Hunter and Wootten, *Atheism,* 221–54. The quotations are on 225.

27. On this point see Burke, "Religion and Secularisation," in Peter Burke, ed., *The New Cambridge Modern History* (Cambridge: Cambridge University Press, 1979), 13: 299–302.

28. Thomas, *The Decline of Magic,* 166–67, 476. David Wootten argues that Febvre's inclination to see the word *atheism* used with abandon overlooks the history of the word and its use by contemporaries. I am not persuaded that Febvre's understanding is as seriously flawed as Wootten argues. In particular, Wootten needs stronger evidence for his assertion that "it was generally agreed in the sixteenth and early seventeenth centuries that an atheist was *either* someone who did not believe in the existence of God *or* someone who held beliefs which made God's existence irrelevant." Wootten, "New Histories of Atheism," in Hunter and Wootten, *Atheism,* 24–28. The quotation is on 24–25; the italics are in the original.

29. Turner, *Without God, without Creed,* 171; Bernard Lightman, *The Origins of Agnosticism: Victorian Unbelief and the Limits of Knowledge*

(Baltimore: Johns Hopkins University Press, 1987), 6–18.

30. In the spirit of the time, Gui Patin described seventeenth-century Italy as the home of "pox, poisoning, and atheism." Quoted in Nicholas Davidson, "Atheism in Italy, 1500–1700," in Hunter and Wootten, *Atheism,* 56.

31. Even those whose thoroughness in the archives brought to light the cases of Menocchio, Valée, and Aikenhead have come away uncertain of how much more historical evidence has not survived. Ginzburg, *The Cheese and the Worms,* xiii–xiv, 128; Wootten, "New Histories of Atheism," in Hunter and Wootten, *Atheism,* 28–31.

32. Discussions can be found in the articles in Hunter and Wootten, *Atheism;* and in Turner, *Without God, without Creed,* esp. 14–22, 42–64.

33. Although a full discussion obviously lies beyond the scope of this study, important representative contributions—in addition to the works cited in the notes above—include David S. Landes, *The Unbound Prometheus: Technological Change and Industrial Development in Western Europe from 1750 to the Present* (Cambridge: Cambridge University Press, 1969), 1–40, esp. 22–26, 30–31; Peter Gay, *The Rise of Modern Paganism,* vol. 1 of *The Enlightenment: An Interpretation* (New York: Knopf, 1966); E. J. Hobsbawm, *The Age of Capital, 1848–1875* (New York: New American Library, 1875), 277–306; Donald Worster, *Nature's Economy: A History of Ecology Ideas* (Cambridge: Cambridge University Press, 1977), 26–55; Lynn White, Jr., *Medieval Religion and Technology* (Berkeley: University of California Press, 1978); Joel Mokyr, *The Lever of Riches: Technological Creativity and Economic Progress* (New York: Oxford University Press, 1990), 170–76, 200–205; Mark Smith, *Religion in Industrial Society: Oldham and Saddleworth, 1740–1865* (Oxford: Clarendon Press, 1994); R. H. Tawney, *Religion and the Rise of Capitalism* (1926; reprint, New York: Penguin, 1990).

34. Mona Ozouf, *Festivals and the French Revolution,* trans. Alan Sheridan (Cambridge, Mass.: Harvard University Press, 1988), 110–18, 262–71. See also Robert M. Isherwood, *Farce and Fantasy: Popular Entertainment in Eighteenth-Century Paris* (New York: Oxford University Press, 1986), 153.

35. Samuel H. Cross, "The Russian Primary Chronicle," *Harvard Studies and Notes in Philology and Literature* 12 (1930): 199, 205, reprinted in Daniel H. Kaiser and Gary Marker, eds., *Reinterpreting Russian History: Readings, 860–1860s* (New York: Oxford University Press, 1994), 66–67.

36. Dorothy Atkinson, "Society and the Sexes in the Russian Past," in Dorothy Atkinson, Alexander Dallin, and Gail Warshofsky Lapidus, eds., *Women in Russia* (Stanford, Calif.: Stanford University Press, 1977), 4–5.

37. A detailed overview is Henrik Birnbaum, "Christianity before Christianization: Christians and Christian Activity in Pre-988 Rus'," in Boris Gasparov and Olga Raevsky-Hughes, eds., *Slavic Cultures in the Middle Ages,* vol. 1 of *Christianity and the Eastern Slavs* (Berkeley: University of California Press, 1993), 42–62.

38. For additional detail, see Janet Martin, *Medieval Russia, 980–1584* (Cambridge: Cambridge University Press, 1995), 9–10, 73–76; N. L.

Pushkareva, "Women in the Medieval Russian Family of the Tenth through Fifteenth Centuries," in Barbara Evans Clements, Barbara Alpern Engel, and Christine D. Worobec, eds., *Russia's Women: Accommodation, Resistance, Transformation* (Berkeley: University of California Press, 1991), 30–33, 37.

39. Kaiser and Marker, *Reinterpreting Russian History,* 27–29, 50–54. On the persistence of the consumption of beaver, horsemeat, and other prohibited items in the sixteenth and seventeenth centuries, see Smith and Christian, *Bread and Salt,* 12–13.

40. For an account that stresses the link between the rise of the church, the ruralization of monasticism, and the enserfment of the Russian peasantry, see I. I. Skvortsov-Stepanov, "Iz istorii russkoi pravoslavnoi tserkvi: Pravoslavnaia tserkov' v epokhu tataro-mongol'skogo vladychestva," in *Ezhegodnik muzeia istorii religii i ateizma* (Moscow-Leningrad: Izdatel'stvo akademii nauk SSSR, 1960), 5: 263–85. A different emphasis appears in Richard Hellie, *Enserfment and Military Change in Muscovy* (Chicago: University of Chicago Press, 1971).

41. The influence of religiosity on forms of expression in this period is explored more fully in William C. Brumfield and Milos M. Velimirovic, eds., *Christianity and the Arts in Russia* (Cambridge: Cambridge University Press, 1992), 3–51.

42. On "Moscow, the Third Rome," see Nancy Shields Kollmann, "Muscovite Russia, 1450–1598," in Gregory L. Freeze, ed., *Russia: A History* (Oxford: Oxford University Press, 1997), 51.

43. Atkinson, "Society and the Sexes," in Atkinson, Dallin, and Lapidus, *Women in Russia,* 13 n. 38.

44. *The Domostroi: Rules for Russian Households in the Time of Ivan the Terrible,* ed. and trans. Carolyn Johnston Pouncy (Ithaca, N.Y.: Cornell University Press, 1994), 69, 71, 85–89, 95–98, 102–7, 124–28, 131–32, 136, 139–43, 145, 147, 151–58, 162, 171, 204, and passim. Students of the *Domostroi,* whose title literally means "house order," disagree on its authorship, particularly the extent of the contribution of Sylvester, priest of the Annunciation Cathedral and advisor to Tsar Ivan IV. See the editor's introduction (37–44). For a different view, see the review by David M. Goldfrank in *Slavic Review* 55 (1996): 478–79.

45. Arthur Voyce, *Moscow and the Roots of Russian Culture* (Norman: University of Oklahoma Press, 1964), 61–94; Smith and Christian, *Bread and Salt,* 10, 94–97, 138–39; *Classic Russian Cooking: Elena Molokhovets' 'A Gift to Young Housewives,'* trans. and intro. Joyce Toomre (Bloomington: Indiana University Press, 1992), 13–15, 50–51.

46. Atkinson, "Society and the Sexes," in Atkinson, Dallin, and Lapidus, *Women in Russia,* 15–16;

47. Nancy Shields Kollmann, "Women's Honor in Early Modern Russia," in Clements, Engel, and Worobec, *Russia's Women,* 60–73.

48. The case for not imposing modern judgments on the past and for reconstructing as far as possible the internal logic of the period under study is

stated succinctly in Darnton, *Great Cat Massacre*, 75–104. For examples of community expectations of Russian male behavior during a later period, see Stephen P. Frank, "Popular Justice, Community, and Culture among the Russian Peasantry, 1870–1900," in Ben Eklof and Stephen P. Frank, eds., *The World of the Russian Peasant: Post-Emancipation Culture and Society* (Boston: Unwin Hyman, 1990), 143–44. For a related treatment in a different context, see Robert A. Nye, "Medicine and Science as Masculine 'Fields of Honor,'" *Osiris* 12 (1997): 66, 68, 71–72.

49. Smith and Christian, *Bread and Salt*, 78–79, 84–85, 92–93, 168–72. On the persistence of ritual fighting in the late nineteenth century, see Daniel R. Brower, *The Russian City between Tradition and Modernity, 1850–1900* (Berkeley: University of California Press, 1990), 147–48. A different perspective on mass fistfights in the early twentieth century is found in Joan Neuberger, *Hooliganism: Crime, Culture, and Power in St. Petersburg, 1900–1914* (Berkeley: University of California Press, 1993), 85–93.

50. George P. Fedotov, *The Russian Religious Mind* (1946; reprint, New York: Harper and Brothers, 1960), 1: 3–4.

51. A historiographical overview of *dvoeverie* is found in Eve Levin, "*Dvoeverie* and Popular Religion," in Stephen K. Batalden, ed., *Seeking God: The Recovery of Religious Identity in Orthodox Russia, Ukraine, and Georgia* (DeKalb: Northern Illinois University Press, 1993), 29–52. Her reconceptualization of the issue (45–46) apparently departs from the position she took in "Childbirth in Pre-Petrine Russia: Canon Law and Popular Traditions," in Clements, Engel, and Worobec, *Russia's Women*, 45. See also James H. Billington, *The Icon and the Axe: An Interpretive History of Russian Culture* (New York: Vintage Books, 1966), 18. A different objection to *dvoeverie* is found in Moshe Lewin, *The Making of the Soviet System* (New York: Pantheon Books, 1985), 69.

52. Gregory L. Freeze, "Rechristianization of Russia: The Church and Popular Religion, 1750–1850," *Studia Slavica Finlandensia* 7 (1990): 101–2.

53. See note 14 above. An alternate interpretation appears in Iu. M. Lotman and B. A. Uspenskii, "The Role of Dual Models in the Dynamics of Russian Culture (Up to the End of the Eighteenth Century)," in Iu. M. Lotman and B. A. Uspenskii, *The Semiotics of Russian Culture*, ed. Ann Shukman, trans. N. F. C. Owen (Ann Arbor: Michigan Slavic Contributions, 1984), 3–35.

54. The historiographical problems of representing elite and peasant beliefs as antithetical monoliths are surveyed in Vera Shevzov, "Chapels and the Ecclesial World of Prerevolutionary Russian Peasants," *Slavic Review* 55 (fall 1996): 585–86.

55. Pushkareva, "Women in the Russian Family," in Clements, Engel, and Worobec, *Russia's Women*, 31–38. Part of the evidence Pushkareva uses for her discussion of medieval weddings comes from fifteenth- and sixteenth-century accounts that stress continuity with earlier customs. Her discussion of sources is on 34–35.

56. Although the church advocated female virginity at the time of marriage, its commitment to increasing the number of sacralized unions was

stronger. The failure to preserve virginity was subject to a fine, not to the loss of the right to marry in the church. Natalia Pushkareva, *Women in Russian History: From the Tenth to the Twentieth Century,* ed. and trans. Eve Levin (Armonk, N.Y.: M. E. Sharpe, 1997), 31, 36–39.

57. Pushkareva, "Women in the Russian Family," in Clements, Engel, and Worobec, *Russia's Women,* 31–38; Levin, "Childbirth in Pre-Petrine Russia," in Clements, Engel, and Worobec, *Russia's Women,* 45–53.

58. Responses by the high church to heresy are treated in Paul Bushkovitch, *Religion and Society in Russia: The Sixteenth and Seventeenth Centuries* (New York: Oxford University Press, 1992), 14–16, 26–27, 157–58, 205–6 n. 54.

59. Eve Levin, "Supplicatory Prayers as a Source for Popular Religious Culture in Muscovite Russia," in Samuel H. Baron and Nancy Shiclds Kollmann, eds., *Religion and Culture in Early Modern Russia and Ukraine* (DeKalb: Northern Illinois University Press, 1997), 108.

60. Michael Cherniavsky, "The Old Believers and the New Religion," in Michael Cherniavsky, ed., *The Structure of Russian History: Interpretive Essays* (New York: Random House, 1970), 142–44; Robert O. Crummey, "Old Belief as Popular Religion: New Approaches," *Slavic Review* 52 (1993): 700–712; Boris A. Uspensky, "The Schism and Cultural Conflict in the Seventeenth Century," in Batalden, *Seeking God,* 106–35; Roy R. Robson, *Old Believers in Modern Russia* (DeKalb: Northern Illinois University Press, 1995), 29–39.

61. For interpretations that feature differing emphases in their analysis of these developments, see Gregory L. Freeze, "Handmaiden of the State? The Church in Imperial Russia Reconsidered," *Journal of Ecclesiastical History* 36 (1985): 81–91; Reginald E. Zelnik, "'To the Unaccustomed Eye': Religion and Irreligion in the Experience of St. Petersburg Workers in the 1870s," in Robert P. Hughes and Irina Paperno, eds., *Russian Culture in Modern Times,* vol. 2 of *Christianity and the Eastern Slavs* (Berkeley: University of California Press, 1994), 52–53.

62. Freeze, "Handmaiden of the State?" 82–102; Freeze, "Rechristianization of Russia," 102; Donald W. Treadgold, "Russian Orthodoxy and Society," in Robert L. Nichols and Theofanis George Stavrou, eds., *Russian Orthodoxy under the Old Regime* (Minneapolis: University of Minnesota Press, 1978), 21–43; Charles E. Timberlake, ed., *Religious and Secular Forces in Late Tsarist Russia: Essays in Honor of Donald W. Treadgold* (Seattle: University of Washington Press, 1992), 5–13, 19–27; Robert L. Nichols, "Church and State in Imperial Russia," *Donald W. Treadgold Papers* 102 (1995): 7–22; Paul Valliere, "Theological Liberalism and Church Reform in Imperial Russia," in Geoffrey A. Hosking, ed., *Church, Nation and State in Russia and Ukraine* (New York: St. Martin's Press, 1991), 108–30; Philip Waters, "The Renovationist Coup: Personalities and Programmes," in Hosking, *Church, Nation and State,* 250.

63. I. S. Belliustin, *Description of the Clergy in Rural Russia,* ed. and trans. Gregory L. Freeze (Ithaca, N.Y.: Cornell University Press, 1985); Gregory

L. Freeze, *The Russian Levites: Parish Clergy in the Eighteenth Century* (Cambridge, Mass.: Harvard University Press, 1977); Gregory L. Freeze, *The Parish Clergy in Nineteenth-Century Russia: Crisis, Reform, Counter-Reform* (Princeton, N.J.: Princeton University Press, 1983). See also Elise Kimerling Wirtschafter, *Social Identity in Imperial Russia* (DeKalb: Northern Illinois University Press, 1997), 49–51.

64. Freeze, "Rechristianization of Russia," 102–8.

65. Gregory L. Freeze, "Bringing Order to the Russian Family: Marriage and Divorce in Imperial Russia, 1760–1860," *Journal of Modern History* 62 (1990): 709–46. The early inability of the church to enforce its strictures against divorce is discussed in Pushkareva, *Women in Russian History,* 34–35.

66. Brenda Meehan-Waters, "To Save Oneself: Russian Peasant Women and the Development of Women's Religious Communities in Prerevolutionary Russia," in Beatrice Farnsworth and Lynne Viola, eds., *Russian Peasant Women* (New York: Oxford University Press, 1992), 121–33, esp. 122–24; Brenda Meehan, "Popular Piety, Local Initiative, and the Founding of Women's Religious Communities in Russia, 1764–1907," in Batalden, *Seeking God,* 83–105.

67. Freeze, "Rechristianization of Russia," 103–4, 112; Lewin, *Making of the Soviet System,* 59–63; Samuel C. Ramer, "Traditional Healers and Peasant Culture in Russia, 1861–1917," in Esther Kingston-Mann and Timothy Mixter, eds., *Peasant Economy, Culture, and Politics of European Russia, 1800–1921* (Princeton, N.J.: Princeton University Press, 1991), 206–32, esp. 231. For elite perceptions, see the description of peasant beliefs based on late-nineteenth- and early-twentieth-century ethnographic materials in Linda J. Ivanits, *Russian Folk Belief* (Armonk, N.Y.: M. E. Sharpe, 1989), 235–44 and passim. One such ethnographic study available in English is Olga Semyonova Tian-Shanskaia, *Village Life in Late Tsarist Russia,* ed. David L. Ransel, trans. David L. Ransel with Michael Levine (Bloomington: Indiana University Press, 1993), 12–13, 33–34, 75–94, and passim.

68. Ben Eklof, *Russian Peasant Schools: Officialdom, Village Culture, and Popular Pedagogy, 1861–1914* (Berkeley: University of California Press, 1986), 29, 31, 32, 39, 53, 54, 69, 156–62, 165, 171, 189, 199, 201, 222, 224, 483, 539 n. 42; Jeffrey Brooks, *When Russia Learned to Read: Literacy and Popular Literature, 1861–1917* (Princeton, N.J.: Princeton University Press, 1985), 250–54; Zelnik, "'To the Unaccustomed Eye,'" 52–56, 59–63. On the propensity of priests both to use and to abuse their specific empowerment under the 1874 Education Statute to maintain the religious and moral orientation of the schools, see Christine Ruane and Ben Eklof, "Cultural Pioneers and Professionals: The Teacher in Society," in Edith W. Clowes, Samuel D. Kassow, and James L. West, eds., *Between Tsar and People: Educated Society and the Quest for Public Identity in Late Imperial Russia* (Princeton, N.J.: Princeton University Press, 1991), 203–5.

69. Gary Marker, *Publishing, Printing, and the Origins of Intellectual Life in Russia, 1700–1800* (Princeton, N.J.: Princeton University Press, 1985),

chaps. 1, 4, 6; Brooks, *When Russia Learned to Read,* chaps. 4, 5; Freeze, "Rechristianization of Russia," 116–17.

70. Indeed, otherworldly concerns predominated. For data on the orientation of the Orthodox sermon in prereform Russia, for example, see Gregory L. Freeze, "The Orthodox Church and Serfdom in Prereform Russia," *Slavic Review* 48 (fall 1989): 363–64.

71. William van den Bercken, *Ideology and Atheism in the Soviet Union* (Berlin: Mouton de Gruyter, 1989), chap. 3; Pospielovsky, *History of Marxist-Leninist Atheism and Soviet Anti-Religious Policies,* 1: chap. 1; Thrower, *Study of Religion and Atheism in the USSR,* chaps. 1–2; Harry Piotrowski, "The League of the Militant Godless, 1924–1941," Ph.D. diss., Syracuse University, 1971, chap. 1; Erwin Adler, "Basic Tendencies in the Atheistic Propaganda Literature of the Eastern Bloc," *Concilium: Pastoral Theology* 3 (March 1967): 66–72. Ironically, even though these authors approach atheism tendentiously as a condition to be corrected (Adler refers to it as "the problem") rather than a historical process to be analyzed, the ideological schema they present closely resembles that offered by official apologists for the Communist antireligious movement. Compare their basic assumption with, for example, the pamphlet by the chief spokesman for Soviet atheism in the 1920s–1930s. Emelian Iaroslavskii, *Kommunisty i religiia* (Moscow: Molodaia gvardiia, 1937).

72. The intelligentsia is the focus of a massive historical literature, among which important works include Martin Malia, *Alexander Herzen and the Birth of Russian Socialism* (Cambridge, Mass.: Harvard University Press, 1961); Franco Venturi, *Roots of Revolution: A History of the Populist and Socialist Movements in Nineteenth Century Russia* (1952; trans. Francis Haskell, New York: Grosset and Dunlap, 1966); Avrahm Yarmolinsky, *Road to Revolution: A Century of Russian Radicalism* (New York: Collier Books, 1962); Philip Pomper, *The Russian Revolutionary Intelligentsia* (Arlington Heights, Ill.: Harlan Davidson, 1970); Abbott Gleason, *Young Russia: The Genesis of Russian Radicalism in the 1860s* (Chicago: University of Chicago Press, 1980).

73. Zelnik, "'To the Unaccustomed Eye,'" 49–52.

74. Venturi, *Roots of Revolution,* 134–35, 184–85, 188, 232–33, 285, 304–5, 449; Gleason, *Young Russia,* 100, 128, 181–83; Christopher Read, *Religion, Revolution and the Russian Intelligentsia, 1900–1912: The Vekhi Debate and Its Intellectual Background* (New York: Barnes and Noble Books, 1979), 78–79; *Pod znamenem Marksizma* 7–8 (July–August 1922). The revolutionary careers of Chernyshevsky and Dobroliubov represent only one choice among many newly opened to sons of priests. See Laurie Manchester, "The Secularization of the Search for Salvation: The Self-Fashioning of Orthodox Clergymen's Sons in Late Imperial Russia," *Slavic Review* 57 (spring 1998): 50–76.

75. Leo Tolstoy, *A Confession and Other Writings,* trans. and intro. Jane Kentish (New York: Penguin Books, 1987), 20–21; Leo Tolstoy, *The Death of Ivan Ilyich,* trans. Lynn Solataroff (New York: Bantam Books, 1981), 102–4 and passim. Another manifestation of religious decline among the upper classes was their reduced observance of fast days, compared to the lower

classes, in the nineteenth century. *Classic Russian Cooking,* 13–15.

76. An extensive, albeit tendentious, account of the intellectual and popular roots of religious nonbelief in nineteenth-century Russia is found in M. I. Shakhnovich, "Kritika legendy o 'Russkom narodne-bogonostse,'" in *Ezhegodnik muzeia istorii religii i ateizma,* 6: 257–90.

77. Examples could be multiplied; extensive treatments of this issue appear in Read, *The Russian Intelligentsia;* Catherine Evtuhov, *The Cross and the Sickle: Sergei Bulgakov and the Fate of Russian Religious Philosophy* (Ithaca, N.Y.: Cornell University Press, 1997).

78. Richard Stites, *Revolutionary Dreams: Utopian Vision and Experimental Life in the Russian Revolution* (New York: Oxford University Press, 1989), 101–5.

79. Zelnik, "'To the Unaccustomed Eye,'" 49–52.

80. On this point, see Gregory L. Freeze, "Subversive Piety: Religion and the Political Crisis in Late Imperial Russia," *Journal of Modern History* 68 (1996): 308–50.

81. Jeffrey Burds, "A Culture of Denunciation: Peasant Labor Migration and Religious Anathematization in Rural Russia, 1860–1905," *Journal of Modern History* 68 (December 1996): 789; Stephen P. Frank, "'Simple Folk, Savage Customs?' Youth, Sociability, and the Dynamics of Culture in Rural Russia, 1856–1914," *Journal of Social History* 25 (1992): 716.

82. Quoted in Jeffrey Burds, "The Social Control of Peasant Labor in Russia: The Response of Village Communities to Labor Migration in the Central Industrial Region, 1861–1905," in Kingston-Mann and Mixter, *Peasant Economy,* 61.

83. The dynamics of out-migration are examined in Barbara Alpern Engel, *Between the Fields and the City: Women, Work, and Family in Russia, 1861–1914* (Cambridge: Cambridge University Press, 1996), 34–63, esp. 50–61. A further challenge to viewing the effects of out-migration in terms of a stark dichotomy of continuity and change is found in Frank, "'Simple Folk, Savage Customs?'" 711–36.

84. Gregory L. Freeze, "'Going to the Intelligentsia': The Church and Its Urban Mission in Post-Reform Russia," in Clowes, Kassow, and West, *Between Tsar and People,* 215; Nichols, "Church and State," 15; Burds, "Culture of Denunciation," 792–93. A discussion of the active role of priests in the normal oversight of morals is found in Jeffrey Burds, *Peasant Dreams and Market Politics: Migration and the Russian Village, 1861–1905* (Pittsburgh: University of Pittsburgh Press, 1998), 188–97. For a comparison with Mexico, see Paul Vanderwood, *The Power of God against the Guns of the Government: Religious Upheaval in Mexico at the Turn of the Nineteenth Century* (Stanford, Calif.: Stanford University Press, 1998), 49–66.

85. Zelnik, "'To the Unaccustomed Eye,'" 53–54, 58; Young, *Power and the Sacred in Revolutionary Russia,* 13, 44–47; Freeze, "Rechristianization of Russia," 115.

86. Burds, "Culture of Denunciation," 799.

87. Ibid., 792–96, 799, 804, 807–8; Burds, *Peasant Dreams and Market Politics,* 214–15; Engel, *The Fields and the City,* 64–66, 77–78, 90–98, 115; V. A. Murin, *Byt i nravy derevenskoi molodezhi* (Moscow: Novaia Moskva, 1926), 11; Semën Ivanovich Kanatchikov, *A Radical Worker in Tsarist Russia: The Autobiography of Semën Ivanovich Kanatchikov,* trans. and ed. Reginald E. Zelnik (Stanford, Calif.: Stanford University Press, 1986), 34–36. The quotation is on 34.

88. This is discussed in Husband, "Soviet Atheism and Russian Orthodox Strategies of Resistance, 1917–1932," 83; William B. Husband, *Revolution in the Factory: The Birth of the Soviet Textile Industry, 1917–1920* (New York: Oxford University Press, 1990), 19, 99.

89. Kanatchikov, *Radical Worker,* 29.

90. Mark D. Steinberg, "Workers on the Cross: Religious Imagination in the Writings of Russian Workers, 1910–1924," *Russian Review* 53 (1994): 213–39, esp. 214.

91. Vera Shevzov, "Universal, National and Local Feasts: Competing Parameters of Orthodox Identity in Rural Russia," paper presented at the National Conference of the American Association of Slavic Studies, Washington, D.C., 27 October 1995 (cited by permission).

92. Zelnik, "'To the Unaccustomed Eye,'" 58. Less persuasive than Zelnik's approach is an interpretation that links the seemingly contradictory evidence of peasant religiosity to the "not wholly reliable" character of available sources. See Stephen P. Dunn and Ethel Dunn, *The Peasants of Central Russia* (New York: Holt, Rinehart and Winston, 1967), 29–30.

93. The program is reprinted in *O religii i tserkvi,* 53–54.

94. Arto Luukkanen, *The Party of Unbelief: The Religious Policy of the Bolshevik Party, 1917–1929* (Helsinki: Societas Historica Finlandiae, 1994), 46–55.

95. Such perceptions of "culture" were in no way confined to Russia at the beginning of the twentieth century. See Lawrence W. Levine, *Highbrow/Lowbrow: The Emergence of Cultural Hierarchy in America* (Cambridge, Mass.: Harvard University Press, 1988), 200–206, 226. For the definition of *culture* employed herein, see note 14, above.

2: REVOLUTION AND ANTIRELIGIOUS POLICY

1. This anti-Bolshevik "sonnet," which contains the common accusation that the Bolsheviks worked in the service of Germany, reached Sovnarkom not later than 4 January 1918. It is one of several criticisms in verse located in GARF by S. B. Vakunov and D. Nokhotovich and reprinted in "Sataninskii Lenin (Stikhotvorenye poslaniia Predsedatel'iu Soveta Narodnykh Kommissarov. 1917–1918 gg.)," in *Neizvestnaia Rossiia: XX vek, IV* (Moscow: Izdatel'stvo Ob"edineniia Mosgorarkhiv, 1993), 389.

2. As noted in the introduction, *propaganda* in this book means the systematic propagation of a particular doctrine or practice and does not carry the

connotation of falsehood as found in American colloquial references.

3. This section draws on William B. Husband, "The New Economic Policy (NEP) and the Revolutionary Experiment, 1921–1929," in Freeze, *Russia: A History,* 264–90.

4. For a full discussion, see William J. Chase, *Workers, Society, and the Soviet State: Labor and Life in Moscow, 1918–1929* (Urbana: University of Illinois Press, 1987); Husband, *Revolution in the Factory.*

5. For an insightful synopsis of the controversy surrounding NEP, see Eric Naiman, *Sex in Public: The Incarnation of Early Soviet Ideology* (Princeton, N.J.: Princeton University Press, 1997), 5–11.

6. Alan Ball, *Russia's Last Capitalists: The Nepmen, 1921–1929* (Berkeley: University of California Press, 1987).

7. The party readmitted Zinoviev and Kamenev in 1928 following a humiliating recantation, but Trotsky was exiled and then forcibly deported in 1929.

8. Called the "scissors crisis" because, when plotted on a graph, these price indices resembled scissors, this relationship of manufacturing to agricultural prices reversed the situation of the previous year. The relationships in both years were, of course, relative, since they occurred in what was still an economy of extreme shortage.

9. See Alexander Erlich, *The Soviet Industrialization Debate, 1924–1928* (Cambridge, Mass.: Harvard University Press, 1960).

10. The deep historical root of the contrast between the frequently acrimonious internal relations of the Russian village and its propensity to unite in the face of the outside world is discussed insightfully in Lynne Viola, *Peasant Rebels under Stalin: Collectivization and the Culture of Peasant Resistance* (New York: Oxford University Press, 1996), 5–8.

11. Typical of this campaign is the poster Iakov Guminer prepared for the Leningrad State Publishing House for Art, which stated that "2 + 2 Plus the Enthusiasm of the Workers = 5," in Leah Dickerman, ed., *Building the Collective: Soviet Graphic Design, 1917–1937* (New York: Princeton Architectural Press, 1996), 29, 116–17.

12. For the extensive and complex historiography of the forced collectivization of Soviet agriculture, see Moshe Lewin, *Russian Peasants and Soviet Power: A Study of Collectivization* (New York: Norton, 1975); R. W. Davies, *The Socialist Offensive: The Collectivisation of Soviet Agriculture, 1929–1930* (Cambridge, Mass.: Harvard University Press, 1980); Robert Conquest, *The Harvest of Sorrow* (New York: Oxford University Press, 1986); Lynne Viola, *The Best Sons of the Fatherland* (New York: Oxford University Press, 1987); Viola, *Peasant Rebels under Stalin;* Sheila Fitzpatrick, *Stalin's Peasants: Resistance and Survival in the Russian Village after Collectivization* (New York: Oxford University Press, 1994).

13. See Sheila Fitzpatrick, ed., *Cultural Revolution in Russia, 1928–1931* (Bloomington: Indiana University Press, 1978), esp. her "Cultural Revolution as Class War" (8–40); S. Frederick Starr, *Red and Hot: The Fate of*

Jazz in the Soviet Union (New York: Oxford University Press, 1983), 79–106; Denise Youngblood, *Movies for the Masses: Popular Cinema and Soviet Society in the 1920s* (Cambridge: Cambridge University Press, 1992).

14. For a classic general articulation of this attitude, see *Vestnik tserkovnogo edineniia* 29 (29 October 1917): 1. Problems predated the Bolshevik revolution. When the Provisional Government attempted to transfer parish schools receiving a state subsidy to the jurisdiction of the Ministry of Popular Education in July 1917, the Holy Synod declared the move "impossible . . . for it deprives the Orthodox Church of one of its means of exerting a religious enlightenment influence on the Russian people." *Vestnik tserkovnogo edineniia* 6 (9 July 1917): 1.

15. Examples of the depth of disagreement even on issues of paramount importance are described in Catherine Evtuhov, "The Church in the Russian Revolution: Arguments for and against Restoring the Patriarchate at the Church Council of 1917–1918," *Slavic Review* 50 (fall 1991): 497–511; O. Iu. Vasil'eva, "Russkaia pravoslavnaia tserkov' i Sovetskaia vlast' v 1917–1927 godakh," *Voprosy istorii* 8 (1993): 40–54, esp. 42.

16. *Dekrety Sovetskoi vlasti, tom I: 25 oktiabria 1917g.–16 marta 1918g.* (Moscow: Gosizdat, 1957), 17–20, 39–41. No fewer than two million desiatins of church land were thus nationalized. M. M. Persits, "Zakonodatel'stvo Oktiabr'skoi revoliutsii o svobode sovesti," in *Voprosy istorii religii i ateizma: Sbornik statei, V* (Moscow: Akademiia Nauk SSSR, 1958), 54.

17. *Sobranie Uzakonenii i rasporiazhenii rabochego i krest'ianskogo pravitel'stva* (hereafter *SU*), 9 (24 December 1917): 131; *Russkaia Pravoslavnaia Tserkov' i Kommunisticheskoe Gosudarstvo, 1917–1941: Dokumenty i Fotomaterialy,* ed. Ia. N. Shchapov, comp. O. Iu. Vasil'eva (Moscow: Bibleisko-Bogoslovskii Institut Sviatogo Apostola Andreia, 1996), 21–22; *Kul'turnoe stroitel'stvo v RSFSR: Dokumentay i materialy, 1917–1921,* ed. M. P. Kim (Moscow: Sovetskaia Rossiia, 1983), 1 (1): 78–79. According to one Soviet source, this affected 4 Russian Orthodox ecclesiastical academies, 56 ecclesiastical seminaries, 185 ecclesiastical schools, 85 women's schools, and more than 40,000 church-parish schools (404). In June 1917, the Provisional Government had already taken steps to begin the secularization of elementary education. See Persits, "Zakonodatel'stvo Oktiabr'skoi revoliutsii o svobode sovesti," in *Voprosy istorii religii i ateizma: Sbornik statei, V,* 54.

18. *SU* 11 (29 December 1917): 160–63; *Dekrety Sovetskoi vlasti, I,* 237–39, 247–49; *Voprosy istorii religii i ateizma: Sbornik statei, V,* 4–5.

19. Vasilii Ivanovich Belavin became Patriarch Tikhon in November 1917, the first to hold the office since the reign of Peter the Great. According to a church decree of 4 November 1917, Tikhon was "first among equals" in relation to the bishops, and he was accountable to the *Sobor. Russkaia Pravoslavnaia Tserkov' v sovetskoe vremia (1917–1991): Materialy i dokumenty po istorii otnoshenii mezhdu gosudarstvom i Tserkov'iu,* book 1, comp. Gerd Shtrikker (Moscow: Propilei, 1995), 105. This delineation of authority was a key point in the protracted debates over the advisability of restoring the Patriarchate.

Evtuhov, "Church in the Russian Revolution," 497–511, esp. 509–11.

20. There is a long-standing contention that violence against Orthodoxy was centrally coordinated from the beginning of Bolshevik rule. See, for example, Philip Walters, "A Survey of Soviet Religious Policy," in Sabrina Petra Ramet, ed., *Religious Policy in the Soviet Union* (Cambridge: Cambridge University Press, 1993), 6. Arto Luukkanen challenges whether such coordination existed. I find Luukkanen's interpretion, based on his exhaustive examination of archival sources, to be the more persuasive. See *The Party of Unbelief,* 64 n. 11.

21. *Russkaia Pravoslavnaia Tserkov' v sovetskoe vremia (1917–1991),* 1: 103–4. The quotation is from Vasil'eva, "Russkaia pravoslavnaia tserkov' i Sovetskaia vlast' v 1917–1927 godakh," 41.

22. *Russkaia Pravoslavnaia Tserkov' v sovetskoe vremia (1917–1991),* 1: 105–6; *Russkaia Pravoslavnaia Tserkov' i Kommunisticheskoe Gosudarstvo, 1917–1941,* 13–15.

23. *Russkaia Pravoslavnaia Tserkov' v sovetskoe vremia (1917–1991),* 1: 110–13; *Russkaia Pravoslavnaia Tserkov' i Kommunisticheskoe Gosudarstvo, 1917–1941,* 23–25.

24. For a discussion of deliberations on the decree, see M. M. Persits, *Otdelenie tserkvi ot gosudarstva i shkoly ot tserkvi v SSSR (1917–1919 gg.)* (Moscow: Izdatel'stvo akademii nauk SSSR, 1958), 104–5. A photocopy of the draft decree, showing Lenin's handwritten replacement of "religion is the private affair of every citizen of the Russian Republic" with "the church is separated from the state," follows p. 104. See also *Kommunisticheskaia partiia i sovetskoe pravitel'stvo o religii i tserkvi* (Moscow: Gosudarstvennoe izdatel'stvo politicheskoi literatury, 1959), 39.

25. *SU* 18 (26 January 1918): 272–73; *Dekrety Sovetskoi vlasti, I,* 371–74; *Voprosy istorii religii i ateizma, V,* 6–8; *Russkaia Pravoslavnaia Tserkov' i Kommunisticheskoe Gosudarstvo, 1917–1941,* 25–30. Because the separation decree was widely publicized, erroneous dates (i.e., the publication date of the organ in which it appears rather than of its issue) have been attributed to it.

26. Luukkanen, *Party of Unbelief,* 70. The nationalization decree signed by Kollontai, located in RTsKhIDNI, is reprinted in *Russkaia Pravoslavnaia Tserkov' i Kommunisticheskoe Gosudarstvo, 1917–1941,* 22–23. Although criticized at the time, the seizure of the monastery was treated in later accounts as a heroic victory over a "White Guard" uprising. E. Iaroslavskii, *Protiv religii i tserkvi* (Moscow: Gosudarstvennoe antireligioznoe izdatel'stvo, 1932), 1: 358 n. 7.

27. *Voprosy istorii religii i ateizma, V,* 26–27. A questioning of the motives of the clergy typical of the period is found in the January 1918 resolution of the Moscow Party Committee in *Uprochenie Sovetskoi vlasti v Moskve i Moskovskoi gubernii: Dokumenty i materialy* (Moscow: Moskovskii rabochii, 1958), 109–10. A declaration published in the mass newspaper *Bednota* that characterized the May demonstration as anti-Soviet agitation masquerading as religion is quoted in Persits, "Zakonodatel'stvo Oktiabr'skoi revoliutsii o svo-

bode sovesti," in *Voprosy istorii religii i ateizma: Sbornik statei, V,* 62.

28. *Russkaia Pravoslavnaia Tserkov' i Kommunisticheskoe Gosudarstvo, 1917–1941,* 37–38; *Voprosy istorii religii i ateizma: Sbornik statei, V,* 44–46.

29. Orlando Figes, *Peasant Russia, Civil War: The Volga Countryside in Revolution, 1917–1921* (Oxford: Clarendon Press, 1989), 147–50. The Liquidation Commission reports from GARF compiled and published by M. I. Odintsov bear out Figes's description. "'Tserkov' otdeliaetsia ot gosudarstva': Doklady eksperta Narkomiusta M. V. Galkina, 1918 g." *Istoricheskii arkhiv* 6 (1993): 164–65, 167; "'Tserkov' otdeliaetsia ot gosudarstva': Doklady eksperta Narkomiusta M. V. Galkina, 1918 g. (okonchanie)," *Istoricheskii arkhiv* 1 (1994): 139–40, 143.

30. *Dekrety Sovetskoi vlasti, I,* 261; "'Tserkov' otdeliaetsia ot gosudarstva': Doklady eksperta Narkomiusta M. V. Galkina, 1918 g. (okonchanie)," 137; *Antireligioznik* 11 (November 1926): 4; Luukkanen, *Party of Unbelief,* 69–70, 73–74, 80; Jonathan W. Daly, "'Storming the Last Citadel': The Bolshevik Assault on the Church, 1922," in Vladimir N. Brovkin, ed., *The Bolsheviks in Russian Society: The Revolution and the Civil Wars* (New Haven, Conn.: Yale University Press, 1997), 235–36.

31. *Russkaia Pravoslavnaia Tserkov' i Kommunisticheskoe Gosudarstvo, 1917–1941,* 24.

32. *Russkaia Pravoslavnaia Tserkov' v sovetskoe vremia (1917–1991),* 1: 115.

33. *Russkaia Pravoslavnaia Tserkov' i Kommunisticheskoe Gosudarstvo, 1917–1941,* 37–38; *Voprosy istorii religii i ateizma: Sbornik statei, V,* 44–46.

34. Luukkanen, *Party of Unbelief,* 74.

35. GARF, f. 393, op. 11, d. 13, ll. 32, 32 ob., 33.

36. RTsKhIDNI, f. 17. op. 85, d. 16, l. 56; op. 60, d. 792, l. 33; GARF, f. 5407, op. 1, d. 5, ll. 4–5; f. 353, op. 4, d. 378, ll. 45–47; *Nash bezbozhnik* 14 (26 November 1925): 1; *Kommunizm i religiia* (Moscow: Moskovskii rabochii, 1922), 3; *Bezbozhnik* 53 (7 December 1923): 6; *Kommunisticheskaia revoliutsiia* 10 (1 July 1923): 53; S. Abramson, "Komsomol'skaia derevnia," in V. G. Tan-Bogoraz, ed., *Komsomol v derevne* (Moscow-Leningrad: Gosudarstvennoe izdatel'stvo, 1926), 16; *Bezbozhnik* 3 (18 January 1925): 8; 33 (16 August 1925): 2; 45 (8 November 1925): 6.

37. Although not endorsed by the church, the belief that the remains of a true saint would not putrefy had deep roots in Russian popular religion. The most frequently cited literary representation of this is the case of Father Zossima in Fëdor Dostoevsky, *The Brothers Karamazov,* trans. Constance Garnett (New York, 1955), part 3, book 7, chap. 1. For photographs of crypt openings in Section VIII files, see GARF, f. 353, op. 2, d. 734, passim. Narkomiust published photographs of the opening of the burial vault of Makarii Zhabynskii in *Revoliutsiia i tserkov'* 2 (1919): 28–32. *Izvestiia VTsIK* reported that in April 1919 the Film Committee of Narkompros filmed the opening of the tomb of Saint Sergei of Radonezh for exhibition during Easter week. Apprised of this development by Krasikov, Lenin urged the rapid dissemination of the film

throughout Moscow. *Kul'turnaia zhizn' v SSSR, 1917–1927: Khronika* (Moscow: Nauka, 1975), 1: 129–130. Photographs taken in connection with the closing of the Sergei Radonezh Monastery were printed in *Revoliutsiia i tserkov'* 6–8 (1919): 56–58. Reflecting the public position of the leadership that such activities be conducted in an orderly way, the NKVD issued instructions on 28 February 1919 for the opening of tombs and disposal of their contents. The fact that the NKVD felt the need to issue an elaboration on 23 April 1919 suggests that the original did not generate a satisfactory level of compliance. *Russkaia Pravoslavnaia Tserkov' i Kommunisticheskoe Gosudarstvo, 1917–1941*, 59.

38. GARF, f. 5407, op. 1, d. 8, l. 26.

39. For example, GARF, f. 5263, op. 1, d. 3, ll. 34, 35; *Antireligioznik* 11 (November 1926): 3.

40. *Russkaia Pravoslavnaia Tserkov' i Kommunisticheskoe Gosudarstvo, 1917–1941*, 23–25.

41. *Zhivaia tserkov'* 2 (23 May 1922): 1.

42. *Revoliutsiia i tserkov'* 1 (1919): 42–45.

43. Ibid.

44. Ibid.

45. For example, see RTsKhIDNI, f. 5, op. 1, d. 2620, l. 1, for a notation of religious hostility. The reports contained in RTsKhIDNI, f. 5, op. 1, dd. 2618–56, focus on problems of security and instability in general, significant regional variations are reflected in them, and in many cases they are silent on issues of religion and atheism. I thank Gregory Freeze for calling these materials to my attention. Published documents of the secret police pertinent to attitudes toward the Soviet state and the problems of maintaining order during the 1920s and early 1930s appear in *Rapports secrets soviétiques: La société russe dans les documents confidentiels, 1921–1991*, comp. and trans. Nicholas Werth and Gaël Moullec (Paris: Gallimard, 1994), 30–43, 186–213. Classified secret police reports on the general political mood of the population during 1922–1929 may also be found there (95–110).

46. See Hoover Institution Archives, Boris I. Nicolaevsky Collection, ser. 114, box 182, folder 14.

47. This aspect of the topic has been so widely covered in existing historiography as to not require elaboration here, although hard data for the actual numbers killed have not been made public and possibly do not exist. Representative of the genre is the characterization of "arrests and brutal murders of dozens of bishops, thousands of the lower clergy and monastics, and uncounted thousands of lay believers." Pospielovsky, *History of Marxist-Leninist Atheism and Soviet Anti-Religious Policies*, 1: 27.

48. *Bezbozhnik* 9 (11 February 1923): 7.

49. Quoted in B. Kandidov, "Uchastie tserkovnikov v grazhdanskoi voiny i interventsii," in *Voinstvuiushchee bezbozhie v SSSR za 15 let, 1917–1932* (Moscow: Gosudarstvennoe antireligioznoe izdatel'stvo, 1932),

101. See also P. V. Verkhovskoi, *Patriarkh Tikhon* (n.p.: Izdatel'stvo Novaia Rossiia, 1919), 3.

50. Iaroslavskii, *Protiv religii i tserkvi*, 1: 45; Peter Kenez, *Civil War in South Russia, 1919–1920* (Berkeley: University of California Press, 1977), 78–80; Kandidov, "Uchastie tserkovnikov v grazhdanskoi voiny i interventsii," in *Voinstvuiushchee bezbozhie v SSSR za 15 let, 1917–1932*, 107–19. A more formulaic assertion of this staple of the Bolshevik position is Vladimir Bonch-Bruevich, *"Zhivaia tserkov'" i proletariat* (Moscow: Zhizn' i znanie, 1929), 7–8.

51. Complaints that local officials monopolized the best resources (not all of which, of course, were former church property) and were indifferent to the plight of the mass were common in 1917–1921. On 8 December 1918, the party disbanded the unrepentant leadership of the pro-Bolshevik Union of Textile Workers in Orekhovo-Zuevo for stealing furniture and occupying excessive living space. GARF, f. 5457, op. 3, d. 26, ll. 12–13. The union's national newspaper noted that entire families inhabited "dirty, smoky rooms while the comfortable buildings are occupied by Soviet institutions and Soviet employees." *Tekstil'shchik* 13–14 (July 1919): 7.

52. *Dekrety Sovetskoi vlasti, tom II: 17 marta–1 iiulia 1918g.* (Moscow: Politizdat, 1959), 35–36. Point 10 of the Sovnarkom decree of 20 January 1918 ended state and local subsidies to the church. In addition, in her official capacity as People's Commissar of State Welfare and her self-appointed role of custodian of church property, Alexandra Kollontai had published a decree on 20 January 1918 that severed church-state economic ties, effective 1 March. Persits, *Otdelenie tserkvi ot gosudarstva i shkoly ot tserkvi v SSSR*, 103.

53. *Dekrety Sovetskoi vlasti, tom IV: 10 noiabria 1918g.–31 marta 1919 g.* (Moscow: Politizdat, 1968), 413; *Dekrety Sovetskoi vlasti, tom V: 1 aprelia–31 iiulia 1919 g.* (Moscow: Politizdat, 1971), 94.

54. *Dekrety Sovetskoi vlasti, I*, 404–5.

55. *Dekrety Sovetskoi vlasti, II*, 553.

56. *Kommunisticheskaia partiia Sovetskogo soiuza v rezoliutsiiakh i resheniiakh s"ezdov, konferentsii i plenumov TsK:* vol. 1, *1918–1925* (Moscow: Izdatel'stvo politicheskoi literatury, 1953), 420–21.

57. GARF, f. 353, op. 3, d. 745, ll. 1, 7–9. So effective were these directives that Narkomiust attributed resistance in Zvengorod and Voznesensk in mid-1919 directly to them. But in October 1919, Tikhon appealed to the clergy to abstain from the political struggle in the country. *Russkaia Pravoslavnaia Tserkov' v sovetskoe vremia (1917–1991)*, 1: 136–37.

58. GARF, f. 353, op. 2, d. 695, ll. 185, 185 ob.

59. Ibid., d. 712, ll. 1, 4, 7, 13, 54.

60. "'Tserkov' otdeliaetsia ot gosudarstva': Doklady eksperta Narkomiusta M. V. Galkina, 1918 g. (okonchanie)," 139–41.

61. GARF, f. 353, op. 2, d. 687, ll. 1, 4; d. 688, ll. 6, 11–19; d. 690, ll. 1, 1 ob., 3–8, 10–12; d. 691, ll. 161–70; *Voprosy istorii religii i ateizma: Sbornik statei, V*, 18–25. Typical of the lack of specific concern, biblical citations,

historical analysis of a purported perversion of the Christian ideal through the link of tsar and clergy, and an explanation of the decree itself run together in one early Soviet explanation of the separation of church and state that was written in May 1918. I. M. Lukin (I. Antonov), *Tserkov' i gosudarstvo* (Moscow: Kommunist, 1918), 3–24, 32.

62. *SU* 62 (1918): 757–65; *Voprosy istorii religii i ateizma: Sbornik statei, V,* 11–17; *Russkaia Pravoslavnaia Tserkov' v sovetskoe vremia (1917–1991),* 1: 128–31. Official Soviet historiography presented this as a logical progression rather than a change. For example, Persits, *Otdelenie tserkvi ot gosudarstva i shkoly ot tserkvi v SSSR,* 110–25.

63. GARF, f. 353, op. 3, d. 749, l. 2.

64. For reportage typical of the period, in this case that the civil war drew the most capable cadres to the front and organs commonly could not pay their staff, see *Revoliutsiia i tserkov'* 3–5 (1919): 61, 107, 118. Because of the absence of fuel at the printing plant, this issue did not appear until 1 May 1920.

65. GARF, f. 393, op. 11, d. 13, ll. 32, 32 ob., 33.

66. *Pravda,* 31 March 1921, 1; *Stenograficheskii otchet vtorogo vsesoiuznogo s"ezda voinstvuiushchikh bezbozhnikov* (Moscow: Bezbozhnik, 1930), 50. The full text of "On the Organization of Antireligious Agitation and Propaganda" is located in RTsKhIDNI, f. 17, op. 60, d. 158, ll. 5–9.

67. *O religii i tserkvi,* 55–56.

68. Material on the organization of Agitprop is located in the introduction to its inventory catalog in the fond of the Central Committee of the Communist Party in RTsKhIDNI, f. 17, op. 60.

69. Luukkanen, *Party of Unbelief,* 99–101, 125–27; *Kommunizm i religiia,* 3. Also, published accounts disagree over the date of the founding of the Antireligious Commission, its leadership, and the moment of its dissolution. Those interested in pursuing the particulars are referred to Luukkanen, *Party of Unbelief,* 126 n. 97; G. V. Vorontsov, "Iz istorii partiinogo rukovodstva propagandoi ateizma v SSSR (1921–1929 gg.)," in V. N. Sherdakov, ed., *Ateizm, religiia, sovremennost'* (Leningrad: Nauka, 1973), 105.

70. *Russkaia Pravoslavnaia Tserkov' v sovetskoe vremia (1917–1991),* 1: 146–47. An assessment of the 1921 Orthodox relief effort more positive than the one herein—and one that reproduces Tikhon's own explanation of the events—appears in Vasil'eva, "Russkaia pravoslavnaia tserkov' i Sovetskaia vlast' v 1917–1927 godakh," 43. Compare this with the main points of the Patriarch's letter of 28 February 1922 in *Russkaia Pravoslavnaia Tserkov' i Kommunisticheskoe Gosudarstvo, 1917–1941,* 74–75. Although not conclusive, descriptions of the Volga famine conditions of September–November 1921 presented by members of the American Relief Administration to the U.S. House of Representatives Committee on Foreign Affairs expressed a low opinion of Soviet relief efforts and did not mention those by the Orthodox Church. Rex A. Wade, ed., *Triumph and Retreat, 1920–1922,* vol. 2 of *Documents of Soviet History* (Gulf Breeze, Fla.: Academic International Press, 1993), 295–300.

71. *Nauka i religiia* 1 (1922): 1, 5–8, 12–15.

72. *Bezbozhnik* 1 (1933): 5.

73. G. Volodin, *Po sledam istorii: Ocherki iz istorii Donetskogo ordena Lenina metallurgicheskogo zavoda imeni V. I. Lenina* (Donetsk: Donbass, 1967), 172.

74. On this point, see the various resolutions passed in 1922 in GARF, f. 5263, op. 1, d. 54, ll. 47–57.

75. E. M. Khenkin, *Ocherki istorii bor'by Sovetskogo gosudartsva s golodom (1921–1922)* (Krasnoiarsk: Izdatel'stvo Krasnoiarskogo universiteta, 1988), 86–88; I. Trifonov, *Ocherki istorii klassovoi bor'by v SSSR v gody NEPa (1921–1937)* (Moscow: Gosudarstvennoe izdatel'stvo politicheskoi literatury, 1960), 31–32; Luukkanen, *Party of Unbelief,* 107–9; *Nauka i religiia* 1 (1922): 38–40. Both church and state used the term *voluntary* imprecisely in this connection. It could refer either to grassroots initiative or to acts performed to preempt forceful confiscation. Moreover, within one week Veniamin retreated from his original position and placed three conditions on his support of surrender. *Russkaia Pravoslavnaia Tserkov' i Kommunisticheskoe Gosudarstvo, 1917–1941,* 80–83. For a recent interpretation that presents the campaign as a singularly rapacious exercise, see Daly, "'Storming the Last Citadel,'" 235–68.

76. A. Kostitsyn, *Trudiashchaia zhenshchina i religiia* (Moscow: Moskovskii rabochii, 1929), 7–8, 10; Husband, *Revolution in the Factory,* 8–9, 16, 59.

77. GMIR, f. 29, op. 2, d. 3, ll. 1–5. The quotation is on l. 1. The report of the incident filed by Korotkov, secretary of the Ivanovo-Voznesensk Provincial Soviet, erroneously listed five soldiers killed rather than beaten and gave the number wounded as fifteen. See the documents published in "Politburo i tserkov', 1922–1923," comp. and intro. N. N. Pokrovskii, *Novyi mir* 8 (1994): 191. GMIR was undergoing reorganization in 1995, and during that time some files that will ultimately receive different permanent designations were identified in the GMIR card catalog only by temporary folder numbers.

78. "K 120–letiiu so dnia rozhdeniia V. I. Lenina: Novye dokumenty (1920–1922 gg.)," *Izvestiia TsK KPSS* 4 (1990): 190–93.

79. Representative examples include GARF, f. 5263, op. 1, d. 54, ll. 69–71; RTsKhIDNI, f. 89, op. 4, d. 115, l. 3. See also the extensive documentation of episodes of the campaign and resistance by the church in *Russkaia Pravoslavnaia Tserkov' i Kommunisticheskoe Gosudarstvo, 1917–1941,* 71–145.

80. See, for example, his communications of 12 and 30 March 1922 in "Politburo i tserkov', 1922–1923," 189–90; *Russkaia Pravoslavnaia Tserkov' i Kommunisticheskoe Gosudarstvo, 1917–1941,* 79.

81. *Rapports secrets soviétiques,* 217–18. For a summary Soviet account of the seizure of church valuables, see N. A. Chemerskii, "Iz"iatie v 1922 g. tserkovnykh tsennosti dlia pomoshchi golodaiushchim," in *Voprosy istorii religii i ateizma: Sbornik statei, X* (Moscow: Izdatel'stvo akademii nauk, 1962), 186–212.

82. The prerevolutionary origins of Renovationism are discussed in

Edward E. Roslof, "The Renovationist Movement in the Russian Orthodox Church, 1922–1946," Ph.D. diss., University of North Carolina at Chapel Hill, 1994, 21–45.

83. *Zhivaia tserkov'* 2 (23 May 1923): 2, 6–7, 9.

84. Coverage of the Living Church varied in *Bezbozhnik*, for example, during the first half of 1923, apparently in direct proportion to the immediate usefulness of the Renovationists on any given issue. See *Bezbozhnik* 5–6 (21 January 1923): 7–8; 9 (11 February 1923): 1; 10 (18 February 1923): 1; 12 (4 March 1923): 1; 15 (25 March 1923): 1, 6; 16 (1 April 1923): 1; 21 (13 May 1923): 1–2, 13; 23 (27 May 1923): 6; 26 (17 June 1923): 1.

85. Luukkanen, *Party of Unbelief,* 133–35; Gregory L. Freeze, "Counter-reformation in Russian Orthodoxy: Popular Response to Religious Innovation, 1922–1925," *Slavic Review* 54 (summer 1995): 305–39; Edward E. Roslof, "The Heresy of 'Bolshevik' Christianity: Orthodox Rejection of Religious Reform during NEP," *Slavic Review* 55 (fall 1996): 614–35. In some rural areas, though, party workers found that peasants knew nothing of this battle between the Renovationists and the followers of Tikhon. N. Rosnitskii, ed., *Polgoda v derevne: Osnovnye itogi obsledovaniia 28 volostei i 32730 krest'ianskikh khoziastv Penzenskoi gub.* (Penza: Izdanie komissii po rabote v derevne pri gubkome RKP[b], 1925), 225. Rival denominations took special pains to distance themselves publicly from Renovationism. *Baptist* 4 (1928): 21–22.

86. RTsKhIDNI, f. 89, op. 4, d. 115, l. 2; d. 118, ll. 1–21.

87. A discussion of this controversy, based on archival documents made available since 1991, appears in Freeze, "Counter-reformation in Russian Orthodoxy," 322–27. A concise and authoritative summary of the much-studied arrest and release of Tikhon, which also makes judicious use of declassified party documents, is found in Luukkanen, *Party of Unbelief,* 129–33. M. I. Odintsov has published documents on the activities of the political police in regard to Tikhon for the years 1919–1925. *Istoricheskii arkhiv* 5–6 (1997): 141–55. Additional relevant documents appear in "Politburo i tserkov', 1922–1923," 195–96, 203–7. The Ninth Congress of Evangelical Christians of the USSR of 1–10 September 1923 took a similar conciliatory step when it sent a resolution to VTsIK that included a reversal of its previous intransigence on the issue of military service for followers. Iaroslavskii, *Protiv religii i tserkvi,* 1: 375 n. 68.

88. *Izvestiia TsK RKP(b)* 51 (1923): 204.

89. V. I. Brudnyi, *Obriady vchera i segodnia* (Moscow: Nauka, 1968), 71–72; S. Makar'ev, "Komsomol Prionezh'ia," in Tan-Bogoraz, *Komsomol v derevne,* 105; Boris Shabalin, *Krasnyi treugol'nik* (Leningrad: Istoriia zavodov, 1953), 243; *Bezbozhnik* 7 (28 February 1923): 2; 1 (4 January 1925): 3; *Nash bezbozhnik* 14–15 (29 July 1924): 3.

90. For an account of a Komsomol Christmas in Kursk, where only an "insufficiency of material means" limited the level of additional accomplishment, see V. E. Sharov et al., eds., *Iz istorii Kurskoi oblastnoi Komsomol'skoi organizatsii (1918–1970 gg.)* (Kursk: Kurskaia pravda, 1972), 76–77. An en-

thusiastic report of the event put on by the Komsomol at the Institute of Oriental Studies appears in *Bezbozhnik* 5–6 (21 January 1923): 2–3. See also *Bezbozhnik* 7 (28 February 1923): 2; 28 (1 July 1923): 6.

91. RTsKhIDNI, f. 89, op. 4, d. 115, l. 3. On 27 February 1923, the commission squelched a suggestion to attempt an additional event to counter Jewish Passover. In a vigorous, if immoderate, attempt to raise the level of antireligious discourse, on 12 June 1923 the commission resolved that each of its members would write no fewer than two articles per month for *Bezbozhnik*. RTsKhIDNI, f. 89, op. 4, d. 115, ll. 7, 24.

92. A. Bakurova, "Komsomol na antireligioznom fronte," in *Voinstvuiushchee bezbozhie v SSSR za 15 let, 1917–1932*, 305–6.

93. Ralph Talcott Fisher, Jr., *Pattern for Soviet Youth: A Study of the Congresses of the Komsomol, 1918–1954* (New York: Columbia University Press, 1959), 130–31.

94. *Bezbozhnik* 5–6 (21 January 1923): 3–4.

95. *Pod znamenem Marksizma* 3 (1922): 6–8.

96. *Revoliutsiia i tserkov'* 1–3 (1923): 31–32.

97. For one harbinger of this shift, see the report of the Antireligious Commission to the Politburo of 28 November 1922, which deals with the closing of *Nauka i religiia* and its replacement with *Krasnaia nov'*, which published antireligious propaganda in a tone more directed to the masses. *Istoricheskii arkhiv* 2 (1993): 83.

98. *Kommunisticheskaia partiia Sovetskogo soiuza v rezoliutsiiakh i resheniiakh:* vol. 1, *1918–1925,* 420–21.

99. *Dvenadtsatyi s"ezd RKP(b): Stenograficheskii otchet, 17–25 aprelia 1923 g.* (Moscow: Izdatel'stvo politicheskoi literatury, 1968), 44.

100. *Kommunisticheskaia partiia Sovetskogo soiuza v rezoliutsiiakh i resheniiakh:* vol. 1, *1918–1925,* 743–45.

101. The VIII Section of Narkomiust published *Revoliutsiia i tserkov'* from 1919 to 1924 in press runs of 30,000–40,000. Press runs of *Nauka i religiia* averaged 25,000–30,000, and it put out additional brochures and seventeen issues of a wall newspaper of the same name in runs of 125,000. *Antireligioznik* 19 (October 1932): 24–25. Examples of the proclivity to speak above the expected level of a mass audience are Genrikh Kunov, *Vozniknovenie religii i very v boga* (Moscow: Kommunist, 1919); *Zapiski nauchnogo obshchestva marksistov* 3 (July–September 1922): 60–85.

102. The monthly *Pod znamenem marksizma* [Under the Banner of Marxism] had begun publication in January 1922, but it never fully followed Lenin's urging that it promote materialism militantly, nor did its level of discourse allow it to address a mass audience.

103. Iaroslavskii cited the circulation of *Antireligioznik* at 15,000 copies and of the journal *Bezbozhnik* at 15,000 in a speech of 10 December 1928 to the Party Central Committee. A journal entitled *Ateist* published two issues during 1922 with a press run of 15,000, but it should not be confused with its more permanent namesake launched in 1925. The initial issue of the latter *Ateist*

published a run of 15,000 but contracted to 4,000 the following year. RTsKhIDNI, f. 89, op. 4, d. 26, l. 5; *Bezbozhnik* 273 (6 May 1928): 1; *Antireligioznik* 19 (October 1932): 29; *Ateist* 1 (1925): 1–3.

104. A. F. Okulov et al., eds., *Ateizm v SSSR: stanovlenie i razvitie* (Moscow: Mysl', 1986), 61–64. See also the Party Antireligious Commission documents of November–December 1922 pertinent to the activities of the Krasnaia nov' press, which initially published *Bezbozhnik,* reproduced in *Istoricheskii arkhiv* 2 (1993): 83, 86. For a compilation of antireligious publications, see Ia. Glan, *Antireligioznaia literatura za 12 let (1917–1929)* (Moscow: Bezbozhnik, 1930); Ia. Glan, *Antireligioznaia literatura po oktiabr'skogo perioda, 1930 (iiul')–1932 (noiabr')* (Moscow: Gosudarstvennoe antireligioznoe izdatel'stvo, 1932).

105. *Antireligioznik* 10 (October 1927), reprinted in Iaroslavskii, *Protiv religii i tserkvi,* 1: 276.

106. In late 1925, for example, 738 of the paper's 1,268 correspondents were peasants. GARF, f. 5407, op. 1, d. 1, l. 11. *Derevenskii bezbozhnik,* which depended on peasant correspondents for data about rural Moscow Province, began publication in March 1928. *Antireligioznik* 6 (1929): 52. The liberal use of illustrations paralleled the heavy reliance of the Bolsheviks on posters. See V. L. Andrianova and S. G. Rutenberg, "Antireligioznyi plakat pervykh let sovetskoi vlasti," in *Ezhegodnik muzeia religii i ateizma,* 5: 188–205.

107. GARF, f. 5407, op. 1, d. 1, l. 11; *Bezbozhnik* 77 (6 July 1924): 1; 106 (1 February 1925): 7; 181 (25 July 1926): 8. In this case, the circulation figures for July and October 1925 are from the record in GARF of the 28 October 1925 meeting of the Central Council of the League of Atheists. They differ slightly from those reported in the paper itself: 210,000 in February 1925 and January 1926, 130,000 in February 1926, 123,000 in March 1926. See *Bezbozhnik* 106 (1 February 1925): 7; 155 (17 January 1926): 8; 159 (14 February 1926): 8; 164 (21 March 1926): 8.

108. *Pod znamenem Marksizma* 5 (May 1930): 56.

109. *Bezbozhnik* 185 (22 August 1926): 2.

110. GARF, f. 353, op. 4, d. 378, l. 6.

111. *Bezbozhnik* 243 (9 October 1927): 7.

112. *Bezbozhnik* 47 (11 November 1923): 1.

113. *Bezbozhnik* 5–6 (21 January 1923): 5; GARF, f. 5407, op. 1, d. 8, ll. 57–60.

114. GARF, f. 5407, op. 1, d. 7, ll. 11–12; *Bezbozhnik* 204 (2 January 1927): 7.

115. *Bezbozhnik* 82 (10 August 1924): 3; RTsKhIDNI, f. 89, op. 4, d. 116, l. 20; Okulov et al., *Ateizm v SSSR,* 61–62. A Society of Militant Materialists informally linked to *Pod znamenem Marksizma* organized in 1924, but it did not hold a national conference until 1929, when it renamed itself the Society of Militant Materialists-Dialecticalists. It pursued the seemingly contradictory objective of bringing mass attention to its preoccupation with questions of Marxist theory and philosophy. At the time of its initial congress, the society

had gone no further than discussing basic organizational issues. *Pod znamenem Marksizma* 12 (December 1926): 236; 5 (May 1929): 129–30. 116. GARF, f. 5407, op. 1, d. 1, ll. 26, 31; d. 2, ll. 25, 27; *Kul'turnoe stroitel'stvo v RSFSR,* 1 (2): 331 n. 77; *Antireligioznik* 4 (April 1926): 61; *Bezbozhnik* 86 (7 September 1924): 2–3; 90 (5 October 1924): 3; 99 (7 December 1924): 3; 111 (8 March 1925): 2–3, 7; 113 (24 March 1925): 1–2; 192 (10 October 1926): 4; *Stenograficheskii otchet vtorogo vsesoiuznogo s"ezda voinstvuiushchikh bezbozhnikov,* 53. A more sympathetic interpretation of this process appears in V. Shishakov, "Soiuz voinstvuiushchikh bezbozhnikov (1925–1931)," in *Voinstvuiushchee bezbozhie v SSSR za 15 let, 1917–1932,* 323–26.

117. *Bezbozhnik* 196 (7 November 1926): 7; 205 (9 January 1927): 8; 222 (15 May 1927): 7; V. Kalinin, "Dinamika rosta i sotsial'nogo sostava SVB," in *Voinstvuiushchee bezbozhie v SSSR za 15 let, 1917–1932,* 345; E. Iaroslavskii, *Ocherednye zadachi antireligioznoi propagandy* (Moscow: Bezbozhnik, 1930), 5.

118. *Bezbozhnik* 181 (25 July 1926): 2–3; 192 (10 October 1926): 4; 205 (9 January 1927): 8; *Uchebnik dlia rabochikh antireligioznykh kruzhkov, 2-e izdanie,* ed. A. Lukachevskii (Moscow: Bezbozhnik, 1928), 3.

119. Reports on two later conferences of this type in Leningrad, in the Rozhkovo-Simonov region of Moscow and in Voronezh, may be found in *Bezbozhnik* 222 (15 May 1927): 7; 320 (31 March 1929): 3; 321 (1 April 1929): 2; 324 (28 April 1929): 2.

120. RTsKhIDNI, f. 89. op. 4, d. 26, l. 4. The comment from Stepanov-Skvortsov is in *Bezbozhnik* 313 (10 February 1929): 1.

121. *Bezbozhnik* 299 (4 November 1928): 1.

122. *Trinadtsatyi s"ezd RKP(b), mai 1924 goda: Stenograficheskii otchet* (Moscow: Izdatel'stvo politicheskoi literatury, 1963), 447–50, 642–43.

123. GARF, f. 5263, op. 1, d. 3, l. 35.

124. *Kommunisticheskaia partiia Sovetskogo soiuza v rezoliutsiiakh i resheniiakh,* vol. 3, *1922–1925,* 301–4.

125. *Bezbozhnik* 74 (15 June 1924): 2.

126. RTsKhIDNI, f. 89, op. 4, d. 115, l. 3.

127. GARF, f. 5407, op. 1, d. 12, ll. 20–21. For a report on using different anti-Christmas strategies for town and countryside in December 1925, see Smolensk Archive, WKP 459: 25.

128. *Bezbozhnik* 268 (1 April 1928): 7.

129. *Bezbozhnik u stanka* 5 (1929): 20; GARF, f. 5407, op. 1, d. 39, l.5. See also *Bezbozhnik u stanka* 23 (1929): passim.

130. GARF, f. 5407, op. 1, d. 35, ll. 97, 97 ob.

131. RTsKhIDNI, f. 17, op. 60, d. 792, l. 95.

132. GARF, f. 5407, op. 1, d. 8, ll. 7–8.

133. Rosnitskii, *Polgoda v derevne,* 218–19.

134. *Uchebnik dlia rabochikh antireligioznykh kruzhkov, 2-e izdanie,* 3.

135. Luukkanen, *Party of Unbelief,* 187–89. Tikhon's testament is

reprinted in *Russkaia Pravoslavnaia Tserkov' i Kommunisticheskoe Gosudarstvo, 1917–1941,* 203–6.

136. *Russkaia Pravoslavnaia Tserkov' v sovetskoe vremia (1917–1991),* 1: 255–59, 267–68.

137. The twelve slogans of the 1930–1931 League of Militant Godless anti-Christmas campaign, for example, concentrated far more on the fulfillment of full collectivization than on atheism. GMIR, folder 34, l. 3.

138. Fitzpatrick, *Cultural Revolution in Russia, 1928–1931,* passim.

139. *SU* 35 (18 May 1929): 353.

140. Daniel Peris, "The 1929 Congress of the Godless," *Soviet Studies* 43 (1991): 711–32, esp. 714–17, 725; Piotrowski, "The League of the Militant Godless," 213–24.

141. GMIR, folder 21, l. 3 ob. On antireligious violence as a result of collectivization, see Viola, *Peasant Rebels under Stalin,* 39–40, 135, 154–58, 161–65, 187–88, 194; Fitzpatrick, *Stalin's Peasants,* 43–45, 49, 59–65, 105, and esp. 204–14, which offers a concise summary of the complex tension between oppression and accommodation on the question of religion in the countryside in the 1930s. Maurice Hindus, in his account of a single village following collectivization, also comments on the contrast between the 1920s and the 1930s regarding religion as well as the survivals of religiosity. *Red Bread: Collectivization in a Russian Village* (1931; Bloomington: Indiana University Press, 1988), 34–35, 44, 186–209, 304–6, 311.

142. Kalinin, "Dinamika rosta i sotsial'nogo sostava SVB," in *Voinstvuiushchee bezbozhie v SSSR za 15 let, 1917–1932,* 345.

143. GARF, f. 5407, op. 1, d. 95, ll. 59–62

3: MATERIALISM AND THE SECULARIZATION OF SOCIETY

1. *Radio v derevne* (11 December 1927) (trial issue): 1.

2. For an analysis of the problems inherent in translating *byt* into English from the perspective of a scholar whose native language is Russian, see Daniel A. Alexandrov, "The Historical Anthropology of Science in Russia," *Russian Studies in History* 34 (fall 1995): 65–66 (a translation of D. A. Alexandrov, "Istoricheskaia antropologiia nauki v Rossii," *Voprosy istorii estestvovaniia i tekhniki* 4 [1994]). The translation problem for a native speaker of English is expressed in Eric Naiman's reference to "what the Russians call *byt:* the category of nitty-gritty detail and everyday life." *Sex in Public,* 27.

3. *Kul'turnoe stroitel'stvo v RSFSR,* 1 (1): 44–45.

4. An application of this definition appears in M. V. Larin, "K voprosu o stanovlenii i razvitii sotsialisticheskoi kul'tury upravleniia (1917–1941 gg.), in Iu. S. Borisov, ed., *Dukhovnyi potentsial SSSR nakanune Velikoi Otechestvennoi Voiny: Iz istorii sovetskoi kul'tury 1917–1941 gg.: Sbornik statei* (Moscow: Nauka, 1985), 7.

5. GARF, f. 5407, op. 1, d. 90, ll. 85–86; *Bezbozhnik* 31 (22 July 1923): 1.

6. RTsKhIDNI, f. 17, op. 60, d. 777, l. 112; *Nash bezbozhnik* 16–17 (19 August 1924): 1; 2 (25 January 1925): 2–4, 1; *Pod znamenem Marksizma* 12 (December 1925): 164–78; *Bezbozhnik* 249 (20 November 1927): 5; *Ateist* 37 (February 1929): 51; *Bezbozhnik u stanka* 2 (1929): 3; A. E. Segal, *Religiia i znakharstvo* (Moscow-Leningrad: Moskovskii rabochii, 1931), 3.

7. *Nash bezbozhnik* 5 (7 March 1925): 1; *Antireligioznik* 6 (June 1930): 53. Believers as well as nonbelievers subscribed to the idea that faith and knowledge were incompatible. In 1925, the religious journal *Baptist* complained that this view had a wide following among its own followers. *Baptist* 2 (February 1925): 21.

8. *Bezbozhnik* 289 (26 August 1928): 1.

9. Iaroslavskii, *Protiv religii i tserkvi,* 1: 257, reprinted from *Bezbozhnik* 36 (19 September 1926).

10. For representative examples of propaganda that promoted aspects of this message generally or counterposed them to religiosity, see GARF, f. 9636, op. 1, d. 13, l. 8; *Rabotnitsa* 3 (March 1923): 18–19; *Bezbozhnik* 26 (17 June 1923): 3; *Nash bezbozhnik* 12–13 (8 July 1924): 1; 7 (18 April 1925): 5; 10–11 (30 August 1925): 7; *Ateist* 1 (January 1926): 3–7; *Bezbozhnik* 165 (28 March 1926): 2; *Voprosy truda* 5–6 (May–June 1926): 36–37; *Nash bezbozhnik* 7 (24 July 1926): 1; *Bezbozhnik* 183 (8 August 1926): 2; *Antireligioznik* 9 (September 1926): 38–54; *Bezbozhnik* 196 (7 November 1926): 1; 263 (26 February 1928): 2; 310 (20 January 1929): 6; *Derevenskii bezbozhnik* 6 (April 1929): 1; *Bezbozhnyi byt* 2 (22 May 1929): 1; *Bezbozhnik* 328 (26 May 1929): 1; *Voprosy truda* 2 (February 1930): 13; *Antireligioznik* 6 (June 1930): 53; *Voprosy truda* 3–4 (March–April 1931): 113–19; *Radio v derevne* 20 (20–30 July 1931): 1; Vladimir F. Zybkovets, *Ot sokhi k traktoru* (Leningrad: Lenpartizdat, 1934), passim.

11. *Sredne-volzhskii bezbozhnik* 5 (9 November 1930): 1. On the future of urban life in a materialist age, see *Voprosy truda* 2 (February 1930): 13–21, esp. 13–14.

12. *Bezbozhnik* 154 (5 January 1926): 2.

13. *Velikaia Oktiabr'skaia sotsialisticheskaia revoliutsiia i stanovlenie sovetskoi kul'tury, 1917–1927,* ed. M. P. Kim (Moscow: Nauka, 1985), 165–73, 431–44; *Bezbozhnik* 136 (30 August 1925): 6.

14. *Bezbozhnik* 26 (17 June 1923): 3.

15. *Velikaia Oktiabr'skaia sotsialisticheskaia revoliutsiia i stanovlenie sovetskoi kul'tury, 1917–1927,* 288–336, esp. 293–94, 297–98, 307–11, 317–19. In his article "Nauka na sluzhbe u kapitala," Vl. Sarab'ianov interprets this approach to science as essentially above class interests; that is, only in the USSR is science employed for the benefit of the whole population. Not all scientists work in their class interests, he concedes, but all bourgeois science is directed toward class orientations. *Antireligioznik* 1 (January 1926): 10–13. Informative treatments of the Soviet scientific-technological establishment can be found in Alexander Vucinich, *Empire of Knowledge: The Academy of Sciences of the USSR, 1917–1970* (Berkeley: University of California Press, 1984); Loren R. Graham, *Science, Philosophy, and Human Behavior in the Soviet*

Union (New York: Columbia University Press, 1987); Anne D. Rassweiler, *The Generation of Power: The History of Dneprostroi* (New York: Oxford University Press, 1988); Jonathan Coopersmith, *The Electrification of Russia, 1880–1926* (Ithaca, N.Y.: Cornell University Press, 1992); Michael David-Fox, *Revolution of the Mind: Higher Learning among the Bolsheviks, 1918–1929* (Ithaca, N.Y.: Cornell University Press, 1997), esp. 201–19.

16. I. S. Gurevich, "Etnografiia i izuchenie istorii kul'turnoi revoliutsii v SSSR," in M. P. Kim, ed., *Kul'turnaia revoliutsiia v SSSR, 1917–1965 gg.* (Moscow: Nauka, 1967), 251–60, esp. 252.

17. *Velikaia Oktiabr'skaia sotsialisticheskaia revoliutsiia i stanovlenie sovetskoi kul'tury, 1917–1927*, 140–41.

18. GME, f. 2, op. 1, d. 343, l. 2.

19. Relevant records are filed in GME, f. 2, op. 1, d. 87 (religious holidays, celebrations, and customs), d. 116 (wedding celebrations), d. 132 (general research), d. 135 (living conditions), d. 143 (religion and the economy); f. 2, op. 2, d. 5 (wedding ceremonies), d. 22 (celebrations and living conditions), d. 30 (weddings), d. 34 (sorcerers and sorcery), d. 35 (weddings and other celebrations), d. 38 (popular tales on the occult), d. 39 (superstitions), d. 40 (weddings), d. 42 (sorcery).

20. Iakov A. Iakovlev, *Derevnia kak ona est'* (Moscow: Krasnaia nov', 1924), vi; Iakov A. Iakovlev, *Nasha derevnia: Novoe v starom i staroe v novom* (Moscow: Krasnaia nov', 1924), 1.

21. Gurevich, "Etnografiia i izuchenie istorii kul'turnoi revoliutsii v SSSR," in Kim, *Kul'turnaia revoliutsiia v SSSR*, 252.

22. *Etnografiia* 1–2 (1926): 45–46; *Antireligioznik* 4 (April 1926): 14–15.

23. *Antireligioznik* 2 (February 1926): 31–32.

24. *Voinstvuiushchii ateizm* 12 (December 1931): 3.

25. RTsKhIDNI, f. 17. op. 60, d. 158, ll. 1–2, 5–9, 17–18, and esp. 23–25.

26. P. Rulin, "Komsomol'tsy dvadtsatogo goda," in *Raduga trekh gor* (Moscow: Moskovskii rabochii, 1967), 179. For representative examples of articles on popular science in antireligious journals, see *Bezbozhnik* 50 (2 December 1923): 2; *Nash bezbozhnik* 11 (25 June 1925): 1; *Bezbozhnik u stanka* 1 (1929): 18–20. Although the full public reaction is impossible to assess, one observer noted that youth were more drawn to novels and works that directly affected agriculture and *byt* than to books of a purely natural-science character. Murin, *Byt i nravy derevenskoi molodezhi*, 27–28.

27. *Na putiakh k novoi shkole* 5 (March 1923): 36.

28. *Rabotnitsa* 1 (January 1923): 20–22; 2 (February 1923): 19–20; 3 (March 1923): 18–19; 4 (April 1923): 22.

29. *Sredne-volzhskii bezbozhnik* 13 (20–30 March 1931): 4.

30. *Radio v derevne* 4 (1–10 February 1930): 2.

31. *Radio v derevne* (11 December 1927) (trial issue): 1, 2, 4; 1 (1 January 1928): 2–3; 2 (8 January 1928): 1; 4 (22 January 1928): 1; 10 (4 March

1928): 1; 52 (23 December 1928): 1; A. N. Bryzgalov, *Onezhskii zavod* (Petrozavodsk: Gosudarstvennoe izdatel'stvo Karel'skoi ASSR, 1957), 29. See also GARF, f. 5407, op. 1, d. 90, l. 21.

32. Segal, *Religiia i znakharstvo,* 9. Beyond the claims made in its content, this source also communicates hostility through the language it uses. For example, to refer to the communion cloth, called a *plat,* the author uses a common term for "rag" [*triapka*].

33. *Nash bezbozhnik* 7–8 (28 May 1924): 6.

34. *Rabochaia gazeta* 2 (3 January 1925): 4.

35. V. E. Ignat'ev, *Gigena v shkole* (Moscow: Rabotnik prosveshcheniia, 1925), 5–16, 27–41.

36. A. M. Bol'shakov, *Ocherki derevnia SSSR, 1917–1927* (Moscow: Rabochii prosveshcheniia, 1928), 173.

37. *Antireligioznik* 1 (January 1928): 32–40; 2 (February 1928): 61–62.

38. A. M. Bol'shakov, *Derevnia, 1917–1927* (Moscow: Rabotnik prosveshcheniia, 1927), 292–95.

39. S. Lapitskaia, "Staryi i novyi byt: Otryvki iz istorii Trekhgornoi manufaktury," in L. Aberbakh, ed., *Shestnadtsat' zavodov* (Moscow: Istoriia zavodov, 1934), 522–25, 528–29.

40. Marietta S. Shaginian, *Fabrika Tornton [Krasnyi tkach]* (Moscow: TsK Soiuza tekstil'shchikov, 1927), 46–50.

41. RTsKhIDNI, f. 17, op. 32, d. 142, ll. 18–19.

42. The full range of resistance to collectivization as cultural conflict is masterfully analyzed in Viola, *Peasant Rebels under Stalin.* The cultural dynamics of resistance to so-called tractorization are discussed in Matt Oja, "*Traktorizatsiia* as Cultural Conflict, 1929–1933," *Russian Review* 51 (July 1992): 343–62.

43. *Ateist* 37 (February 1929): 48–53, 71. In an effort to battle Egor'ev Day practices, the journal *Bezbozhnik* devoted its entire first page to a depiction of a priest administering incense to a field while holding his other hand cupped to receive surreptitious payment from a peasant. *Bezbozhnik* 1 (January 1925): 1.

44. For example, see the pictorial representation in *Bezbozhnik* 43 (14 October 1923): 1. This print, which covers two-thirds of the cover, shows a peasant whose tractor grinds up a church over the impotent protests of the priest. Also, an instruction of 1 December 1924 from the Party Central Committee to the Komsomol specifically called for linking antireligious work to the teaching of agriculture and natural science. *Kommunisticheskaia partiia Sovetskogo soiuza v rezoliutsiiakh:* vol. 3, *1922–1925,* 307. *Bezbozhnik* 28 (1 July 1923): 6 suggests an emphasis on agricultural instruction as a preferred mechanism for injecting "antireligious propaganda with requisite caution in the countryside."

45. GARF, f. 5407, op. 1, d. 11, l. 7.

46. RTsKhIDNI, f. 17, op. 60, d. 791, ll. 4–5, 11.

47. *Spravochnik partiinogo rabotnika, vyp.* 5 (Moscow-Leningrad: Gosudarstvennoe izdatel'stvo , 1926), 424.

48. *Bezbozhnik* 165 (28 March 1926): 2.

49. *Bezbozhnik* 166 (4 April 1926): 7.

50. *Bezbozhnik* 80 (27 July 1924): 3; *Nash bezbozhnik* 4 (22 February 1925): 4; 8 (31 May 1925): 4; 3 (9 April 1926): 1.

51. F. Oleshchuk, *XVII s"ezd VKP(b) i zadachi antireligioznoi raboty* (Moscow: Gosudarstvennoe antireligioznoe izdatel'stvo, 1934), 28–29.

52. *Derevenskii bezbozhnik* 1 (March 1928): 1.

53. *Bezbozhnik u stanka* 1 (1929): 3.

54. Rosnitskii, *Polgoda v derevne,* 183.

55. On the separation of these spheres, see G. A. Bordiugov, "Nekotorye problemy kul'tury byta v kontse 20-kh–30-e gody," in Borisov, *Dukhovnyi potentsial SSSR nakanune Velikoi Otechestvennoi Voiny: Iz istorii sovetskoi kul'-tury 1917–1941 gg.,* 172–78, 181–82; R. F. Filippova, "K istorii otdeleniia shkoly i tserkvi," in *Po etapam razvitiia ateizma v SSSR* (Leningrad: Nauka, 1967), 92–93.

56. *Kul'turnoe stroitel'stvo v RSFSR,* 1 (1):2–25.

57. *Kommunisticheskaia partiia Sovetskogo soiuza v rezoliutsiiakh:* vol. 2, *1918–1922,* 114; Okulov et al., *Ateizm v SSSR,* 125; Larry E. Holmes, *The Kremlin and the Schoolhouse: Reforming Education in Soviet Russia, 1917–1931* (Bloomington: Indiana University Press, 1991), 27–43 and passim.

58. Okulov et al., *Ateizm v SSSR,* 123.

59. *O religii i tserkvi,* 55–56, 122–23; *Kommunisticheskaia partiia i sovetskoe pravitel'stvo o religii i tserkvi,* 44.

60. V. A. Kozlov, *Kul'turnaia revoliutsiia i krest'ianstvo, 1921–1927 (Po materialam Evropeiskoi chasti RSFSR)* (Moscow: Nauka, 1983), 21–22.

61. Okulov et al., *Ateizm v SSSR,* 124. See also P. G. Ryndziunskii, "Bor'ba za preodolenie religioznykh vliianii v sovetskoi shkole (1917–1919 gg.)," in *Voprosy istorii religii i ateizma: Sbornik statei, III* (Moscow: Izdatel'stvo akademii nauk, 1955), 47–86.

62. I. G. Batiuk, "Preodoelnie religioznykh perezhitkov v soznanii liudei," in Kim, *Kul'turnaia revoliutsiia v SSSR,* 237; Persits, *Otdelenie tserkvi ot gosudarstva i shkoly ot tserkvi v SSSR,* 39. Chronic shortages of paper inhibited textbook publication not only at the outset but for the entire decade of the 1920s. See *Stenograficheskii otchet vtorogo vsesoiuznogo s"ezda voinstvuiushchikh bezbozhnikov,* 132.

63. Persits, *Otdelenie tserkvi ot gosudarstva i shkoly ot tserkvi v SSSR,* 39–40, 126; *Russkaia Pravoslavnaia Tserkov' i Kommunisticheskoe Gosudarstvo, 1917–1941,* ed. Shchapov, comp. Vasil'eva, 32; Filippova, "K istorii otdeleniia shkoly i tserkvi," in *Po etapam razvitiia ateizma v SSSR,* 89–90.

64. *Vestnik prosveshcheniia* 1–3 (1919): 67.

65. *Revoliutsiia i kul'tura* 15 (1927): 22; Okulov et al., *Ateizm v SSSR,* 120; Batiuk, "Preodoelnie religioznykh perezhitkov v soznanii liudei," in Kim, *Kul'turnaia revoliutsiia v SSSR,* 238–40.

66. Kostitsyn, *Trudiashchaia zhenshchina i religiia,* 76.

67. RTsKhIDNI, f. 17, op. 2, d. 142, l. 27.

68. Larry E. Holmes, "Fear No Evil: Schools and Religion in Soviet Russia, 1917–1941," in Ramet, *Religious Policy in the Soviet Union*, 135–36. I thank Professor Holmes for sharing his essay with me while it was still in press.

69. A. Kanva, "Obraztsovaia iacheika," in Tan-Bogoraz, *Komsomol v derevne*, 23; *Kommunisticheskaia partiia Sovetskogo soiuza v rezoliutsiiakh i resheniiakh:* vol. 2, *1918–1922*, 448–51; *Bezbozhnik* 243 (9 October 1927): 7; N. A. Krylov, "Iz istorii propagandy ateizma v SSSR (1923–1925 gg.)," in *Voprosy istorii religii i ateizma: Sbornik statei, VIII* (Moscow: Akademiia Nauk SSSR, 1960), 172; M. Ia. Fenomenov, *Izuchenie byta derevni v shkole (Issledovatel'skaia kraevedcheskaia rabota po obshchestvovedeniiu)* (Moscow: Rabotnik prosveshcheniia, 1926), 48–50.

70. Okulov et al., *Ateizm v SSSR*, 121.

71. GARF, f. 5407, op. 1, d. 8, l. 10.

72. *Na putiakh k novoi shkole* 2 (September 1922): 35–36; Holmes, "Fear No Evil," in Ramet, *Religious Policy in the Soviet Union*, 131.

73. *Bezbozhnik* 102 (4 January 1925): 6.

74. *Trinadtsatyi s"ezd RKP(b), mai 1924 goda: Stenograficheskii otchet*, 470–71.

75. GMIR, folder 81, l. 14; Kostitsyn, *Trudiashchaia zhenshchina i religiia*, 76–78; *Bezbozhnik* 284 (22 July 1928): 1; 293 (23 September 1928): 1.

76. RTsKhIDNI, f. 89, op. 4, d. 26, l. 3; f. 17, op. 32, d. 142, l. 27; *Antireligioznik* 3 (March 1928): 59–60. Those familiar with the role of teachers in the attempts to secularize education in Mexico and France will note important differences from the Russian case. During the early 1930s, the Mexican Ministry of Education and various state committees purged thousands of teachers and civil servants solely on the basis of their religious beliefs, and teachers played an instrumental role in the effort to undermine religion. As in Russia, antireligious teachers were vulnerable to terrorism, especially in rural areas. Adrian Bantjes, "Idolatry and Iconoclasm in Revolutionary Mexico: The Dechristianization Campaigns, 1929–1940," *Mexican Studies/Estudios Mexicanos* 13 (winter 1997): 108–13, 116. See also Jean Meyer, *La Cristiada* (1974; reprint, Mexico City: Siglo Veintiuno Editores, S.A., 1979), 3:272–75; David C. Bailey, *¡Viva Cristo Rey! The Cristero Rebellion and Church-State Conflict in Mexico* (Austin: University of Texas Press, 1974), 296. During the nineteenth century in France, Restoration authorities sided with the church and ecclesiastical education. Local populations most often supported lay teachers when they encountered pressures exerted by local notables. Once carried out, though, the reestablishment of clerical elementary education did not necessarily provoke sharp local opposition, especially as nuns replaced lay female teachers, and working-class anticlericalism proved frequently to be grounded in economic rather than religious concerns. Roger Magraw, "The Conflict in the Villages: Popular Anticlericalism in the Isère (1852–70)," in Theodore Zeldin, ed., *Conflicts in French Society: Anticlericalism, Education and Morals in the Nineteenth Century* (London: Allen and Unwin, 1970), 169–227, esp. 193–202, 217–19.

77. *Narodnoe prosveshchenie* 39–41 (1918): 4.

78. Smolensk Archive, WKP 458: 44, 44 ob., 45; RTsKhIDNI, f. 89, op. 4, d. 116, ll. 10–13; Okulov et al., *Ateizm v SSSR,* 120; Holmes, "Fear No Evil," in Ramet, *Religious Policy in the Soviet Union,* 128, 134; Batiuk, "Preodoelnie religioznykh perezhitkov v soznanii liudei," in Kim, *Kul'turnaia revoliutsiia v SSSR,* 239–40.

79. Kostitsyn, *Trudiashchaia zhenshchine i religiia,* 74–75.

80. Bol'shakov, *Derevnia, 1917–1927,* 228, 233.

81. Iakovlev, *Derevnia kak ona est',* 8.

82. *Sredne-volzhskii bezbozhnik* 31 (20–30 September 1931): 1.

83. *Derevnia na novykh putiakh: Andreevskaia volost' Kostromskoi gubernii i uezda (Materialy obsledovaniia)* (Kostroma: Izdanie Kostromskogo Gubkoma RKP[b], 1925), 173–77.

84. Iakovlev, *Derevnia kak ona est',* 95.

85. *Bezbozhnik* 298 (28 October 1928): 6.

86. V. G. Tan-Bogoraz, "Staryi i novyi byt," in Tan-Bogoraz, ed., *Staryi i novyi byt: Sbornik* (Leningrad: Gosudarstvennoe izdatel'stvo, 1924), 23.

87. Holmes, "Fear No Evil," in Ramet, *Religious Policy in the Soviet Union,* 136.

88. RTsKhIDNI, f. 17, op. 85, d. 16, l. 167; Rosnitskii, *Polgoda v derevne,* 172–76; *Voprosy truda* 9 (September 1924): 24.

89. *Sredne-volzhskii bezbozhnik* 5 (9 November 1930): 1.

90. GARF, f. 5407, op. 1, d. 14, ll. 5–9; RTsKhIDNI, f. 89, op. 4, d. 124, ll. 1, 2, 2 ob.

91. *Bezbozhnik* 243 (9 October 1927): 1. Nadezhda Krupskaia defended her approach in "O bezreligioznoi vospitanii v shkole," *Antireligioznik* 10 (October 1927): 20–22. Beginning with the March 1928 issue, *Antireligioznik* instituted a special section on antireligious education in the schools, which continued until the end of the Cultural Revolution.

92. RTsKhIDNI, f. 89, op. 4, d. 26, ll. 6–9.

93. Rosnitskii, *Polgoda v derevne,* 184; *Bezbozhnik* 294 (30 September 1928): 1.

94. GARF, f. 5407, op. 1, d. 48, ll. 50–82, esp. 50–53, 66, 70, 77, 80–82.

95. *Bezbozhnik u stanka* 8 (1929): 2.

96. GMIR, folder 81, l. 1.

97. *Bezbozhnik* 4 (February 1930): 5.

98. Holmes, "Fear No Evil," in Ramet, *Religious Policy in the Soviet Union,* 139–44; *Bezbozhnik u stanka* 8 (1929): 22.

99. Rosnitskii, *Polgoda v derevne,* 186.

100. GARF, f. 5263, op. 1, d. 21, ll. 179 ob., 180.

101. *Bezbozhnik* 102 (4 January 1925): 6.

102. Rosnitskii, *Polgoda v derevne,* 177–79.

103. *Na putiakh k novoi shkole* 3 (November 1922): 79–81.

104. Rosnitskii, *Polgoda v derevne,* 183–85.

105. *Pravda,* 16 May 1934, 1.

106. Okulov et al., *Ateizm v SSSR*, 164–67, 170, 175–76.

107. V. V. Veresaev, *Polnoe sobranie sochinenii* (Moscow: Nedra, 1929), 8:201–4, 220–21.

108. Nikolai K. Amosov, *O p'ianykh prazdnikakh* (Moscow: Bezbozhnik, 1929), 5–6.

109. Nikolai N. Rumiantsev, *O prestol'nykh prazdnikakh* (Moscow: GAIZ, 1939), 4.

110. *Prazdniki i sviatye russkogo pravoslaviia* (Moscow: Soros, 1992), 1. For the feasts of Ivan Kupalo and other pagan survivals, see Ivanits, *Russian Folk Belief,* 1–18 and passim.

111. Shevzov, "Universal, National and Local Feasts," passim.

112. *Prazdniki i sviatye russkogo pravoslaviia,* 1.

113. Segal, *Religiia i znakharstvo,* 11.

114. TsGAMO, f. 66, d. 631, ll. 1–2, 4. See also Neil Weissman, "Prohibition and Alcohol Control in the USSR: The 1920s Campaign against Illegal Spirits," *Soviet Studies* 3 (July 1986): 349–68; Helena Stone, "The Soviet Government and Moonshine, 1917–1929," *Cahiers du monde russe et soviétique* 3–4 (July–December 1986): 359–80; Stephen White, *Russia Goes Dry: Alcohol, State and Society* (Cambridge: Cambridge University Press, 1996), 15–27.

115. *Bezbozhnik* 13 (25 March 1928): 5.

116. Amosov, *O p'ianykh prazdnikakh,* 3–5, 10 (the quotation is on 4); Kostitsyn, *Trudiashchaia zhenshchina i religiia,* 60, 62–65. For a vivid and detailed description of holiday celebrations in Tver' province, see Helmut Altrichter, "Insoluble Conflicts: Village Life between Revolution and Collectivization," in Sheila Fitzpatrick, Alexander Rabinowitch, and Richard Stites, eds., *Russia in the Era of NEP: Explorations in Soviet Society and Culture* (Bloomington: Indiana University Press, 1991), 195–200; Helmut Altrichter, *Die Bauern von Tver: Vom Leben auf dem russichen Dorge zwischen Revolution und Kollektivierung* (Munich: R. Oldenbourg Verlag, 1984), 100–111.

117. *Volzhskii bezbozhnik* 30 (10–20 September 1931): 2. For an example of antialcohol propaganda from a newspaper of another type, see *Radio v derevne* 44 (28 October 1928): 1.

118. *Bezbozhnik* 1 (January 1931): 4–5.

119. *Sredne-volzhskii bezbozhnik* 2 (22 August 1930): 2.

120. *Volzhskii bezbozhnik* 11 (20–30 February 1931): 3; *Antireligioznik* 2 (January 1932): 31.

121. GARF, f. 5457, op. 3, d. 57, l. 21.

122. Kostitsyn, *Trudiashchaia zhenshchina i religiia,* 42–46.

123. *Bezbozhnik* 273 (6 May 1928): 5. Similar gains for the anti-Christmas campaign of 1928 were reported in *Bezbozhnik u stanka* 3 (1929): 2.

124. Kostitsyn, *Trudiashchaia zhenshchina i religiia,* 62.

125. GARF, f. 5407, op. 1, d. 14, l. 4; *Antireligioznik* 12 (December 1926): 41. The journal does not present evidence to support its further opinion: that the majority who participated might not be far from atheism. See also GARF, f. 5407, op. 1, d. 7, l. 38.

126. Murin, *Byt i nravy derevenskoi molodozhi,* 38–39; S. Abramson, "Komsomol'skaia derevnia," in Tan-Bogoraz, *Komsomol v derevne,* 10; S. Makar'ev, "Komsomol Prionezh'ia," in Tan-Bogoraz, *Komsomol v derevne,* 92.

127. GARF, f. 5263, op. 1, d. 21, ll. 179 ob., 180.

128. GMIR, folder 202, l. 1.

129. Okulov et al., *Ateizm v SSSR,* 171.

130. The mass festivities attached to Bolshevik holidays, including the transformation of public festivals and symbols, is the subject of James von Geldern, *Bolshevik Festivals, 1917–1920* (Berkeley: University of California Press, 1993), 46–47, 61, 79–86, 137, 145, 154–55, and passim.

131. GARF, f. 353, op. 7, d. 2, l. 4; *Voprosy truda* 1 (January 1924): 12, 14, 16. On the reaction of the peasantry, see Fitzpatrick, *Stalin's Peasants,* 207. The calendar of proposed legal holidays in 1929 included New Year's (three days); Day of the 1905 Revolution (one day); Overthrow of the Autocracy (one day); Paris Commune (one day); May Day (three days); Constitution Day (three days); and the Anniversary of the Revolution (three days). *Bezbozhnik u stanka* 6 (1929): 20.

132. *Nash bezbozhnik* 10 (27 October 1927): 3; 12 (22 December 1927): 3; *Volzhskii bezbozhnik* 15 (1–10 April 1931): 1; 18 (1–10 May 1931): 3; 32 (1–10 December 1931): 1; Murin, *Byt i nravy derevenskoi molodozhi,* 42; Shabalin, *Krasnyi treugol'nik,* 191; Abramson, "Komsomol'skaia derevnia," in Tan-Bogoraz, *Komsomol v derevne,* 16; Amosov, *O p'ianykh prazdnikakh,* 24. Complaints that appeared in the antireligious press as late as 1941 indicate that the rural dimension of the problem was not easily eradicated. Drunkenness associated with summer religious holidays actually increased after collectivization and was considered more serious, since whole collectives and not just individual farms participated. *Bezbozhnik* 19 (11 May 1941): 1.

133. Kanva, "Obraztsovaia iacheika," in Tan-Bogoraz, *Komsomol v derevne,* 42–43.

134. Okulov et al., *Ateizm v SSSR,* 173.

135. Makar'ev, "Komsomol Proinezh'ia," in Tan-Bogoraz, *Komsomol v derevne,* 105; *Antireligioznik* 7 (1929): 91; *Nash Bezbozhnik* 2 (25 January 1925): 2; Murin, *Byt i nravy derevenskoi molodozhi,* 47.

136. *Radio v derevne* 52 (23 December 1928): 1.

137. *Sredne-volzhskii bezbozhnik* 3 (20 September 1930): 2. For a similar assessment by the chairman of the rural soviet in Kemennyi raion, see *Kommunisticheskaia molodezh'* 9–10 (May 1933): 23.

138. *Sredne-volzhskii bezbozhnik* 1 (11 August 1930): 3.

139. *Voprosy truda* 1 (January 1924): 11–12.

140. *Bezbozhnik* 35 (19 August 1923): 1; *Antireligioznik* 2 (1930): 19–22.

141. GARF, f. 5263, op. 1, d. 2, ll. 12–13, 13 ob., 15–18; d. 7, l. 18; d. 14, l. 75; d. 19, l. 143.

142. *Sredne-volzhskii bezbozhnik* 1 (11 August 1930): 1.

143. GMIR, folder 202, l. 9.

144. *Volzhskii bezbozhnik* 10 (1–10 February 1931): 3.

145. *Bezbozhnik* 31 (22 July 1923): 3; A. Gagarin, *Khoziaistvo, zhizn' i nastroenie derevni (Po itogam obsledovaniia Pochinkovskoi volosti Smolenskoi gubernii)* (Moscow-Leningrad: Gosudarstvennoe izdatel'stvo, 1925), 83; *Derevnia na novykh putiakh*, 226–28.

146. Bol'shakov, *Derevnia, 1917–1927*, 389–99; M. Ia. Fenomenov, *Sovremennaia derevnia: Opyt kraevedcheskogo obsledovaniia odnoi derevni*, part 2 (Moscow-Leningrad: Gosudarstvennoe izdatel'stvo, 1925), 20–27.

147. *Pravda* quoted in Veresaev, *Polnoe sobranie sochinenii*, 8:212–13.

148. Iakovlev, *Derevnia kak ona est'*, 97.

149. Okulov et al., *Ateizm v SSSR*, 169.

150. *Khudozhestvennyi fol'klor* 2–3 (1927): 96–102.

151. Okulov et al., *Ateizm v SSSR*, 169.

152. *Revoliutsiia i tserkov'* 1–3 (1923): 35.

153. Soviet authorities refused all three requests. *Revoliutsiia i tserkov'* 2 (1919): 37.

154. Gregory L. Freeze, "L'ortodossia russe e la crisi delle famiglie. Il divorzio in Russia tra la rivoluzione e la guerre (1917–1921)" [Russian Orthodoxy and Family Breakdown: Divorce in Revolution and War, 1917–1921], in Adalberto Mainardi, ed., *L'Autunno della Santa Russia, 1917–1945. Atti del VI Convegno ecumenico internazionale spiritualita russa, Bose 16–19 settembre* (Magnano, Italy: Qigajou, 1999).

155. Nina Tumarkin, *Lenin Lives! The Lenin Cult in Soviet Russia* (Cambridge, Mass.: Harvard University Press, 1983), 174–76.

156. Brudnyi, *Obriady vchera i segodnia*, 67; Murin, *Byt i nravy derevenskoi molodozhi*, 43–44, 46.

157. GARF, f. 5263, op. 1, d. 12, ll. 8, 8 ob.; f. 5407, op. 1, d. 158, l. 43.

158. L. A. Tul'tseva, *Sovremennye prazdniki i obriady narodov SSSR* (Moscow: Nauka, 1985), 14–31; Brudnyi, *Obriady vchera i segodnia*, 68–71; Murin, *Byt i nravy derevenskoi molodozhi*, 45; Shabalin, *Krasnyi treugol'nik*, 256–57; *Ocherki istorii Leningradskoi organizatsii VLKSM* (Leningrad: Lenizdat, 1969), 128; *Bezbozhnik* 31 (22 July 1923): 1; 48 (18 November 1923): 2. See also GARF, f. 5407, op. 1, d. 7, l. 55.

4: SOVIET FAMILY VALUES

1. See Bol'shakov, *Derevnia, 1917–1927*, ii, vi; *Bezbozhnik* 102 (2 January 1925): 6; Iakovlev, *Nasha derevnia*, 127–35; V. Nikol'skii, *Sueverie, zhakharstvo, religioznye predrassudki i sovetskaia meditsina* (Moscow: Zhizn' i znanie, 1926), 5; Iakovlev, *Derevnia kak ona est'*, 79; Tan-Bogoraz, *Staryi i novyi byt*, 12; GARF, f. 5407, op. 1, d. 52, ll. 40–41. See also Mark von Hagen, *Soldiers in the Proletarian Dictatorship: The Red Army and the Soviet Socialist State, 1917–1930* (Ithaca, N.Y.: Cornell University Press, 1990), 298–303. One example of a stereotype based on age portrays an elderly peasant employing

labor-intensive agriculture while a young atheist sits aboard a tractor. *Bezbozh-nik* 223 (10 May 1927): 1. Other stereotypes did not stand up so consistently. Although the allegiance of the poorest peasant [*bedniak*] to Bolshevism was a stock element of public discourse, internal party studies on the mood of the peasantry conveyed a different picture to the leadership. A 1926 report on the situation in Kursk province, for example, notes a strong correlation between poverty and a lack of enthusiasm for Soviet power. RTsKhIDNI, f. 17. op. 85, d. 16, ll. 29–32.

2. *Radio v derevne* 46 (11 November 1928): 1; 52 (23 December 1928): 1; 26 (30 June 1929): 1; 45 (7 November 1929): 1; *Bezbozhnik* 316 (3 March 1929): 4; *Bezbozhnik u stanka* 2 (1929): 3; *Bezbozhnik* 1 (January 1934): 2–3; *Antireligioznik* 1 (January 1926): 8–11; Amosov, *O p'ianykh prazdnikakh,* 1–2; F. Oleshchuk, "Stroite i krepite Soiuz Bezbozhnikov!" in *Antireligioznyi sbornik* (Moscow: Bezbozhnik, 1928), 28–29; A. I. Gukovskii and O. V. Trakht-enberg, *Kratkii uchebnik po istorii razvitiia obshchestvennykh form, II-e izdanie* (Moscow: Izdatel'stvo kommunisticheskogo universiteta imemi Ia. M. Sverdlova, 1928), 90.

3. See the reports for 1919–1923 in RTsKhIDNI, f. 5, op. 1, dd. 2618–56.

4. Tan-Bogoraz, *Staryi i novyi byt,* 5.

5. For an illustration of both the extent of the influence of the analytical categories of the 1920s and the degree to which they came to dominate later So-viet scholarship, see Kozlov, *Kul'turnaia revoliutsiia i krest'ianstvo, 1921–1927,* 143, and the works cited in 143 n. 118.

6. Similar assumptions, especially regarding the religiosity of women, informed the antireligious aspirations of the Mexican and French Revolutions. See Bantjes, "Idolatry and Iconoclasm in Revolutionary Mexico," 87–120, esp. 94–96; Jim Tuck, *The Holy War in Los Altos: A Regional Analysis of Mexico's Cristero Rebellion* (Tucson: University of Arizona Press, 1982), 12–13. See also Adrian A. Bantjes, *As If Jesus Walked on Earth: Cardenismo, Sonora, and the Mexican Revolution* (Wilmington, Del.: Scholarly Resources, 1988); Robert E. Quirk, *The Mexican Revolution and the Catholic Church, 1910–1929* (Bloomington: Indiana University Press, 1973).

7. A. Kanva, "Obraztsovaia iacheika," in Tan-Bogoraz, *Komsomol v derevne,* 23–32.

8. S. Makar'ev, "Komsomol Prionezh'ia," in Tan-Bogoraz, *Komsomol v derevne,* 104–5.

9. For an example of such thinking, see A. L. Akulov and I. T. Vlasov, *Trudovoi stazh—60 let* (Moscow: Legkaia industriia, 1968), 39. The authors virtually equate culture with technical competence, characterize the majority of female migrants to the factories in the 1920s as illiterate, and complain that the new arrivals "didn't know production."

10. Wendy Z. Goldman, *Women, the State and Revolution: Soviet Family Policy and Social Life, 1917–1936* (Cambridge: Cambridge University Press, 1993), 56, 104, 208; David Hoffmann, *Peasant Metropolis: Social Identities in*

Moscow, 1929–1941 (Ithaca, N.Y.: Cornell University Press, 1994), 3, 31, 72, 87, 89–90, 115, 131, 133, 183–84. On the general issue of the passage from task-oriented to time-oriented labor and its social ramifications, the definitive argument is E. P. Thompson, "Time, Work-Discipline and Industrial Capitalism," in Thompson, *Customs in Common,* 352–403, esp. 358–59, 373–82.

11. *Tekstil'shchik* 9–10 (25 December 1918): 9–10; Goldman, *Women, the State and Revolution,* chap. 4.

12. [Rabkor] Glukhov, "O lenintse, sem'e i religii," *Rabochaia gazeta* 48 (27 February 1925): 6; *Rabochaia gazeta* 52 (4 March 1925): 5; Kostitsyn, *Trudiashchaia zhenshchina i religiia,* 79–93.

13. So persistently did the party publicize the idea that religion opposed the liberation of females, failed to recognize their rights, and belittled their dignity that the leading Baptist journal felt compelled to respond with three pages of biblical citations supportive of female equality. *Baptist* 3–4 (February 1926): 15–17.

14. *Nash bezbozhnik* 2 (25 January 1925): 1; *Bezbozhnik* 59 (17 February 1924): 2; 113 (24 March 1925): 2; 129 (19 June 1925): 3; 162 (7 March 1926): 6; 242 (2 October 1927): 1, 3; 248 (13 November 1927): 2; Oleshchuk, *XVII s"ezd VKP(b) i zadachi antireligioznoi raboty,* 21–22; L. Rakusheva, *Komsomol protiv religii* (Leningrad: Izdatel'stvo Leningradskogo soveta RKiKD, 1939), 29. See also *Stenograficheskii otchet vtorogo vsesoiuznogo s"ezda voinstvuiushchikh bezbozhnikov,* 7; *Antireligioznik* 2 (February 1927): 3–6; 1 (January 1932): 5; *Sredne-volzhskii bezbozhnik* 12 (1–10 March 1931): 1. Gender stereotypes were a staple of cartoons in *Bezbozhnik* and other publications. In "The Old and the New," elderly women cluster in the background of a peasant hut surrounded by icons and other religious objects. In the foreground, a healthy young male peasant sits before a hearth over which hangs a portrait of Lenin. He reads *Bezbozhnik* to the son who sits on his knee. *Bezbozhnik* 81 (3 August 1924): 8.

15. *Nash bezbozhnik* 1 (10 April 1924): 1; *Bezbozhnik* 143 (18 October 1925): 2.

16. Kostitsyn, *Trudiashchaia zhenshchina i religiia,* 49, 72.

17. GARF, f. 5407, op. 1, d. 24, l. 57. For more on the successful work of sectarians among women, see the coverage of the Fourteenth All-Russian Congress of Soviets in *Bezbozhnik* 329 (2 June 1929): 4.

18. *Antireligioznik* 2 (February 1930): 50–51. See also G. N. Serebrennikov, *Zhenskii trud v SSSR* (Moscow-Leningrad: Gosudarstvennoe sotsial'no-ekonomicheskoe izdatel'stvo, 1924), 93–108.

19. Kostitsyn, *Trudiashchaia zhenshchina i religiia,* 233–34. The delegate Kol'chevskaia gave a more generous assessment of *Rabotnitsa* and *Krest'ianka* at the second plenum of the Central Council of the League of Militant Atheists on 21 March 1930. She praised them for devoting the entirety of their most recent issues to antireligious matters. GARF, f. 5407, op. 1, d. 48, l. 30.

20. TsGAMO, f. 66, op. 18, d. 618, l. 2.

21. *Antireligioznik* 1 (January 1932): 5. No third all-union congress of the league ever took place.

22. *Nash bezbozhnik* 9 (24 June 1925): 1; *Bezbozhnik* 2 (January 1931): 7–8. Common estimates listed women as no more than one-fourth of the antireligious cadre, and there were frequent complaints that their proportion was decreasing. See, for example, GARF, f. 5407, op. 1, d. 8, l. 6.

23. V. Nosov, *Komsomol' i delegatka krest'ianka* (Moscow-Leningrad: Gosudarstvennoe izdatel'stvo, 1927).

24. Shabalin, *Krasnyi treugol'nik*, 243–46.

25. See the report on political work among women delivered to the Party Central Committee by one Comrade Kikolaeva. *Rabochaia gazeta* 6 (18 January 1925): 7.

26. Andrei Shokhin, *Komsomol'skaia derevnia* (Moscow-Leningrad: Molodaia gvardiia, 1923), 82–87. A *chastushka* is a topical song composed of couplets. Originated by peasants, these popular rhymes later entered urban mass culture, where, as in their village variation, they were used to express diverse emotions of love, humor, and social criticism. In the most common form, two thematically linked couplets constituted a verse. A *chastushka* could consist of a single verse; the most elaborate *chastushki* might contain dozens.

27. Murin, *Byt i nravy derevenskoi molodezhi*, 15–16.

28. GARF, f. 5407, op. 1, d. 35, ll. 85–86.

29. Kostitsyn, *Trudiashchaia zhenshchina i religiia*, 34–37.

30. GARF, f. 353, op. 5, d. 64, l. 3.

31. *Revoliutsiia i kul'tura* 3–4 (1928): 5–7.

32. *Voprosy truda* 12 (December 1925): 69–76.

33. Rakusheva, *Komsomol protiv religii*, 52.

34. *Derevnia na novykh putiakh*, 121.

35. V. Ershov, "Komsomolets v sem'e," in Tan-Bogoraz, *Komsomol v derevne*, 114.

36. See, for example, the sources from the 1920s cited uncritically in Kozlov, *Kul'turnaia revoliutsiia i krest'ianstvo, 1921–1927*, 150–54 nn. 149–64.

37. For example, Shokhin, *Komsomol'skaia derevnia*, 104; *Nash bezbozhnik* 18–19 (September 1924): 1.

38. *Antireligioznik* 10 (October 1929): 96–99.

39. *Bezbozhnik* 52 (16 December 1923): 3.

40. *Stenograficheskii otchet vtorogo vsesoiuznogo s"ezda voinstvuiushchikh bezbozhnikov*, 8, 9–10, 11–15; Peris, "The 1929 Congress of the Godless," 711–32; Piotrowski, "The League of the Militant Godless," 169–72.

41. *Bezbozhnik* 187 (5 September 1926): 4.

42. *Bezbozhnik* 162 (7 March 1926): 6.

43. S. Lapitskaia, *Byt rabochikh Trekhgornoi manufaktury* (Moscow: Istoriia zavodov, 1935), 71–77.

44. Ibid.; Kostitsyn, *Trudiashchaia zhenshchina i religiia*, 42–46.

45. *Bezbozhnik u stanka* 1 (1929): 21.

46. Lapitskaia, *Byt rabochikh Trekhgornoi manufaktury*, 128–38; S. Lapitskaia, "Staryi i novyi byt," in Aberbakh, *Shestnadtsat' zavodov*, 525, 528; Shabalin, *Krasnyi treugolnik*, 238. About half of the Prokhorov workers lived at

the plant before 1917, and the remainder found accommodations outside the enterprise in the Krasnaia Presnia section of the city. The nationalization of homes and apartments after 1917 influenced many to abandon the barracks; as a result, both the absolute numbers and the proportion of workers in the factory quarters fell. In spite of the influx of new laborers during the 1920s, fewer people (3,627) lived at the former Prokhorov factory in 1927 than had in 1913 (4,494).

47. S. Kostiuchenko, I. Khrepov, and Iu. Fedorov, *Istoriia Kirovskogo zavoda, 1917–1945* (Moscow: Mysl', 1966), 212–18.

48. Kostitsyn, *Trudiashchaia zhenshchina i religiia*, 42–46.

49. RTsKhIDNI, f. 17, op. 60, d. 791, ll. 31, 107–8.

50. *Voinstvuiushchii ateizm* 4 (April 1931): 47–50. See also Rassweiler, *Generation of Power*, 8, 85, 92–93, 110–15, 129.

51. Kostitsyn, *Trudiashchaia zhenshchina i religiia*, 39–40; *Bezbozhnik* 241 (25 September 1927): 7; *Antireligioznyi sbornik*, 28.

52. *Antireligioznik* 6 (June 1929): 89–93.

53. *Klub i revoliutsiia* 21–22 (November 1930): 41–42.

54. Tan-Bogoraz, *Staryi i novyi byt*, 11.

55. RTsKhIDNI, f. 17, op. 60, d. 777, ll. 112–14.

56. Tan-Bogoraz, *Staryi i novyi byt*, 17. For further discussion, see Altrichter, *Die Bauern von Tver*, 118–22.

57. *Bezbozhnik* 5 (March 1929): 7–9.

58. Kostitsyn, *Trudiashchaia zhenshchina i religiia*, 66–71. For a discussion of divination derived from dreams and random events, see Stephen P. Dunn and Ethel Dunn, *The Peasants of Central Russia* (New York: Holt, Rinehart and Winston, 1967), 27–29.

59. For example, *Nash bezbozhnik* 7 (18 April 1925): 5.

60. *Bezbozhnik* 1 (January 1925): 4; 2 (April 1925): 1–2. See also Frances L. Bernstein, "Envisioning Health in Revolutionary Russia: The Politics of Gender in Sexual-Enlightenment Posters of the 1920s," *Russian Review* 57 (April 1998): 213–15.

61. GARF, f. 5407, op. 1, d. 5, ll. 11–15.

62. *Bezbozhnik* 248 (13 November 1927): 2. Despite their reputation for trust in magical healers, peasants often included the inadequacy of rural medical care among the complaints they expressed in letters in the 1930s. Fitzpatrick, *Stalin's Peasants*, 217. On popular medicine, see Fenomenov, *Sovremennaia derevnia:* part 2, 83–87.

63. RTsKhIDNI, f. 17, op. 32, d. 142, ll. 25–27.

64. *Voprosy truda* 2 (February 1930): 13–14; Shaginian, *Fabrika Tornton*, 53.

65. Fitzpatrick, *Stalin's Peasants*, 204.

66. RTsKhIDNI, f. 89, op. 4, d. 26, l. 3.

67. *Revoliutsiia i tserkov'* 2 (1919): 37; 6–8 (1919): 15–17.

68. *O religii i tserkvi*, 56–57; *Pravda*, 31 March 1921, 1; *Stenograficheskii otchet vtorogo vsesoiuznogo s"ezda voinstvuiushchikh bezbozhnikov*, 222.

69. *Bezbozhnik* 63 (16 March 1924): 2.

70. *Bezbozhnik* 102 (4 January 1925): 6.

71. Kostitsyn, *Trudiashchaia zhenshchina i religiia,* 84–86.

72. *Rabochaia gazeta* 48 (25 February 1925): 6.

73. *Rabochaia gazeta* 52 (4 March 1925): 5.

74. *Stenograficheskii otchet vtorogo vsesoiuznogo s"ezda voin-stvuiushchikh bezbozhnikov,* 92.

75. Smolensk Archive, WKP 459: 1; *Derevnia na novykh putiakh,* 219–23.

76. Fisher, *Pattern for Soviet Youth,* 130–31.

77. S. Abramson, "Komsomol'skaia derevnia," in Tan-Bogoraz, *Komsomol v derevne,* 16.

78. *Nash bezbozhnik* 14 (26 November 1925): 1. See also *Nash bezbozhnik* 9 (24 September 1926): 1.

79. Kostitsyn, *Trudiashchaia zhenshchina i religiia,* 72–75. A noticeable number of Pioneers had also been in attendance when the railway workers' club of the Briansk Station (Moscow) in 1926 sponsored a lecture, "Are Miracles Possible?" *Antireligioznik* 9 (September 1926): 71. A different representation of Pioneers appears in G. A. Bordiugov, "Nekotorye problemy kul'tury byta v kontse 20-kh–30-e gody," in Borisov, *Dukhovnyi potentsial SSSR nakanune Velikoi Otechestvennoi Voiny: Iz istorii sovetskoi kul'tury 1917–1941 gg.,* 179.

80. Abramson, "Komsomol'skaia derevnia," in Tan-Bogoraz, *Komsomol v derevne,* 17; P. Bedov and N. Tumanov, *Kostromskii ekskavatornyi* (Kostroma: Rabochii metallist, 1965), 13–14; Murin, *Byt i nravy derevenskoi molodezhi,* 39–41.

81. GARF, f. 5407, op. 1, d., 12, ll. 19–21.

82. *Stenograficheskii otchet vtorogo vsesoiuznogo s"ezda voin-stvuiushchikh bezbozhnikov,* 71.

83. Ibid., 61. See also 50.

84. GARF, f. 353, op. 3, d. 739, l. 19; RTsKhIDNI, f. 17, op. 85, d. 16, l. 29; GARF, f. 5407, op. 1, d. 1, ll. 14 ob., 15.

85. *Bezbozhnik* 79 (20 July 1920): 3; *Nash bezbohnik* 14–15 (29 July 1924): 3; *Bezbozhnik u stanka* 5 (1929): 6, 20.

86. GMIR, folder 81, l. 19.

87. N. Bogdanova, "Navolotskaia durka (Ocherk s natury)," in Tan-Bogoraz, *Staryi i novyi byt,* 84.

88. Kostitsyn, *Trudiashchaia zhenshchina i religiia,* 82–86; *Derevnia na novykh putiakh,* 173–77; Rosnitskii, *Polgoda v derevne,* 219–27.

89. Veresaev, *Polnoe sobranie sochinenii,* 8:213.

90. For example, see *Nash bezbozhnik* 14–15 (29 July 1924): 3.

91. Tan-Bogoraz, *Staryi i novyi byt,* 18–24; Murin, *Byt i nravy derevenskoi molodezhi,* 33–38; Makar'ev, "Komsomol Prionezh'ia," in Tan-Bogoraz, *Komsomol v derevne,* 92–93; Iakovlev, *Nasha derevnia,* 127–35. Important work on the nexus of the behavior of urban and rural youth in the immediate prerevolutionary period is found in Neuberger, *Hooliganism,* 25–70, 107, 120, 125–28, and passim.

92. Tan-Bogoraz, *Staryi i novyi byt,* 18–24; Murin, *Byt i nravy dereven-skoi molodezhi,* 33–38; Makar'ev, "Komsomol Prionezh'ia," in Tan-Bogoraz, *Komsomol v derevne,* 92–93.

93. Tan-Bogoraz, *Staryi i novyi byt,* 18–24. There is intentional wordplay in the third line of the *chastushka* derived from the verb *pereviazat',* which can mean either to bandage or to tie up.

94. Murin, *Byt i nravy derevenskoi molodezhi,* 35–38.

95. *Derevnia na novykh putiakh,* 226–28; Iakovlev, *Derevnia kak ona est',* 97; Makar'ev, "Komsomol Prionezh'ia," in Tan-Bogoraz, *Komsomol v derevne,* 103.

96. This analysis is consistent with the view of mass advertising presented in Sally West, "The Material Promised Land: Advertising's Modern Agenda in Late Imperial Russia," *Russian Review* 57 (July 1998): 347. As West correctly notes, we cannot today measure accurately the actual influence even of mass messages.

97. GMIR, folder 202, ll. 48–50.

5: RESISTANCE, CIRCUMVENTION, ACCOMMODATION

1. Hindus, *Red Bread,* 34. The quotation is condensed without ellipses.

2. L. D., "Korennye sdvigi v mirovozzrenii trudiashchikhsia mass SSSR (Po materialam ikh neposredstvennykh vyskazyvanii)," in *Voinstvuiushchee bezbozhie v SSSR za 15 let, 1917–1932,* 221.

3. The extent and limitations of the success of this are discussed in von Hagen, *Soldiers in the Proletarian Dictatorship.*

4. Iakovlev, *Derevnia kak ona est',* 79.

5. *Antireligioznik* 11 (November 1926): 4; *Revoliutsiia i tserkov'* 3–5 (1919): 47–61.

6. GARF, f. 5407, op. 1, d. 5, l. 31; d. 7, ll. 88–93; d. 8, l. 19; d. 11, l. 7; RTsKhIDNI, f. 17, op. 60, d. 791, ll. 4–5. See also *Bezbozhnik* 20 (9 May 1923): 1.

7. GARF, f. 5263, op. 1, d. 3, ll. 35 ob.–36.

8. Iakovlev, *Derevnia kak ona est',* 12.

9. GARF, f. 5407, op. 1, d. 5, l. 9.

10. *Kommunisticheskaia revoliutsiia* 10 (1 July 1923): 48–53.

11. RTsKhIDNI, f. 89, op. 4, d. 115, l. 31.

12. Okulov et al., *Ateizm v SSSR,* 87.

13. GARF, f. 5407, op. 1, d. 8, l. 12.

14. *Bezbozhnik* 139 (20 September 1925): 7. Atheistic publications criticized the entire Soviet film establishment in 1928 for commercialism and catering to the "merchant public" instead of producing films of antireligious substance. *Antireligioznik* 5 (May 1928): 22–23.

15. *Bezbozhnik* 50 (2 December 1923): 2. A little more than a year later, Gorev, criticizing a lack of progress in producing a fully antireligious repertoire

and a reliance on vulgar songs popular in 1917–1918, revised his initial positive assessment and declared the level unworthy of the conditions of 1925. *Bezbozhnik* 104 (18 January 1925): 8. See also Stites, *Revolutionary Dreams,* 107–8.

16. GARF, f. 5407, op. 1, d. 2, l. 28; RTsKhIDNI, f. 89, op. 4, d. 116, ll. 3–5.

17. *Bezbozhnik* 125 (14 June 1925): 7; *Antireligioznik* 1 (January 1926): 5.

18. RTsKhIDNI, f. 89, op. 4, d. 116, ll. 10–13; f. 17, op. 60, d. 755, ll. 2–3.

19. *Bezbozhnik* 225 (5 June 1927): 7.

20. *Stenograficheskii otchet vtorogo vsesoiuznogo s"ezda voinstvuiushchikh bezbozhnikov,* 29.

21. *Pod znamenem Marksizma* 5 (May 1930): 56–57. Iaroslavskii expressed exactly the same point in *Antireligioznyi sbornik,* 3.

22. *Antireligioznik* 3 (March 1928): 3–24.

23. GARF, f. 5263, op. 1, d. 3, l. 55.

24. See, for example, GARF, f. 5263, op. 1, d. 2, l. 3; d. 3, l. 3; GMIR, folder 81, l. 1.

25. Typical of the course this new genre had run by the end of the Cultural Revolution is Zybkovets, *Ot sokhi k traktoru.*

26. Although the document could give no precise number of illegal church closings, at the end of the Cultural Revolution VTsIK chairman Mikhail Kalinin and VTsIK secretary A. Kiselev described the problem as extensive. GARF, f. 5263, op. 1, d. 21, l. 16.

27. GARF, f. 5263, op. 1, d. 15, ll. 1–14. GARF, f. 5263, op. 1, contains multiple files pertinent to church closings: Voronezh *oblast',* dd. 344–434; Vostochno-Sibirskii *krai,* dd. 435–52; Gor'kov *krai,* dd. 453–582; Dal'nye-Vostochnyi *krai,* dd. 583–87; Zapadnaia *oblast',* dd. 588–647; Leningrad *oblast',* dd. 988–1148; Moscow *oblast',* dd. 1149–427; Saratov *krai,* dd. 1468–85.

28. GARF, f. 5263, op. 1, d. 7, ll. 71–73.

29. Ibid., d. 6, ll. 12–16; d. 7, ll. 7, 72, 74.

30. Ibid., d. 7, ll. 5–5 ob., 9, 30, 70; d. 8, ll. 29–29 ob., 31.

31. Examples of rhetoric to this effect could be multiplied endlessly, but models typical of the genre are in *Derevenskii bezbozhnik* 1 (March 1928): 1; *Radio v derevne* 52 (23 December 1928): 1; *Bezbozhnik u stanka* 1 (1929): 6. When the League of Militant Atheists issued instructions on antireligious propaganda on 23 January 1930, the directive specifically spoke of religious organizations opposing the elimination of the kulaks as a class, and it ordered the liberation of *bedniaks* and *seredniaks* from "kulak religious influence." GARF, f. 5407, op. 1, d. 41, l. 1.

32. GARF, f. 5407, op. 1, d. 23, ll. 1–2; d. 90, l. 25; A. Bakurova, "Komsomol na antireligioznom fronte," in *Voinstvuiushchee bezbozhie v SSSR za 15 let, 1917–1932,* 310. Iaroslavskii is quoted in *Antireligioznyi sbornik,* 4.

33. GARF, f. 5407, op. 1, d. 39, ll. 12 ob.–13, 72; GMIR, folder 34, ll. 2–3, 5, 7–15, 18, 21; Smolensk Archive, WKP 460: 1–3; *Antireligioznik* 1 (Jan-

uary 1931): 6–8; 4 (April 1931): 3–4. According to A. Lukachevskii, there were 3,200 *bezbozhnik* shock brigades working in the countryside by 1931, 61 godless shops, 7 factories, and 300 collective farms. *Antireligioznik* 7 (July 1931): 3–4.

34. GARF, f. 5407, op. 1, d. 51, l. 210; RTsKhIDNI, f. 89, op. 4, d. 30, l. 1; d. 122, ll. 6, 6 ob.; *Bezbozhnik* 289 (26 August 1928): 1. For an example of the public face of antireligious activism, see the feature on the Matorin collective farm that declared its complete acceptance of atheism in *Bezbozhnik* 8 (August 1933): 12–15.

35. *Sredne-volzhskii bezbozhnik* 1 (11 August 1930): 3.

36. GARF, f. 5407, op. 1, d. 72, l. 80; S. Abramson, "Komsomol'skaia derevnia," in Tan-Bogoraz, *Komsomol v derevne,* 16–18; *Derevenskii bezbozhnik* 4 (June 1928): 5.

37. GARF, f. 5407, op. 1, d. 23, ll. 1–3.

38. Ibid., d. 87, l. 31; *Bezbozhnik u stanka* 7 (1929): 2; *Bezbozhnik* 271 (22 April 1928): 1; *Ocherki istorii Leningradskoi organizatsii VLKSM,* 192–95, 210–15; *Bezbozhnik u stanka* 10 (1929): 2. The mobilization of workers for collectivization is described in Viola, *Best Sons of the Fatherland.* For party members in antireligious work, see also GARF, f. 5407, op. 1, d. 14, l. 1.

39. *Bezbozhnik* 2 (January 1929): 11.

40. RTsKhIDNI, f. 89, op. 4, d. 129, ll. 7–19; GARF, f. 5407, op. 1, d. 87, l. 25; d. 95, ll. 59–62; *Antireligioznik* 1 (January–February 1933): 45.

41. For a discussion see Viola, *Peasant Rebels under Stalin,* 39–40.

42. *Bezbozhnik u stanka* 7 (1929): 17.

43. *Sredne-volzhskii bezbozhnik* 1 (11 August 1930): 3; GARF, f. 5407, op. 1, d. 41, ll. 1–3; d. 48, ll. 1–2; f. 5263, op. 1, d. 3, ll. 5–5 ob.; GMIR, folder 21, l. 3 ob. For a description of a specific incident of this type, see *Antireligioznik* 1 (1930): 33.

44. *Pod znamenem Marksizma* 5 (May 1930): 57–59; 10–12 (October–December 1930): 3–5. See, for example, GARF, f. 5407, op. 1, d. 48, l. 2.

45. GARF, op. 2, f. 353, d. 691, l. 160. In response to this question in the document cited here, the rapporteur listed two such incidents.

46. *Revoliutsiia i tserkov'* 1 (1919): 47.

47. *Bezbozhnik* 5–6 (21 January 1923): 1; 26 (17 June 1923): 1. See also *Antireligioznik* 6 (June 1929): 5; Iaroslavskii, *Protiv religii i tserkvi,* 1: 249, 363–64 n. 32.

48. RTsKhIDNI, f. 17. op. 85, d. 217, l. 92.

49. RTsKhIDNI, f. 89, op. 4, d. 26, ll. 1–2.

50. *Stenograficheskii otchet vtorogo vsesoiuznogo s"ezda voinstvuiushchikh bezbozhnikov,* 71; RTsKhIDNI, f. 17, op. 32, d. 142, l. 24. Other examples appear in GARF, f. 5407, op. 1, d. 45, ll. 32–33; *Pravda,* 6 February 1926, cited in *Bezbozhnik* 165 (28 March 1926); *Sredne-volzhskii bezbozhnik* 5 (9 November 1930): 4.

51. *Sredne-volzhskii bezbozhnik* 2 (22 August 1930): 2–3.

52. GMIR, folder 21, l. 8.

53. *Sredne-volzhskii bezbozhnik* 1 (11 August 1930): 3.

54. *Sredne-volzhskii bezbozhnik* 2 (22 August 1930): 2–3.

55. GARF, f. 5407, op. 1, d. 52, l. 61. See also Lynne Viola, *"Bab'i bunty* and Peasant Women's Protest during Collectivization," *Russian Review* 45 (1986).

56. *Antireligioznik* 1 (January 1930): 5.

57. RTsKhIDNI, f. 17, op. 32, d. 142, l. 24.

58. GARF, f. 5263, op. 1, d. 14, l. 126.

59. Ibid., d. 19, l. 211.

60. Ibid., d. 7, l. 59.

61. S. Kogen, ed., *Antireligioznyi sbornik* (Moscow: Moskovskii rabochii, 1940), 107.

62. See Lynne Viola, "The Peasant Nightmare: Visions of the Apocalypse in the Soviet Countryside," *Journal of Modern History* 62 (December 1990): 747–70.

63. *Kommunisticheskaia revoliutsiia* 10 (1 July 1923): 48–53.

64. GARF, f. 2306, op. 2, d. 402, ll. 70–76, cited in *Kul'turnoe stroitel'stvo v RSFSR,* 1 (1):106.

65. Kenez, *Civil War in South Russia,* 80.

66. *Nash bezbozhnik* 20–21 (4 October 1924): 5; 22–23 (29 November 1924): 1, 7.

67. *Antireligioznik* 7 (July 1926): 50.

68. GMIR, folder 81, l. 17.

69. Kostitsyn, *Trudiashchaia zhenshchina i religiia,* 49.

70. Examples of Bolshevik complaints regarding this practice can be found in GARF, f. 5263, op. 1, d. 22, l. 11; f. 5263, op. 1, d. 36, l. 84.

71. *Sredne-volzhskii bezbozhnik* 2 (22 August 1930): 2.

72. GMIR, folder 21, l. 6. For additional assessments of the role of apocalyptic rumor during collectivization, see GMIR, folder 81, l. 26.

73. *Sredne-volzhskii bezbozhnik* 5 (9 November 1930): 3.

74. GMIR, folder 21, l. 3. For further examples, see GMIR, folder 21, ll. 1 ob., 2, 2 ob.

75. GARF, f. 5407, op. 1, d. 52, l. 42.

76. Ibid., d. 35, l. 63; d. 8, l. 36. For an accusation that groups of Socialist-Revolutionaries and Mensheviks were also masquerading as cells of the Society of the Friends of the Newspaper *Bezbozhnik,* see GARF, f. 5407, op. 1, d. 7, l. 65.

77. E. Iaroslavskii, *Zadachi antireligioznoi propagandy v rekonstruktivnyi period* (Moscow-Leningrad: Moskovskii rabochii, 1931), 31.

78. In a broader sense, revolutionary legality, or socialist legal consciousness, was tied to issues of judicial discretion and the dictates of experience. For a discussion, see Peter H. Solomon, Jr., *Soviet Criminal Justice under Stalin* (Cambridge: Cambridge University Press, 1996), 25, 32.

79. GARF, f. 5263, op. 1, d. 3, l. 36.

80. Ibid., d. 3, ll. 35–36; d. 21, l. 16.

81. GARF, f. 5407, op. 1, d. 31, ll. 42, 42 ob.

82. GARF, f. 5263, op. 1, d. 19, ll. 10, 12–15, 21, 23–24, 33, 106.

83. TsGIAgM, f. 1215, op. 1, d. 344, ll. 3, 3 ob. See also ll. 4–61 for similar resolutions.

84. GARF, f. 353, op. 2, d. 706, ll. 46–47, 49, 49 ob., 64. Babaevo included settlements of railroad workers at Iashkomlevo, Rystsevo, Shiglino, and Nikol'skii Zavod.

85. This propensity to appeal directly to high authority, the report continues, thwarted the closing of churches even in industrial areas where the majority of workers had ceased observing religion. *Bezbozhnik* 23 (12 June 1929): 4. From the other camp, the *bezbozhnik* Golovkin complained to the league leadership in January 1930 that the constraints the soviet in Ivanovo-Voznesensk imposed upon activists in closing churches undermined all party goals. GARF, f. 5407, op. 1, d. 52, ll. 30–33. For classified reports by the political police on the mood of the population during collectivization and dekulakization, which include appeals to Kalinin, see *Rapports secrets soviétiques,* 112–48. Materials on Kalinin appear on 132, 134, 136, 137, 138, 140.

86. GARF, f. 353, op. 3, d. 737, ll. 11, 12, 12 ob. For a similar case in 1929, see GARF, f. 5263, op. 1, d. 4, l. 2.

87. TsGAMO, f. 4998, op. 1, d. 4, ll. 1–3.

88. TsGIAgM, f. 1215, op. 1, d. 339, ll. 6, 8–11.

89. TsGIAgM, f. 1215, op. 2, dd. 75–170; TsGAMO, f. 66, op. 18, dd. 320–44; GARF, f. 353, op. 4, d. 378, l. 102.

90. TsGIAgM, f. 1215, op. 3, dd. 1–128 all relate to the registration of churches or religious communes. See especially dd. 2, 6, 21, 101, 124. To compare the wording, see TsGIAgM, f. 1215, op. 1, d. 350, l. 11.

91. GARF, f. 5263, op. 1, d. 9, ll. 3, 7–10.

92. To trace the evolution of the Bolshevik reaction and the ways in which the party elected to publicize its concerns, see RTsKhIDNI, f. 89, op. 4, d. 115, ll. 26, 31, 49, 68; d. 119, ll. 9–37; d. 122, l. 6; f. 17, op. 60, d. 777, l. 113; d. 791, l. 5; GARF, f. 5407, op. 1, d. 20, ll. 25–50; *Bezbozhnik* 39 (16 September 1923): 1; 40 (23 September 1923): 1; 51 (9 December 1923): 2; 54 (6 January 1924): 7; 55 (13 January 1924): 6; 150 (6 December 1925): 2, 3–4; 217 (3 April 1927): 6; 261 (12 February 1928): 1; 289 (26 August 1928): 6; *Radio v derevne* 52 (23 December 1928): 1; *Bezbozhnik u stanka* 1 (1929): 17; 14 (1929): 14; *Kommunisticheskaia partiia i sovetskoe pravitel'stvo o religii i tserkvi,* 67–68.

93. RTsKhIDNI, f. 89, op. 4, d. 26, ll. 1–4. See also GARF, f. 5407, op. 1, d. 20, ll. 107, 148; *Bezbozhnik u stanka* 4 (1929): 9; 7 (1929): 17.

94. RTsKhIDNI, f. 89, op. 4, d. 124, ll. 1, 1 ob., 2.

95. GARF, f. 353, op. 2, d. 690, ll. 110–11; op. 5, d. 20, passim; f. 5407, op. 1, d. 9, l. 43; f. 5263, op. 1, d. 19, ll. 217–19; *Bezbozhnik* 23 (27 May 1923): 6; 52 (25 December 1927): 7; *Revoliutsiia i tserkov'* 1–3 (1923): 13–15; *Baptist* 1 (1927): 19; 3 (1927): 23–24. Accusations of opportunism came not

only from Soviet power but from denominations themselves, as when Baptists called attention to individuals and communes who appealed to the Union of Baptists for support; in some cases the appeals were from people who had come to the Union in the expectation that it would provide their train fare home. *Baptist* 4–5 (April–May 1925): 57.

96. GARF, f. 5407, op. 1, d. 7, l. 89.

97. GARF, f. 5263, op. 1, d. 3, ll. 100–101, 105, 109–13 ob.

98. Ibid., d. 7, l. 71.

99. Ibid., d. 7, l. 14.

100. Ibid., d. 27, ll. 84, 91–94. See also TsGAMO, f. 4570, op. 1, d. 29, passim.

101. GARF, f. 5263, op. 1, d. 8, ll. 52, 60. The order to correct this loophole was issued by the VTsIK Secretariat only on 13 December 1934.

102. Ibid., d. 3, ll. 53–54.

103. Ibid. The quotation is on ll. 53.

104. Ibid., d. 3, l. 47. This report illustrates that local Bolsheviks also knew how to manipulate the prejudices of their superiors. In addition to their mention of anti-Semitism, emphasizing that the demonstrators were predominantly female played directly on the prevailing party assumption that rural women were the most backward element in society and, not coincidentally, the chief repository of religiosity.

105. Ibid., d. 30, ll. 66, 66 ob., 67. Charges of listing even babes in arms as petitioners and appealing to superordinate organs in order to circumvent the decision of the factory committee also appeared in the church closure at the former Putilov Factory described in chapter 4. See Kostiuchenko, Khrepov, and Fedorov, *Istoriia Kirovskogo zavoda,* 212.

106. GARF, f. 5263, op. 1, d. 21, ll. 197–99.

107. On accommodation, see also Barbara Evan Clements, "Accommodation, Resistance, Transformation," in Clements, Engel, and Worobec, *Russia's Women,* 5–7; Christine D. Worobec, "Accommodation and Resistance," in Clements, Engel, and Worobec, *Russia's Women,* 27–28. I alone bear responsibility for any flaws in the discussion of accommodation presented here.

108. Félicité de Lamennais, *Essai sur l'indifférence en matière de religion* (Paris: Garnier, 1817), 1: 29, quoted in Vincenzo Miano, "L'indifférence religieuse: Étude théologique," *La Point Théologique* 41 (1983): 29.

109. Charles Moeller, "The Theology of Unbelief as an Hypothesis for the Principles underlying the Salvic Action of the Church," *Concilium: Pastoral Theology* 3 (March 1967): 14–23; Theodore Steeman, "Psychological and Sociological Aspects of Modern Atheism," *Concilium: Pastoral Theology* 3 (March 1967): 24–30; Jules Girardi, "Reflections on Religious Indifference," *Concilium: Pastoral Theology* 3 (March 1967): 31–35; Paul W. Pruyser, *Between Belief and Unbelief* (New York: Harper and Row, 1974); C. Stephen Evans, *Subjectivity and Religious Belief: An Historical, Critical Study* (Washington, D.C.: University Press of America, 1978); C. F. Delaney, ed., *Rationality and Reli-*

gious Belief (Notre Dame, Ind.: University of Notre Dame Press, 1979); Dennis Michael Doyle, "The Distinction between Faith and Belief and the Question of Religious Truth: The Contributions of Wilfred Cantwell Smith and Bernard Longeran," Ph.D. diss., Catholic University of America, 1984; Stanley M. Harrison and Richard C. Taylor, eds., *The Life of Religion: A Marquette University Symposium on the Nature of Religious Belief* (Lanham, Md.: University Press of America, 1986); Jean-Pierre Deconchy, "Religious Belief Systems: Their Ideological Representations and Practical Constraints," *International Journal for the Psychology of Religion* 1 (1991): 5–21; Jozef Corveleyn and Dirk Hutsebaut, eds., *Belief and Unbelief: Psychological Perspectives* (Amsterdam: Rodopi, 1994); George Wall, *Religious Experience and Religious Belief* (Lanham, Md.: University Press of America, 1995); Ilkka Pyysiäinen, *Belief and Beyond: Religious Categorization of Reality* (Åbo: Åbo Akademi, 1996); Benjamin Beit-Hallahmi and Michael Argyle, *The Psychology of Religious Behavior, Belief and Experience* (London: Routledge, 1997); A. Vergote, *Religion, Belief and Unbelief: A Psychological Study* (Amsterdam: Leuven University Press, 1997).

110. Geertz, "Religion as a Cultural System," in Banton, *Anthropological Approaches to the Study of Religion,* 3.

111. GARF, f. 5263, op. 1, d. 3, l. 63.

112. GMIR, folder 81, l. 2. Large petitions to close churches appeared in other periods, of course, but their number—in combination with the quantum increase in and aggressive character of public antireligious acts and demonstrations—set the Cultural Revolution apart.

113. GARF, f. 5407, op. 1, d. 52, ll. 40–41.

114. GARF, f. 5263, op. 1, d. 3, l. 68.

115. *Antireligioznik* 1 (January 1928): 6–9.

116. On the use of electoral politics to this end, see Young, *Power and the Sacred in Revolutionary Russia,* 193–209 and passim.

117. *Bezbozhnik* 329 (2 June 1929): 4.

118. Hindus, *Red Bread,* 39–44.

119. GME, f. 2, op. 2, ll. 5–8.

120. GMIR, folder 202, l. 2.

121. The questions asked and information requested included (1) Biography; (2) What were your living conditions while growing up? (3) Where did you receive your education? (4) When did you begin production work? (5) Are you in the party? (6) Do you participate in social work? (7) What is your work history? (8) What is your family situation? (9) Are you bringing up your children in the spirit of atheism? (10) Is your salary sufficient? (11) Describe your living conditions now; (12) Does your work give you satisfaction? (13) What is your attitude toward religion? (14) Do you go to church? (15) Are there icons in your home? (16) Do you support religion financially? (17) How do you spend your free time? GMIR, folder 202, l. 4.

EPILOGUE

1. The quotation is condensed without ellipses.

2. For a detailed discussion, see Peris, *Storming the Heavens,* 197–221; Dawn Priscilla Mann, "The League of Militant Godless, 1924–1941," master's thesis, Georgetown University, 1986, 84–102.

3. A detailed examination appears in Gregory L. Freeze, "The Stalinist Assault on the Parish, 1929–1941," in Manfred Hildermeier, ed., *Schriften des Historischen Kollegs: Kolloquien 43* (Munich: Oldenburg Verlag, 1998), 209–32, esp. 221–31.

4. Fitzpatrick, *Stalin's Peasants,* 204–6. The figure on rural churches closed during collectivization is from Viola, *Peasant Rebels under Stalin,* 40.

5. For a full discussion, see Anderson, *Religion, State and Politics in the Soviet Union and Successor States.*

Selected Bibliography

PRIMARY SOURCES

Archives

Archive of the State Museum of the Ethnography of the Peoples of the USSR (GME), Saint Petersburg.
   f. 2   Rural Expeditions, 1890s–1920s

Archive of the State Museum of the Political History of Russia (GMPIR), Saint Petersburg.
   Document fond, drawer 19
   Negative fond, drawers 29, 31, 42
   Poster fond

Central State Archive of the City of Moscow (TsGIAgM), Moscow.
   f. 1215   Administrative Department of the Moscow City Soviet

Central State Archive of the Moscow Region (TsGAMO), Moscow.
   f. 66   Nationalization of Church Property
   f. 4570   Moscow Oblast' Soviet Commission on Religious
          Denominations
   f. 4998   Moscow Soviet Department of Justice

Hoover Institution Archives, University of Illinois at Urbana-Champaign.
   Boris I. Nicolaevsky Collection

Russian Center for the Preservation and Study of Documents on Recent History (RTsKhIDNI), Moscow.
   f. 5   Vladimir I. Lenin fond
   f. 17   Party Central Committee
   f. 89   Emelian Iaroslavskii fond

Smolensk Archive, University of Illinois at Urbana-Champaign.
   Antireligious Campaigns, 1924, 1925, 1930: WKP 10, 22, 23, 25, 27, 458, 459, 460

State Archive of the Russian Federation (GARF), Moscow.
    f. 353   People's Commissariat of Justice
    f. 393   NKVD
    f. 5263   Central Commission on Religious Questions
    f. 5407   League of Militant Atheists
    f. 5457   Union of Textile Workers

State Museum of the History of Religion (GMIR), Saint Petersburg.
    f. 29   Central Council of the League of Militant Godless
    folder 21   "On Resistance by Believers to Collectivization," 1931
    folder 41   "On Fulfilling the Five-Year-Plan in Four Years"
    folder 55   "Recommendations on the Organization of Local Anti-religious Work," 1929
    folder 81   "Reports on Religious Life in the Country for 1930"
    folder 197 The Newspaper *Ateist,* February 1922
    folder 202 Interviews on Workers' Attitudes toward Religion, 1930
    folder 380 "On the Eradication of Illiteracy"

Periodicals

Antireligioznik
Ateist (replaced by *Voinstvuiushchii ateizm,* 1931)
Baptist (Russian)
Bezbozhnik (journal)
Bezbozhnik (newspaper)
Bezbozhnik u stanka
Bezbozhnyi byt
Derevenskii bezbozhnik
Etnografiia
Istoricheskii arkhiv
Izvestiia
Izvestiia VtsIK
Khudozhestvennyi fol'klor
Klub i revoliutsiia
Kommunisticheskaia molodezh'
Kommunisticheskaia revoliutsiia
Komsomol'skaia pravda
Krest'ianka
Na putiakh k novoi shkole
Narodnoe prosveshchenie
Nash bezbozhnik (supplement to *Tambovskaia pravda*)
Nauka i religiia (replaced by *Krasnaia nov',* 1922)
Pechat' i revoliutsiia
Pod znamenem Marksizma
Pravda

Rabochaia gazeta
Rabotnitsa
Radio v derevne
Revoliutsiia i kul'tura
Revoliutsiia i tserkov'
Sobranie Uzakonenii i rasporiazhenii rabochego i krest'ianskogo pravitelstva
Sredne-volzhskii bezbozhnik (replaced by *Volzhskii bezbozhnik,* 1931)
Tekstil'shchik
Trud
Vestnik prosveshcheniia
Vestnik tserkovnogo edineniia
Voprosy istorii religii i ateizma
Voprosy truda
Zapiski nauchnogo obshchestva marksistov
Zhivaia tserkov'

Published Documents and Records

Belliustin, I. S. *Description of the Clergy in Rural Russia.* Edited and translated by Gregory L. Freeze. Ithaca, N.Y.: Cornell University Press, 1985.
Dekrety Sovetskoi vlasti. Vols. 1–5 (1917–1919). Moscow: Politizdat, 1959–1971.
Dekrety Sovetskoi vlasti, tom I: 25 oktiabria 1917g.–16 marta 1918g. Moscow: Gosizdat, 1957.
The Domostroi: Rules for Russian Households in the Time of Ivan the Terrible. Edited and translated by Carolyn Johnston Pouncy. Ithaca, N.Y.: Cornell University Press, 1994.
Dvenadtsatyi s"ezd RKP(b): Stenograficheskii otchet, 17–25 aprelia 1923 g. Moscow: Izdatel'stvo politicheskoi literatury, 1968.
Iz istorii Kurskoi oblastnoi organizatsii (1918–1970 gg.). Edited by V. E. Shapov et al. Kursk: Kurskaia pravda, 1972.
"K 120-letiiu so dnia rozhdeniia V. I. Lenina: Novye dokumenty (1920–1922 gg.)." *Izvestiia TsK KPSS* 303 (April 1990): 174–97.
Kanatchikov, Semën Ivanovich. *A Radical Worker in Tsarist Russia: The Autobiography of Semën Ivanovich Kanatchikov.* Translated and edited by Reginald E. Zelnik. Stanford, Calif.: Stanford University Press, 1986.
Kommunisticheskaia partiia i sovetskoe pravitel'stvo o religii i tserkvi. Moscow: Gosudarstvennoe izdatel'stvo politicheskoi literatury, 1959, 1961.
Kommunisticheskaia partiia Sovetskogo soiuza v rezoliutsiiakh i resheniiakh s"ezdov, konferentsii i plenumov TsK. Vols. 1–3. Moscow: Izdatel'stvo politicheskoi literatury, 1953–1984.
Kul'turnaia zhizn' v SSSR, 1917–1927: Khronika. Vol. 1. Moscow: Nauka, 1975.
Kul'turnoe stroitel'stvo v RSFSR: Dokumentay i materialy, 1917–1921. Vol. 1,

parts 1–2. Edited by M. P. Kim. Moscow: Sovetskaia Rossiia, 1983–1984.

Marx, Karl, and Friedrich Engels. *The Communist Manifesto.* New York: Penguin Books, 1967.

Neizvestnaia Rossiia: XX vek, IV. Moscow: Izdatel'stvo Ob"edineniia Mosgorarkhiv, 1993.

"'Ne stesniaias' nikakim sredsvami': Materialy Komissii TsK VKP(b) po voprosam otdeleniia tserkvi ot gosudarstva, Oktiabr'–dekabr' 1922 g." *Istoricheskii arkhiv* 2 (1993): 76–89.

O religii i tserkvi: Sbornik vyskazyvanii klassikov Marksizma-Leninizma, dokumentov KPSS i Sovetskogo gosudarstva. Moscow: Politizdat, 1981.

"'Podvergnut' arestu i privlech' k sudebnoi otvetstvennosti': VChK-GPU i patriarkh Tikhon, 1917–1925 gg." *Istoricheskii arkhiv* 5–6 (1997): 141–55.

"Poezdka na Vserossiiskii tserkovnyi sobor: Dnevnik nastoiatelia Sukhumskogo kafedral'nogo sobora protoiereia G. S. Golubtsova, Ianvar'–aprel' 1918 g." *Istoricheskii arkhiv* 5 (1994): 165–95.

"Politburo i tserkov', 1922–1923: Tri arkhivnykh dela." Compiled and with an introduction by N. N. Pokrovskii. *Novyi mir* 8 (1994): 186–213.

Rapports secrets soviétiques: La société russe dans les documents confidentiels, 1921–1991. Compiled and translated into French by Nicholas Werth and Gaël Moullec. Paris: Gallimard, 1994.

Russkaia Pravoslavnaia Tserkov' i Kommunisticheskoe Gosudarstvo, 1917–1941: Dokumenty i Fotomaterialy. Edited by Ia. N. Shchapov. Compiled by O. Iu. Vasil'eva. Moscow: Bibleisko-Bogoslovskii Institut Sviatogo Apostola Andreia, 1996.

Russkaia Pravoslavnaia Tserkov' v sovetskoe vremia (1917–1991): Materialy i dokumenty po istorii otnoshenii mezhdu gosudarstvom i Tserkov'iu. Book 1. Compiled by Gerd Shtrikker. Moscow: Propilei, 1995.

Stenograficheskii otchet vtorogo vsesoiuznogo s"ezda voinstvuiushchikh bezbozhnikov. Moscow: Bezbozhnik, 1930.

Tolstoy, Leo. *A Confession and Other Writings.* Translated and with an introduction by Jane Kentish. New York: Penguin Books, 1987.

———. *The Death of Ivan Ilyich.* Translated by Lynn Solataroff. New York: Bantam Books, 1981.

Trinadtsatyi s"ezd RKP(b), mai 1924 goda: Stenograficheskii otchet. Moscow: Izdatel'stvo politicheskoi literatury, 1963.

"Tserkov' otdeliaetsia ot gosudarstva: Doklady eksperta Narkomiusta M. V. Galkina, 1918 g." *Istoricheskii arkhiv* 6 (1993): 162–70; 1 (1994): 136–47.

The Unknown Lenin: From the Secret Archive. Edited by Richard Pipes. New Haven, Conn.: Yale University Press, 1996.

Uprochenie sovetskoi vlasti v Moskve i moskovskoi gubernii: Dokumenty i materialy. Moscow: Moskovskii rabochii, 1958.

Velikaia Oktiabr'skaia sotsialisticheskaia revoliutsiia i stanovlenie sovetskoi kul'tury, 1917–1927. Edited by M. P. Kim. Moscow: Nauka, 1985.

Wade, Rex A., ed. *Documents of Soviet History.* Vol. 2, *Triumph and Retreat, 1920–1922.* Gulf Breeze, Fla.: Academic International Press, 1993.

Antireligious Publications, Ethnography, and Social Propaganda

Amosov, Nikolai K. *O p'ianykh prazdnikakh.* Moscow: Bezbozhnik, 1929.

Antireligioznyi sbornik. Moscow: Bezbozhnik, 1928.

Bol'shakov, A. M. *Derevnia, 1917–1927.* Moscow: Rabotnik prosveshcheniia, 1927.

———. *Ocherki derevnia SSSR, 1917–1927.* Moscow: Rabochii prosveshcheniia, 1928.

Bonch-Bruevich, Vladimir. *"Zhivaia tserkov'" i proletariat.* Moscow: Zhizn' i znanie, 1929.

Brykin, N. *V novoi derevne: Ocherki derevenskoi byta.* Moscow: Gosudarstvennoe izdatel'stvo, 1925.

Derevnia na novykh putiakh: Andreevskaia volost' Kostromskoi gubernii i uezda (Materialy obsledovaniia). Kostroma: Izdanie Kostromskogo Gubkoma RKP(b), 1925.

Fenomenov, M. Ia. *Izuchenie byta derevni v shkole (Issledovatel'skaia kraevedcheskaia rabota po obshchestvovedeniiu).* Moscow: Rabotnik prosveshcheniia, 1926.

———. *Sovremennaia derevnia: Opyt kraevedcheskogo obsledovaniia odnoi derevni.* Moscow-Leningrad: Gosudarstvennoe izdatel'stvo, 1925.

Gagarin, A. *Khoziaistvo, zhizn' i nastroenie derevni (Po itogam obsledovaniia Pochinkovskoi volosti Smolenskoi gubernii).* Moscow-Leningrad: Gosudarstvennoe izdatel'stvo, 1925.

Grigorov, Leonid M. *Ocherki sovremennoi derevni: Kniga pervaia.* Moscow: Gosudarstvennoe izdatel'stvo, 1924.

———. *Ocherki sovremennoi derevni: Kniga vtoraia.* Moscow-Leningrad: Gosudarstvennoe izdatel'stvo, 1925.

Gukovskii, A. I., and O. V. Trakhtenberg. *Kratkii uchebnik po istorii razvitiia obshchestvennykh form, II-e izdanie.* Moscow: Izdatel'stvo kommunisticheskogo universiteta imemi Ia. M. Sverdlova, 1928.

Iakovlev, Iakov A. *Derevnia kak ona est'.* Moscow: Krasnaia nov', 1924.

———. *Nasha derevnia: Novoe v starom i staroe v novom.* Moscow: Krasnaia nov', 1924.

Iaroslavskii, Emelian. *Kommunisty i religiia.* Moscow: Molodaia gvardiia, 1937.

———. *Ocherednye zadachi antireligioznoi propagandy.* Moscow: Bezbozhnik, 1930.

———. *Protiv religii i tserkvi.* Vol. 1. Moscow: Gosudarstvennoe antireligioznoe izdatel'stvo, 1932.

————. *Zadachi antireligioznoi propagandy v rekonstruktivnyi period*. Moscow-Leningrad: Moskovskii rabochii, 1931.

Ignat'ev, V. E. *Gigena v shkole*. Moscow: Rabotnik prosveshcheniia, 1925.

Kogen, S., ed. *Antireligioznyi sbornik*. Moscow: Moskovskii rabochii, 1940.

Kommunizm i religiia. Moscow: Moskovskii rabochii, 1922.

Kostitsyn, A. *Trudiashchaia zhenshchina i religiia*. Moscow: Moskovskii rabochii, 1929.

Kozlov, V. A. *Kul'turnaia revoliutsiia i krest'ianstvo, 1921–1927 (Po materialam Evropeiskoi chasti RSFSR)*. Moscow: Nauka, 1983.

Kunov, Genrikh. *Vozniknovenie religii i very v boga*. Moscow: Kommunist, 1919.

Lukin, I. M. (I. Antonov). *Tserkov' i gosudarstvo*. Moscow: Kommunist, 1918.

Murin, V. A. *Byt i nravy derevenskoi molodezhi*. Moscow: Novaia Moskva, 1926.

Nikol'skii, V. *Sueverie, zhakharstvo, religioznye predrassudki i sovetskaia meditsina*. Moscow: Zhizn' i znanie, 1926.

Nosov, V. *Komsomol' i delegatka krest'ianka*. Moscow-Leningrad: Gosudarstvennoe izdatel'stvo, 1927.

Oleshchuk, F. *XVII s"ezd VKP(b) i zadachi antireligioznoi raboty*. Moscow: Gosudarstvennoe antireligioznoe izdatel'stvo, 1934.

Rakusheva, L. *Komsomol protiv religii*. Leningrad: Izdatel'stvo Leningradskogo soveta RKiKD, 1939.

Rosnitskii, N., ed. *Polgoda v derevne: Osnovnye itogi obsledovaniia 28 volostei i 32730 krest'ianskikh khoziastv Penzenskoi gub*. Penza: Izdanie komissii po rabote v derevne pri gubkome RKP(b), 1925.

Rumiantsev, Nikolai Vasil'evich. *O prestol'nykh prasdnikakh*. Moscow: GAIZ, 1939.

Segal, A. E. *Religiia i znakharstvo*. Moscow-Leningrad: Moskovskii rabochii, 1931.

Serebrennikov, G. N. *Zhenskii trud v SSSR*. Moscow-Leningrad: Gosudarstvennoe sotsial'no-ekonomicheskoe izdatel'stvo, 1924.

Shokhin, Andrei. *Komsomol'skaia derevnia*. Moscow-Leningrad: Molodaia gvardiia, 1923.

Shuvaev, K. M. *Staraia i novaia derevnia*. Moscow: Sel'khozgiz, 1937.

Spravochnik partiinogo rabotnika, vyp. 5. Moscow-Leningrad: Gosudarstvennoe izdatel'stvo, 1926.

Tan-Bogoraz, V. G., ed. *Komsomol v derevne*. Moscow-Leningrad: Gosudarstvennoe izdatel'stvo, 1926.

————, ed. *Staryi i novyi byt: Sbornik*. Leningrad: Gosudarstvennoe izdatel'stvo, 1924.

Uchebnik dlia rabochikh antireligioznykh kruzhkov, 2-e izdanie. Edited by A. Lukachevskii. Moscow: Bezbozhnik, 1928.

Veresaev, V. V. *Polnoe sobranie sochinenii*. Vol. 8. Moscow: Nedra, 1929.

Voinstvuiushchee bezbozhie v SSSR za 15 let, 1917–1932. Moscow: Gosudarstvennoe antireligioznoe izdatel'stvo, 1932.

Zybkovets, Vladimir F. *Ot sokhi k traktoru.* Leningrad: Lenpartizdat, 1934.
————. *Religiia i krest'ianskoe khoziaistvo.* 3d ed. Moscow: Bezbozhnik, 1930.

SECONDARY SOURCES

Adler, Erwin. "Basic Tendencies in the Atheistic Propaganda Literature of the Eastern Bloc." *Concilium: Pastoral Theology* 3 (March 1967): 66–77.

Altrichter, Helmut. *Die Bauern von Tver: Vom Leben auf dem russichen Dorge zwischen Revolution und Kollektivierung.* Munich: Oldenbourg Verlag, 1984.

Anderson, John. *Religion, State and Politics in the Soviet Union and Successor States.* Cambridge: Cambridge University Press, 1994.

Anokhina, L. A., and M. N. Shmeleva. *Kul'tura i byt kolkhoznikov Kalininskoi oblasti.* Moscow: Nauka, 1964.

Atkinson, Dorothy, Alexander Dallin, and Gail Warshofsky Lapidus, eds. *Women in Russia.* Stanford, Calif.: Stanford University Press, 1977.

Badone, Ellen ed. *Religious Orthodoxy and Popular Faith in European Society.* Princeton, N.J.: Princeton University Press, 1990.

Bailey, David C. *¡Viva Cristo Rey! The Cristero Rebellion and Church-State Conflict in Mexico.* Austin: University of Texas Press, 1974.

Ball, Alan M. *And Now My Soul Is Hardened: Abandoned Children in Soviet Russia, 1918–1930.* Berkeley: University of California Press, 1994.

————. *Russia's Last Capitalists: The Nepmen, 1921–1929.* Berkeley: University of California Press, 1987.

Bantjes, Adrian A. *As If Jesus Walked on Earth: Cardenismo, Sonora, and the Mexican Revolution.* Wilmington, Del.: Scholarly Resources, 1988.

————. "Idolatry and Iconoclasm in Revolutionary Mexico: The Dechristianization Campaigns, 1929–1940." *Mexican Studies/Estudios Mexicanos* 13 (winter 1997): 87–120.

Banton, Michael, ed. *Anthropological Approaches to the Study of Religion.* London: Tavistock Publications, 1965.

Baron, Samuel H., and Nancy Shields Kollmann, eds. *Religion and Culture in Early Modern Russia and Ukraine.* DeKalb: Northern Illinois University Press, 1997.

Batalden, Stephen K., ed. *Seeking God: The Recovery of Religious Identity in Orthodox Russia, Ukraine, and Georgia.* DeKalb: Northern Illinois University Press, 1993.

Bedov, P., and N. Tumanov. *Kostromskii ekskavatornyi.* Kostroma: Rabochii metallist, 1965.

Bernstein, Frances L. "Envisioning Health in Revolutionary Russia: The Politics of Gender in Sexual-Enlightenment Posters of the 1920s." *Russian Review* 57 (April 1998): 191–217.

Billington, James H. *The Icon and the Axe: An Interpretive History of Russian Culture.* New York: Vintage Books, 1966.

Borisov, Iu. S., ed. *Dukhovnyi potentsial SSSR nakanune Velikoi Otechestvennoi Voiny: Iz istorii sovetskoi kul'tury 1917–1941 gg.: Sbornik statei.* Moscow: Nauka, 1985.

Bourdeaux, Michael, ed. *The Politics of Religion in Russia and the New States of Eurasia.* New York: M. E. Sharpe, 1995.

Bouwsma, William J. *A Usable Past: Essays in European Cultural History.* Berkeley: University of California Press, 1990.

Braudel, Fernand. *A History of Civilizations.* Translated by Richard Mayne. New York: Penguin, 1987.

Brooks, Jeffrey. *When Russia Learned to Read: Literacy and Popular Literature, 1861–1917.* Princeton, N.J.: Princeton University Press, 1985.

Brovkin, Vladimir N., ed. *The Bolsheviks in Russian Society: The Revolution and the Civil Wars.* New Haven, Conn.: Yale University Press, 1997.

Brown, Judith C. *Immodest Acts: The Life of a Lesbian Nun in Renaissance Italy.* New York: Oxford University Press, 1986.

Brudnyi, V. I. *Obriady vchera i segodnia.* Moscow: Nauka, 1968.

Brumfield, William C., and Milos M. Velimirovic, eds. *Christianity and the Arts in Russia.* Cambridge: Cambridge University Press, 1992.

Bryzgalov, A. N. *Onezhskii zavod.* Petrozavodsk: Gosudarstvennoe izdatel'stvo Karel'skoi ASSR, 1957.

Burds, Jeffrey. "A Culture of Denunciation: Peasant Labor Migration and Religious Anathematization in Rural Russia, 1860–1905." *Journal of Modern History* 68 (December 1996): 786–818.

―――. *Peasant Dreams and Market Politics: Migration and the Russian Village, 1861–1905.* Pittsburgh: University of Pittsburgh Press, 1998.

Burke, Peter. *Popular Culture in Early Modern Europe.* 1978. Rev. ed., Brookfield, Vt.: Scolar, 1994.

―――, ed. *The New Cambridge Modern History.* vol. 13. Cambridge: Cambridge University Press, 1979.

Bushkovitch, Paul. *Religion and Society in Russia: The Sixteenth and Seventeenth Centuries.* New York: Oxford University Press, 1992.

Chartier, Roger, ed. *A History of Private Life: Passions of the Renaissance.* Translated by Arthur Goldhammer. Cambridge, Mass.: Belknap Press, 1989.

Chase, William J. *Workers, Society, and the Soviet State: Labor and Life in Moscow, 1918–1929.* Urbana: University of Illinois Press, 1987.

Cherniavsky, Michael, ed. *The Structure of Russian History: Interpretive Essays.* New York: Random House, 1970.

Clark, Gillian. *Women in Late Antiquity: Pagan and Christian Lifestyles.* Oxford: Clarendon Press, 1993.

Classic Russian Cooking: Elena Molokhovets' 'A Gift to Young Housewives.' Translated by and with an introduction by Joyce Toomre. Bloomington: Indiana University Press, 1992.

Clements, Barbara Evans, Barbara Alpern Engel, and Christine D. Worobec, eds. *Russia's Women: Accommodation, Resistance, Transformation.* Berkeley: University of California Press, 1991.

Clowes, Edith W., Samuel D. Kassow, and James L. West, eds. *Between Tsar and People: Educated Society and the Quest for Public Identity in Late Imperial Russia.* Princeton, N.J.: Princeton University Press, 1991.

Coopersmith, Jonathan. *The Electrification of Russia, 1880–1926.* Ithaca, N.Y.: Cornell University Press, 1992.

Crummey, Robert O. "Old Belief as Popular Religion: New Approaches." *Slavic Review* 52 (1993): 700–712.

Curtiss, John. *The Russian Church and the Soviet State, 1917–1950.* Boston: Little, Brown, 1953.

Dahm, Helmut. "The Problems of Atheism in Recent Soviet Publications." *Studies in Soviet Thought* 41 (March 1991): 85–126.

Darnton, Robert. *The Great Cat Massacre and Other Episodes of French Cultural History.* New York: Basic Books, 1984.

———. *The Kiss of Lamourette: Reflections in Cultural History.* New York: W. W. Norton, 1990.

David-Fox, Michael. *Revolution of the Mind: Higher Learning among the Bolsheviks, 1918–1929.* Ithaca, N.Y.: Cornell University Press, 1997.

Davies, R. W. *The Socialist Offensive: The Collectivisation of Soviet Agriculture, 1929–1930.* Cambridge, Mass.: Harvard University Press, 1980.

Davis, Natalie Zemon. "From 'Popular Religion' to Religious Cultures." In Steven Ozment, ed. *Reformation Europe: A Guide to Research.* St. Louis: Center for Reformation Research, 1982.

———. *Society and Culture in Early Modern France.* Stanford, Calif.: Stanford University Press, 1975.

———. "Some Tasks and Themes in the Study of Popular Religion." In Charles Trinkaus and Heiko A. Oberman, eds. *The Pursuit of Holiness in Late Medieval and Renaissance Religion.* Leiden: E. J. Brill, 1974.

Davis, Nathaniel. *A Long Walk to Church: A Contemporary History of Russian Orthodoxy.* Boulder: Westview Press, 1995.

de Lamennais, Félicité. *Essai sur l'indifférence en matière de religion.* Vol. 1. Paris: Garnier, 1817.

Dickerman, Leah, ed. *Building the Collective: Soviet Graphic Design, 1917–1937.* New York: Princeton Architectural Press, 1996.

Eklof, Ben. *Russian Peasant Schools: Officialdom, Village Culture, and Popular Pedagogy, 1861–1914.* Berkeley: University of California Press, 1986.

Eklof, Ben, and Stephen P. Frank, eds. *The World of the Russian Peasant: Post-Emancipation Culture and Society.* Boston: Unwin Hyman, 1990.

Emeliakh, L. I., ed. *Ateisticheskie traditsii russkogo naroda: Sbornik nauchnykh trudov.* Leningrad: Izdanie Gosudarstvennogo muzeia istorii religii i ateizma, 1982.

———. *Krest'iane i tserkov' nakanune oktiabria.* Leningrad: Nauka, 1976.

Engel, Barbara Alpern. *Between the Fields and the City: Women, Work, and Family in Russia, 1861–1914.* Cambridge: Cambridge University Press, 1996.

Erlich, Alexander. *The Soviet Industrialization Debate, 1924–1928.* Cambridge, Mass.: Harvard University Press, 1960.

Evtuhov, Catherine. "The Church in the Russian Revolution: Arguments for and against Restoring the Patriarchate at the Church Council of 1917–1918." *Slavic Review* 50 (fall 1991): 497–511.

———. *The Cross and the Sickle: Sergei Bulgakov and the Fate of Russian Religious Philosophy.* Ithaca, N.Y.: Cornell University Press, 1997.

Ezhegodnik muzeia istorii religii i ateizma, I–VII. Moscow-Leningrad: Izdatel'stvo akademii nauk SSSR, 1957–1964.

Farnsworth, Beatrice, and Lynne Viola, eds. *Russian Peasant Women.* New York: Oxford University Press, 1992.

Febvre, Lucien. *The Problem of Unbelief in the Sixteenth Century: The Religion of Rabelais.* 1942. Translated by Beatrice Gottlieb, Cambridge, Mass.: Harvard University Press, 1982.

Fedotov, George P. *The Russian Religious Mind.* Vol. 1. 1946. Reprint, New York: Harper and Brothers, 1960.

Figes, Orlando. *Peasant Russia, Civil War: The Volga Countryside in Revolution, 1917–1921.* Oxford: Clarendon Press, 1989.

Fisher, Ralph Talcott, Jr. *Pattern for Soviet Youth: A Study of the Congresses of the Komsomol, 1918–1954.* New York: Columbia University Press, 1959.

Fitzpatrick, Sheila. *Stalin's Peasants: Resistance and Survival in the Russian Village after Collectivization.* New York: Oxford University Press, 1994.

———, ed. *Cultural Revolution in Russia, 1928–1931.* Bloomington: Indiana University Press, 1978.

Fitzpatrick, Sheila, Alexander Rabinowitch, and Richard Stites, eds. *Russia in the Era of NEP: Explorations in Soviet Society and Culture.* Bloomington: Indiana University Press, 1991.

Foucault, Michel. *Discipline and Punish: The Birth of the Prison.* Translated by Alan Sheridan. New York: Vintage Books, 1995.

———. *The History of Sexuality: An Introduction.* Vol. 1. 1976. Translated by Robert Hurley. New York: Vintage Books, 1990.

———. *Madness and Civilization: A History of Insanity in the Age of Reason.* 1961. Translated by Richard Howard. New York: Vintage Books, 1988.

Frank, Stephen P. "'Simple Folk, Savage Customs?' Youth, Sociability, and the Dynamics of Culture in Rural Russia, 1856–1914." *Journal of Social History* 25 (1992): 711–36.

Freeze, Gregory L. "Bringing Order to the Russian Family: Marriage and Divorce in Imperial Russia, 1760–1860." *Journal of Modern History* 62 (1990): 709–46.

———. "Counter-reformation in Russian Orthodoxy: Popular Response to Religious Innovation, 1922–1925." *Slavic Review* 54 (summer 1995): 305–39.

———. "Handmaiden of the State? The Church in Imperial Russia Reconsidered." *Journal of Ecclesiastical History* 36 (1985): 82–102.

———. "The Orthodox Church and Serfdom in Prereform Russia." *Slavic Review* 48 (fall 1989): 361–87.

———. "L'ortodossia russe e la crisi delle famiglie: Il divorzio in Russia tra la rivoluzione e la guerre (1917–1921)." In A. Mainardi, ed., *L'Autunno della Santa Russia, 1917–1945: Atti del VI Convegno ecumenico internazionale spiritualita russa, Bose 16–19 settembre.* Magnano, Italy: Qigajou, 1999.

———. *The Parish Clergy in Nineteenth-Century Russia: Crisis, Reform, Counter-Reform.* Princeton, N.J.: Princeton University Press, 1983.

———. "Rechristianization of Russia: The Church and Popular Religion, 1750–1850." *Studia Slavica Finlandensia* 7 (1990): 101–36.

———. *The Russian Levites: Parish Clergy in the Eighteenth Century.* Cambridge, Mass.: Harvard University Press, 1977.

———. "The Stalinist Assault on the Parish, 1929–1941." In *Schriften des Historischen Kollegs: Kolloquien 43.* Edited by Manfred Hildermeier. Munich: Oldenburg Verlag, 1998.

———. "Subversive Piety: Religion and the Political Crisis in Late Imperial Russia." *Journal of Modern History* 68 (1996): 308–50.

———, ed. *Russia: A History.* Oxford: Oxford University Press, 1997.

Gasparov, Boris, and Olga Raevsky-Hughes, eds. *Christianity and the Eastern Slavs.* Vol. 1., *Slavic Cultures in the Middle Ages.* Berkeley: University of California Press, 1993.

Gay, Peter. *The Enlightenment: An Interpretation.* Vol. 1, *The Rise of Modern Paganism.* New York: W. W. Norton, 1966.

Geertz, Clifford. *The Interpretation of Cultures.* New York: Basic Books, 1973.

Ginzburg, Carlo. *The Cheese and the Worms: The Cosmos of a Sixteenth-Century Miller.* 1976. Translated by John and Anne Tedeschi. Baltimore: Johns Hopkins University Press, 1980.

Gleason, Abbott. *Young Russia: The Genesis of Russian Radicalism in the 1860s.* Chicago: University of Chicago Press, 1980.

Gnatovskaia, D. Iu., and M. P. Zezina. "Bytovye kommuny rabochei i studencheskoi molodezhi vo vtoroi polovine 20-kh-nachale 30-kh godov." *Vestnik Moskovskogo universiteta, series 8, istoriia* 1 (January–February 1998): 42–58.

Goldman, Wendy Z. *Women, the State and Revolution: Soviet Family Policy and Social Life, 1917–1936.* Cambridge: Cambridge University Press, 1993.

Gould, Stephen Jay. "On Heroes and Fools in Science." In *Ever since Darwin: Reflections in Natural History.* New York: W. W. Norton, 1977.

Graham, Loren R. *Science, Philosophy, and Human Behavior in the Soviet Union.* New York: Columbia University Press, 1987.

Hindus, Maurice. *Red Bread: Collectivization in a Russian Village.* 1931. Reprint, Bloomington: Indiana University Press, 1988.

Hobsbawm, Eric J. *The Age of Capital, 1848–1875.* New York: New American Library, 1875.

Hobsbawm, Eric J., and Terence Ranger, eds. *The Invention of Tradition.* Cambridge: Cambridge University Press, 1983.

Hoffmann, David. *Peasant Metropolis: Social Identities in Moscow,*

1929–1941. Ithaca, N.Y.: Cornell University Press, 1994.

Holmes, Larry E. *The Kremlin and the Schoolhouse: Reforming Education in Soviet Russia, 1917–1931.* Bloomington: Indiana University Press, 1991.

Hosking, Geoffrey A., ed. *Church, Nation and State in Russia and Ukraine.* New York: St. Martin's Press, 1991.

Hunter, Michael, and David Wootten, eds. *Atheism from the Reformation to the Enlightenment.* Oxford: Clarendon Press, 1992.

Husband, William B. *Revolution in the Factory: The Birth of the Soviet Textile Industry, 1917–1920.* New York: Oxford University Press, 1990.

———. "Soviet Atheism and Russian Orthodox Strategies of Resistance, 1917–1932." *Journal of Modern History* 70 (March 1998): 74–107.

Hutchison, Keith. "What Happened to Occult Qualities in the Scientific Revolution?" *Isis* 73 (1982): 233–53.

Ivanits, Linda J. *Russian Folk Belief.* Armonk, N.Y.: M. E. Sharpe, 1989.

Kaiser, Daniel H., and Gary Marker, eds. *Reinterpreting Russian History: Readings, 860–1860s.* New York: Oxford University Press, 1994.

Kenez, Peter. *Cinema and Soviet Society, 1917–1953.* Cambridge: Cambridge University Press, 1992.

———. *Civil War in South Russia, 1919–1920.* Berkeley: University of California Press, 1977.

Khenkin, E. M. *Ocherki istorii bor'by Sovetskogo gosudarstva s golodom (1921–1922).* Krasnoiarsk: Izdatel'stvo Krasnoiarskogo universiteta, 1988.

Kim, M. P., ed. *Kul'turnaia revoliutsiia v SSSR, 1917–1965 gg.* Moscow: Nauka, 1967.

Kingston-Mann, Esther, and Timothy Mixter, eds. *Peasant Economy, Culture, and Politics of European Russia, 1800–1921.* Princeton, N.J.: Princeton University Press, 1991.

Kline, George. *Religious and Anti-Religious Thought in Russia.* Chicago: University of Chicago Press, 1968.

Kors, Alan Charles. *Atheism in France, 1650–1729.* Princeton, N.J.: Princeton University Press, 1990.

Kostiuchenko, S., I. Khrepov, and Iu. Fedorov. *Istoriia Kirovskogo zavoda, 1917–1945.* Moscow: Mysl', 1966.

Kozlov, V. A. *Kul'turnaia revoliutsiia i krest'ianstvo, 1921–1927 (Po materialam Evropeiskoi chasti RSFSR).* Moscow: Nauka, 1983.

Kristeller, Paul Oskar. "The Myth of Renaissance Atheism and the French Tradition of Free Thought." *Journal of the History of Philosophy* 6 (1968): 233–43.

Kuhn, Thomas S. *The Structure of Scientific Revolutions.* 2d ed. Chicago: University of Chicago Press, 1970.

Landes, David S. *The Unbound Prometheus: Technological Change and Industrial Development in Western Europe from 1750 to the Present.* Cambridge: Cambridge University Press, 1969.

Lapitskaia, S. *Byt rabochikh Trekhgornoi manufaktury.* Moscow: Istoriia zavodov, 1935.

————. "Staryi i novyi byt: otryvki iz istorii Trekhgornoi manufaktury." In L. Aberbakh, ed., *Shestnadtsat'zavodov*. Moscow: Istoriia zavodov, 1934.

Le Roy Ladurie, Emmanuel. *Montaillou: The Promised Land of Error*. 1975. Translated by Barbara Bray, New York: George Braziller, 1978.

Lewin, Moshe. *The Making of the Soviet System*. New York: Pantheon Books, 1985.

Lightman, Bernard. *The Origins of Agnosticism: Victorian Unbelief and the Limits of Knowledge*. Baltimore: Johns Hopkins University Press, 1987.

Lotman, Iu. M., and B. A. Uspenskii. *The Semiotics of Russian Culture*. Edited by Ann Shukman. Translated by N. F. C. Owen. Ann Arbor: Michigan Slavic Contributions, 1984.

Luukkanen, Arto. *The Party of Unbelief: The Religious Policy of the Bolshevik Party, 1917–1929*. Helsinki: Societas Historica Finlandiae, 1994.

Malia, Martin. *Alexander Herzen and the Birth of Russian Socialism*. Cambridge, Mass.: Harvard University Press, 1961.

Manchester, Laurie. "The Secularization of the Search for Salvation: The Self-Fashioning of Orthodox Clergymen's Sons in Late Imperial Russia." *Slavic Review* 57 (spring 1998): 50–76.

Mann, Dawn Priscilla. "The League of Militant Godless, 1924–1941." Master's thesis, Georgetown University, 1986.

Marker, Gary. *Publishing, Printing, and the Origins of Intellectual Life in Russia, 1700–1800*. Princeton, N.J.: Princeton University Press, 1985.

Marshall, Richard H., ed. *Aspects of Religion in the Soviet Union, 1917–1967*. Chicago: University of Chicago Press, 1971.

Meyer, Jean. *La Cristiada*. 3 vols. 1973–1974. Reprint, Mexico City: Siglo Veintiuno Editores, S.A., 1979–1980.

Midgley, Graham. *University Life in Eighteenth-Century Oxford*. New Haven, Conn.: Yale University Press, 1996.

Mokyr, Joel. *The Lever of Riches: Technological Creativity and Economic Progress*. New York: Oxford University Press, 1990.

Naiman, Eric. *Sex in Public: The Incarnation of Early Soviet Ideology*. Princeton, N.J.: Princeton University Press, 1997.

Neuberger, Joan. *Hooliganism: Crime, Culture, and Power in St. Petersburg, 1900–1914*. Berkeley: University of California Press, 1993.

Nichols, Robert L. "Church and State in Imperial Russia." *Donald W. Treadgold Papers* 102 (1995): 7–22.

Nichols, Robert L., and Theofanis George Stavrou, eds. *Russian Orthodoxy under the Old Regime*. Minneapolis: University of Minnesota Press, 1978.

Obshchestvo i priroda: Istoricheskie etapy i formy vzaimodeistviia. Moscow: Nauka, 1981.

Ocherki istorii Leningradskoi organizatsii VLKSM. Leningrad: Lenizdat, 1969.

Oja, Matt. "*Traktorizatsiia* as Cultural Conflict, 1929–1933." *Russian Review* 51 (July 1992): 343–62.

Okulov, A. F., et al., eds. *Ateizm v SSSR: Stanovlenie i razvitie*. Moscow: Mysl', 1986.

Osler, Margaret J., and Paul Lawrence Farber, eds. *Religion, Science, and Worldview: Essays in Honor of Richard S. Westfall.* Cambridge: Cambridge University Press, 1985.

Ozouf, Mona. *Festivals and the French Revolution.* Translated by Alan Sheridan. Cambridge, Mass.: Harvard University Press, 1988.

Peris, Daniel. "The 1929 Congress of the Godless." *Soviet Studies* 43 (1991): 711–32.

———. "Commissars in Red Cassocks: Former Priests in the League of Militant Godless." *Slavic Review* 54 (summer 1995): 340–64.

———. *Storming the Heavens: The Soviet League of the Militant Godless.* Ithaca, N.Y.: Cornell University Press, 1998.

Persits, M. M. *Ateizm russkogo rabochego (1870–1905 gg.).* Moscow: Nauka, 1965.

———. *Otdelenie tserkvi ot gosudarstva i shkoly ot tserkvi v SSSR (1917–1919 gg.).* Moscow: Izdatel'stvo akademii nauk SSSR, 1958.

Piotrowski, Harry. "The League of the Militant Godless, 1924–1941." Ph.D. diss., Syracuse University, 1971.

Plaggenborg, Stefan. "Volksreligiosistätund antireligiöse Propaganda in der frühen Sowjetunion." *Arkhiv für Sozialgeschichte* 26 (1992): 95–130.

Platonov, N. F. "Pravoslavnaia tserkov v 1917–1935 gg." In *Ezhegodnik muzeia istorii religii i ateizma, V,* 206–71. Moscow-Leningrad: Izdatel'stvo akademii nauk, 1961.

Po etapam razvitiia ateizma v SSSR. Leningrad: Nauka, 1967.

Pomper, Philip. *The Russian Revolutionary Intelligentsia.* Arlington Heights, Ill.: Harlan Davidson, 1970.

Pospielovsky, Dmitry V. *A History of Marxist-Leninist Atheism and Soviet Anti-Religious Policies.* 3 vols. New York: St. Martin's Press, 1987–1988.

Powell, David E. *Antireligious Propaganda in the Soviet Union: A Study of Mass Persuasion.* Cambridge, Mass.: MIT Press, 1975.

Prazdniki i sviatye russkogo pravoslaviia. Moscow: Soros, 1992.

Pushkareva, Natalia. *Women in Russian History: From the Tenth to the Twentieth Century.* Edited and translated by Eve Levin. Armonk, N.Y.: M. E. Sharpe, 1997.

Quirk, Robert E. *The Mexican Revolution and the Catholic Church, 1910–1929.* Bloomington: Indiana University Press, 1973.

Ramet, Pedro. *Cross and Commissar: The Politics of Religion in Eastern Europe and the USSR.* Bloomington: Indiana University Press, 1987.

Ramet, Sabrina Petra, ed. *Religious Policy in the Soviet Union.* Cambridge: Cambridge University Press, 1993.

Rassweiler, Anne D. *The Generation of Power: The History of Dneprostroi.* New York: Oxford University Press, 1988.

Read, Christopher. *Religion, Revolution and the Russian Intelligentsia, 1900–1912: The Vekhi Debate and Its Intellectual Background.* New York: Barnes and Noble Books, 1979.

Richards, Jeffrey. *Sex, Dissidence and Damnation: Minority Groups in the Middle Ages.* London: Routledge, 1991.

Robson, Roy R. *Old Believers in Modern Russia.* DeKalb: Northern Illinois University Press, 1995.

Roslof, Edward E. "The Heresy of 'Bolshevik' Christianity: Orthodox Rejection of Religious Reform during NEP." *Slavic Review* 55 (fall 1996): 614–35.

———. "The Renovationist Movement in the Russian Orthodox Church, 1922–1946." Ph.D. diss., University of North Carolina, Chapel Hill, 1994.

Rulin, P. "Komsomol'tsy dvadtsatogo goda." In *Raduga trekh gor.* Moscow: Moskovskii rabochii, 1967.

Scott, James C. *Domination and the Arts of Resistance: Hidden Transcripts.* New Haven, Conn.: Yale University Press, 1990.

———. *The Moral Economy of the Peasant: Rebellion and Subsistence in Southeast Asia.* New Haven, Conn.: Yale University Press, 1976.

———. *Weapons of the Weak: Everyday Forms of Peasant Resistance.* New Haven, Conn.: Yale University Press, 1985.

Shabalin, Boris. *Krasnyi treugol'nik.* Leningrad: Istoriia zavodov, 1953.

Shaginian, Marietta S. *Fabrika Tornton [Krasnyi tkach].* Moscow: TsK Soiuza tekstil'shchikov, 1927.

Sharov, V. E., et al., eds. *Iz istorii Kurskoi oblastnoi Komsomol'skoi organizatsii (1918–1970 gg.).* Kursk: Kurskaia pravda, 1972.

Sherdakov, V. N., ed. *Ateizm, religiia, sovremennost'.* Leningrad: Nauka, 1973.

Shevzov, Vera. "Chapels and the Ecclesial World of Prerevolutionary Russian Peasants." *Slavic Review* 55 (fall 1996): 585–613.

———. "Universal, National and Local Feasts: Competing Parameters of Orthodox Identity in Rural Russia." Paper presented at the National Conference of the American Association of Slavic Studies, Washington, D.C., 27 October 1995.

Siegelbaum, Lewis H. *Soviet State and Society between Revolutions, 1918–1929.* Cambridge: Cambridge University Press, 1992.

Smirnov, N. A., and A. P. Kazhdan, eds. *Tserkov' v istorii Rossii (IX v.–1917 g.): Kriticheskie ocherki.* Moscow: Nauka, 1967.

Smith, Mark. *Religion in Industrial Society: Oldham and Saddleworth, 1740–1865.* Oxford: Clarendon Press, 1994.

Smith, R. E. F., and David Christian. *Bread and Salt: A Social and Economic History of Food and Drink in Russia.* Cambridge: Cambridge University Press, 1984.

Solomon, Peter H., Jr. *Soviet Criminal Justice under Stalin.* Cambridge: Cambridge University Press, 1996.

Spinka, Matthew. *The Church in Soviet Russia.* New York: Oxford University Press, 1956.

Starr, S. Frederick. *Red and Hot: The Fate of Jazz in the Soviet Union.* New York: Oxford University Press, 1983.

Steinberg, Mark D. "Workers on the Cross: Religious Imagination in the Writings of Russian Workers, 1910–1924." *Russian Review* 53 (1994): 213–39.

Stites, Richard. *Revolutionary Dreams: Utopian Vision and Experimental Life in the Russian Revolution.* New York: Oxford University Press, 1989.

Tawney, R. H. *Religion and the Rise of Capitalism.* 1926. Reprint, New York: Penguin, 1990.

Thomas, Keith. *Religion and the Decline of Magic.* New York: Scribner's, 1971.

Thompson, E. P. *Customs in Common.* New York: New Press, 1993.

Thrower, James. *Marxist-Leninist "Scientific Atheism" and the Study of Religion and Atheism in the USSR.* Berlin: Mouton, 1983.

Tian-Shanskaia, Olga Semyonova. *Village Life in Late Tsarist Russia.* Edited by David L. Ransel. Translated by David L. Ransel with Michael Levine. Bloomington: Indiana University Press, 1993.

Timberlake, Charles E. "The Fate of Russian Orthodox Monasteries and Convents since 1917." *Donald W. Treadgold Papers* 103 (May 1995): 7–62.

———, ed. *Religious and Secular Forces in Late Tsarist Russia: Essays in Honor of Donald W. Treadgold.* Seattle: University of Washington Press, 1992.

Tirado, Isabel A. "The Revolution, Young Peasants, and the Komsomol's Antireligious Campaigns (1920–1928)." *Canadian-American Slavic Studies* 26 (1992): 97–117.

Trifonov, I. Ia. *Klassy i klassovaia bor'ba v SSSR v nachale NEPa (1921–1925 gg.), chast' II.* Leningrad: Izdatel'stvo Leningradskogo universiteta, 1969.

———. *Klassy i klassovaia bor'ba v SSSR v nachale NEPa (1921–1923 gg.), chast' I.* Leningrad: Izdatel'stvo Leningradskogo universiteta, 1964.

———. *Ocherki istorii klassovoi bor'by v SSSR v gody NEPa (1921–1937).* Moscow: Gosudarstvennoe izdatel'stvo politicheskoi literatury, 1960.

Tul'tseva, L. A. *Sovremennye prazdniki i obriady narodov SSSR.* Moscow: Nauka, 1985.

Tumarkin, Nina. *Lenin Lives! The Lenin Cult in Soviet Russia.* Cambridge, Mass.: Harvard University Press, 1983.

Turner, James. *Without God, without Creed: The Origins of Unbelief in America.* Baltimore: Johns Hopkins University Press, 1985.

van den Bercken, William. *Ideology and Atheism in the Soviet Union.* Berlin: Mouton de Gruyter, 1989.

Vanderwood, Paul. *The Power of God against the Guns of the Government: Religious Upheaval in Mexico at the Turn of the Nineteenth Century.* Stanford, Calif.: Stanford University Press, 1998.

Vasil'eva, O. Iu. "Russkaia pravoslavnaia tserkov' i Sovetskaia vlast' v 1917–1927 godakh." *Voprosy istorii* 8 (1993): 40–54.

Venturi, Franco. *Roots of Revolution: A History of the Populist and Socialist Movements in Nineteenth Century Russia.* 1952. Translated by Francis Haskell, New York: Grosset and Dunlap, 1966.

Viola, Lynne. *The Best Sons of the Fatherland.* New York: Oxford University Press, 1987.

———. "The Peasant Nightmare: Visions of the Apocalypse in the Soviet Countryside." *Journal of Modern History* 62 (December 1990): 747–70.

————. *Peasant Rebels under Stalin: Collectivization and the Culture of Peasant Resistance.* New York: Oxford University Press, 1996.

Volodin, G. *Po sledam istorii: Ocherki iz istorii Donetskogo ordena Lenina metallurgicheskogo zavoda imeni V. I. Lenina.* Donetsk: Donbass, 1967.

von Geldern, James. *Bolshevik Festivals, 1917–1920.* Berkeley: University of California Press, 1993.

von Hagen, Mark. *Soldiers in the Proletarian Dictatorship: The Red Army and the Soviet Socialist State, 1917–1930.* Ithaca, N.Y.: Cornell University Press, 1990.

Voprosy istorii religii i ateizma: Sbornik statei, III–X. Moscow: Izdatel'stvo akademii nauk SSSR, 1955–1962.

Voyce, Arthur. *Moscow and the Roots of Russian Culture.* Norman: University of Oklahoma Press, 1964.

Vucinich, Alexander. *Empire of Knowledge: The Academy of Sciences of the USSR, 1917–1970.* Berkeley: University of California Press, 1984.

Wagner, William G. *Marriage, Property, and Law in Late Imperial Russia.* Oxford: Clarendon Press, 1994.

Weber, Max. *The Protestant Ethic and the Spirit of Capitalism.* 1930. Translated by Talcott Parsons, London: Routledge, 1995.

————. *The Sociology of Religion.* 1922. Translated by Ephraim Fischoff, Boston: Beacon Press, 1963.

West, Sally. "The Material Promised Land: Advertising's Modern Agenda in Late Imperial Russia." *Russian Review* 57 (July 1998): 345–63.

White, Lynn, Jr. *Medieval Religion and Technology.* Berkeley: University of California Press, 1978.

Wootten, David. "Lucien Febvre and the Problem of Unbelief in the Early Modern Period." *Journal of Modern History* 60 (1988): 695–730.

Worster, Donald. *Nature's Economy: A History of Ecology Ideas.* Cambridge: Cambridge University Press, 1977.

Yarmolinsky, Avrahm. *Road to Revolution: A Century of Russian Radicalism.* New York: Collier Books, 1962.

Young, Glennys. *Power and the Sacred in Revolutionary Russia: Religious Activists in the Village.* University Park: Pennsylvania State University Press, 1997.

Youngblood, Denise. *Movies for the Masses: Popular Cinema and Soviet Society in the 1920s.* Cambridge: Cambridge University Press, 1992.

Zeldin, Theodore, ed. *Conflicts in French Society: Anticlericalism, Education and Morals in the Nineteenth Century.* London: Allen and Unwin, 1970.

Zelnik, Reginald E. "'To the Unaccustomed Eye': Religion and Irreligion in the Experience of St. Petersburg Workers in the 1870s." In Robert P. Hughes and Irina Paperno, eds., *Christianity and the Eastern Slavs.* Vol. 2, *Russian Culture in Modern Times.* Berkeley: University of California Press, 1994.

Zybkovets, V. *Natsionalizatsiia monastyrskikh imushchestv v Sovetskoi Rossii (1917–1921 gg.).* Moscow: Nauka, 1975.

Index

complaints from believers,
136–37, 146–50
See also Mikhail Kalinin

Weber, Max, 10, 152
Westernizers, 28
William I of Aquitane, 5
Wisdom of Solomon, The, 2
witchcraft. *See* popular religion
Woman Worker, The. See Rabotnitsa
women
  education of, 19, 84–85, 108
  prerevolutionary social status of,
    16–20
  Soviet philosophy regarding, 70,
    100–1, 104–11
  spirituality among, 25–26,
    102–5, 112–13, 125–28,
    156–58
  See also marriage and divorce;
    sexuality
Women's Section. *See Zhenotdel*
Working Class Moscow. See
  Rabochaia Moskva
Workers' Newspaper. See Rabochaia
  gazeta
Wycliffe, John, 5–6

Zaichnevsky, P. G., 29
Zelnik, Reginald, 31
zemliachestvo, 106
Zhenotdel, 104–5, 108–9, 133
Zinoviev, Grigorii, 36, 40–41, 60,
  119–20
Zwingli, Ulrich, 9